Tolstoy, My Father

reminiscences

by Ilya Tolstoy

Translated from the Russian
by Ann Dunnigan

COWLES BOOK COMPANY, INC.
A subsidiary of Henry Regnery Company • Chicago

Contents

The Tolstoy Family

Lev [Leo] Nikolayevich Tolstoy ("Lyovochka") (1828–1910)
Sofya Andreyevna ("Sonya") his wife (1844–1919)

Their children:

Sergei Lvovich ("Seryozha") (1863–1947)
Tatyana Lvovna ("Tanya") (1864–1950)
Ilya Lvovich ("Ilyusha") (1866–1933)
Lev Lvovich ("Lyolya") (1869–1945)
Maria Lvovna ("Masha") (1871–1906)
Pyotr Lvovich ("Petya") (1872–1873)
Nikolai Lvovich ("Nikolenka") (1874–1875)
Andrei Lvovich ("Andryusha") (1877–1916)
Mikhail Lvovich ("Misha") (1879–1944)
Aleksei Lvovich ("Alyosha") (1881–1886)
Aleksandra Lvovna ("Sasha") (1884–   )
Ivan Lvovich ("Vanechka") (1888–1895)

Tolstoy, My Father
reminiscences

I

The Legends

Yasnaya Polyana!—Clear Glade—who gave you your lovely name? Who first chose that wondrous spot, and by his own toil lovingly consecrated it? And when?

Yes, you are truly clear and luminous. Bounded on the north, east, and west by the dense woodlands of the Koslov forest reserve, you bask in the sunshine for days on end. There the sun rises at the very edge of the forest—in summer a little to the left, in winter closer to the forest fringe—and drifts over its favorite glade all day, till by evening it reaches the other side of the woods and sinks from sight.

Though there were days when the sun could not be seen, though there were mists and thunderstorms and driven snow, in my mind you remain forever bright and sunny, a place of enchantment. And may that ray of sunshine which I still see falling upon Yasnaya Polyana shed its warm light on these memoirs.

There was a time when Yasnaya Polyana was one of Tula's outposts of defense against the Tatar invasion. When those mounted hordes drew near, the forest was transformed into an abatis, that is, trees were felled and stacked with their tops pointing toward the enemy to form an impassable thicket. In the interspaces where there were no trees the inhabitants dug huge ditches and built ramparts. The remains of one such rampart can still be seen between Tula and Yasnaya Polyana.

Centuries have elapsed and the Tatar raids have long been forgotten. The abatis became Crown property, and at Yasnaya Polyana the country estate and villages of the Princes Volkonsky sprang up.[1]

At the time of Maria Nikolayevna Volkonskaya's marriage, Yasnaya Polyana came into the possession of the Counts Tolstoy, and there, on the twenty-eighth of August, 1828, was born the Tolstoys' youngest son, Lyovochka, who was to become one of the world's greatest writers—Lev Nikolayevich Tolstoy.

Before speaking of my personal memories, I should like to relate several family legends, some of which I learned from my father.

Twenty versts from Yasnaya Polyana, in the village of Solosovka, lived Aleksandr Pavlovich Ofrosimov, an extremely charming man who died only recently. I could write a whole volume about this "typical Russian nobleman." He used to drop in now and then to pay a neighborly visit to my father, whom he deeply respected. Later, when I was a grown man, he and I became close friends and saw a great deal of each other in Tula. As a lover of gypsies he was depicted by my father in The Living Corpse, *and it was he who gave the name* The Funeral *to one of the most famous of those roisterous gypsy songs.[2]*

Once when I was leaving Tula to go to Yasnaya, Ofrosimov stopped me on the staircase of the inn.

"Are you off to see your father, Ilyusha?"

"Yes."

"Go, go and tell him that Ofrosimov says that Lev Nikolayevich is a regular poet—understand, a regular poet!"

"All right, Uncle Sasha, I'll tell him."

I once asked this same Uncle Sasha, as we all called him, how my father had first become acquainted with the Behrses, my mother's family.

"That friendship goes way back. And it wasn't with the Behrses that he first became acquainted, and it wasn't your father but your grandfather, the late Nikolai Ilyich, who became acquainted with your mother's grandfather, the late Aleksandr Mikhailovich Islenyev. And I'll tell you how it happened." Uncle Sasha spoke with a certain deliberate huskiness affected by many of the old-time squires. "My late-lamented father, Pavel Aleksandrovich Ofrosimov, gave to your grandfather, Nikolai Ilyich Tolstoy, a black-spotted hound. One day Nikolai Ilyich rode into a covert after a litter of wolves. They put up a she-wolf. Naturally he coursed her for about twenty versts. The hound strayed from the pack and next day turned up at the country estate of Aleksandr Mikhailovich Islenyev at Krasnoe, near Sergiev. That's how far he'd got! Aleksandr Mikhailovich sees that it's one of the Ofrosimov dogs and sends it back to my father with a letter. Father, Pavel Aleksandrovich, looks at it and writes to Aleksandr Mikhailovich: 'This hound is not mine, I gave it to Count Nikolai Ilyich.' And that's how Count Nikolai Ilyich became acquainted with Islenyev— through that spotted hound of the Ofrosimovs."

I remember my great-grandfather Islenyev, of whom Ofrosimov told this story. He lived to be over eighty, and I can still see him, an old man in a skullcap, going horseback riding with papa, the wolfhounds running alongside them.

He was said to have been a terrific gambler, winning and losing whole fortunes at cards, and this passion endured to the very end of his life. His children, all by Princess Kozlovskaya and therefore illegitimate, bore the fictitious name Islavin. The story is told that once when he was playing cards with her husband, the Prince had proposed that he stake the legitimization of all his children on one card. "Take the card, and all your children will be legitimate Princes Kozlovsky." Aleksandr Mikhailovich took the card, but nobly declined the legitimization of his children.

Few legends concerning my father's family have survived. All I know of Nikolai Ilyich is that he had once been an officer in the army, was taken prisoner by the French in 1813 or '14, and had had a personal interview with Napoleon in Paris.[3] *He died unexpectedly when my father was nine years old.*

Still less is known about my grandmother, Maria Nikola-yevna, born Princess Volkonskaya. She died when my father was only two and he knew nothing about her but the stories told to him by her relatives. She was said to have been ex-tremely kind and clever, and although short of stature and quite plain, had large clear luminous eyes. Her skill as a story-teller was unrivaled, and papa *used to say that his elder brother Nikolai had inherited this talent from her.*[4]

Papa *spoke of no one with as much love and respect as his "Mamma," and it always evoked a particularly tender and gentle mood in him. We could hear in his voice such reverence for her memory that to us she was like a saint.*

The most interesting family legends were those about the so-called "American" Tolstoy, who was Father's uncle once re-moved.[5] *Much of what was told about him was in all probabil-ity rather exaggerated, some of it perhaps intentionally; never-theless, I will relate what I know or have heard about him.*

He once decided to take a trip around the world and went to America. In the course of the voyage he organized a mutiny against the captain of the ship, which resulted in his being set ashore on an uninhabited island. There he made friends with a large monkey, which is said to have served him as a wife. Eventually the ship returned and a boat was put out for him. The monkey, having grown quite attached to him by then, threw itself into the water and swam after him when he left, whereupon Tolstoy calmly picked up his rifle and shot his faith-ful friend. It is further alleged that he then pulled the carcass out of the water and took it on board, where he had it roasted and ate it.

When I studied Ilovaisky's history as a child, I was always vexed by his way of narrating various legends of ancient times and then ending the chapter with, "However, all that probably belongs to the realm of myth." I am afraid that this story too is only a myth. Tolstoy was set down somewhere in the Aleutian Islands, where there are no monkeys. In Woe from Wit *Griboyedov says of him, "He returned an Aleut."*

But there is more about him. He brought an enormous crocodile back to Russia with him. The crocodile ate only live fish and showed a preference for sturgeon and sterlet. Tolstoy used to go around borrowing money from all his friends and acquaintances to pay for the fish. "Just kill the crocodile," one of them advised him. But this was far too simple a solution for Tolstoy, and he probably would have ruined himself eventually had not the crocodile died of its own accord.

He was a very talented man and in addition to his physical prowess was an excellent musician. When he conducted an orchestra, he would be so carried away by emotion that he sometimes seized a huge bronze candelabrum and wielded it like a baton.

A friend once came up to him at a ball and drawing him aside asked him to be his second in a duel. Tolstoy readily consented and the time was set for eight o'clock the next morning. It was agreed that the friend would bring the pistols to his house at exactly seven and they would leave the city together. But when he arrived at the appointed hour, to his horror he found Tolstoy in bed asleep.

"Get up at once and dress!"

"What? . . . What for?"

"Have you forgotten that I'm fighting a duel at eight o'clock and that you promised to be my second?"

"Fighting a duel? With whom?"

The friend gave his adversary's name.

"N.N? Ah, yes . . . Well, don't worry about it, I've already killed him."

It seems that during the night Tolstoy had gone to the man, challenged him to a duel at sunrise, and, having killed him, calmly went home to bed.

The daughter of the "American" Tolstoy, Praskovya Fyodorovna, was married to Perfilev, the Governor of Moscow. Father

*had been very friendly with her at one time, and his brother,
Sergei Nikolayevich, had been so much in love with her that
he had burned her initials on his arm—but in French, a language he considered more appropriate to the venture.* (Honi
soit qui mal y pense.) *By a strange freak of chance Praskovya
Fydorovna also had a pet monkey, Yashka, which she loved
more than anything in the world.* Papa *used to tell us about the
exploits of this monkey.*

*Are the stories I heard as a child about the youth and child-
hood of* papa *and Uncle Sergei (Sergei Nikolayevich Tolstoy)
to be consigned to the realm of legend? They are so much later
in time that they can hardly be considered legendary.*

*To the query "Where were you born?" papa wrote in my
sister Tanya's Book of Questions, "At Yasnaya Polyana, on the
leather sofa."* [6] *This venerable leather-covered walnut sofa, on
which we three eldest children were born too, still stands
where it always stood in my father's room.*

*Unfortunately, I never saw at close range the house where
he was born and spent his childhood. It was originally situated
between two wings, but had been sold for five thousand rubles
by Valerian Petrovich Tolstoy, one of his relatives, and moved
elsewhere at the time Father was with the army in the Caucasus. I do not know the exact story of the sale of the old house.* [7]
*Father was always reluctant to talk about it, and I could never
bring myself to question him in detail about what had happened. I have heard that it was sold to cover his losses at cards.
He himself told me that he had been a passionate card player
at one time and that as a result of losing heavily his property
affairs had become very much entangled.*

*He had planted maple trees and larches where the old house
once stood, and when anyone asked him about the location of
his mother's room—the room in which he was born—he would
look up at one of the larch trees and say, "Right there, in the
topmost branches of that tree, is where I was born."*

*The thirty-six-room house had been moved intact to a site
some twenty versts from Yasnaya, and I saw it only once, and
then no more than a fleeting glimpse as I rode by in a hunt. The*

present house at Yasnaya, which was gradually enlarged as the family increased in size, grew out of one of the original two-story wings.

Papa rarely talked about his childhood. He sometimes reminisced about his grandmother, Pelageya Nikolayevna. She was evidently a queer old woman and he seemed not to have been very fond of her. He used to tell us how she liked to put herself to sleep listening to fairy tales and had bought herself a blind storyteller for the purpose, which was quite suitable as she had no compunction about undressing and going to bed in his presence. Like Scheherazade, the storyteller told one tale after another in a monotonous, singsong voice, ever mindful of her breathing, and the moment she fell asleep silently stole away, and next night took up where he had left off. "And so Aladdin took his wonderful lamp, and went to . . ." and so on till the Countess again fell asleep.

Maman had fewer family legends, and hers were all of more recent origin. She was the daughter of the Court physician Behrs and had been born in the Moscow Kremlin. Her family traditions were essentially those practical, vital principles which she had introduced at Yasnaya Polyana and firmly maintained to the end of her life. Dinner had to be "ordered" every day. One must always wear shoes with French heels. In summer jam had to be made, mushrooms pickled, and clothing put away in tobacco and sprinkled with camphor against moths. On every name-day and birthday there was the traditional cake, and cracknels with morning tea. Guests must always be served appetizers of herring and cheese. When wine was spilled on the tablecloth, salt must be sprinkled on it at once. There always had to be a Christmas tree, and so on. Everyone in the family gladly complied with these customs, especially since the burden of maintaining them fell almost entirely on maman alone, while the rest of us only enjoyed the pleasure they afforded.

II

**Characteristics of the Children. Early Childhood
Impressions. Maman, Papa, Grandmother,
Hannah, the Three Dunyashas. Beginning of
Lessons and School**

C$_{\text{HILDHOOD}}$ memories—a starlit firmament in
which there gleams an infinitude of golden points, some bright,
some dim, some near, some far, all sweetly twinkling and beck-
oning. There is no strict sequence in our memories of childhood: what came early, what late—does it matter? It happened. And that glimmering little star is now remote.

In a letter to Aleksandra Andreyevna Tolstaya, his cousin
once removed, this is how my father described our family:

"The eldest, Sergei, is fair-haired and rather handsome.
There is something weak, forbearing, and very gentle in his expression. His laughter is not infectious, but when he cries it is
all I can do to keep from crying with him. Everyone says he is
like my eldest brother. I am afraid to believe it; that would be
too good to be true. In my brother's character there was neither
egotism nor self-renunciation, but a golden mean between the
two: he never sacrificed himself for anyone, but neither did he

9

harm or interfere with anyone. He kept both his joy and his sorrow to himself. Seryozha is clever, has a mathematical mind, is sensitive to art, good at his lessons, lively and athletic, but *gauche* and absent-minded. Shows little originality. He is much influenced by his physical condition and, depending on whether he is sick or well, is two different boys.

"Ilya, the third, has never been sick. Big-boned, fair, rosy, beaming. Bad at lessons. Always thinks about what he's been told not to think about. Invents his own games. Tidy and frugal: 'mine' is very important to him. Hot-tempered and *violent,** quick to fight, but also tender and extremely sensitive. Sensuous—fond of eating and of lying down in comfort. When he eats currant jelly and buckwheat kasha it makes his lips tingle. Original in everything. When he cries he becomes furious and obnoxious, but when he laughs everyone laughs with him. Anything forbidden holds a fascination for him and he is quick to recognize it. He found out, when only a toddler, that a pregnant woman feels the baby move. For a long time his favorite game was putting something round under his jacket and stroking it with a taut hand as he smiled and whispered, 'That's the little baby.' He would also stroke all the bulges in the furniture where the springs were broken, saying over and over again, 'Little baby.'

"Not long ago when I was writing stories for my *ABC Book,* he made up one of his own. 'A certain boy asked: Does God _____ too? So God punished him and he had to _____ all his life.' If I were to die, Ilya would come to grief without a strict and *loving* guardian.

"During the summer, when we went bathing, Seryozha rode his own horse and I sat Ilya behind me on my horse. One morning I came out to find them both waiting for me, Ilya with hat and towel, beaming and ready to go, Seryozha running up from somewhere, hatless and out of breath. 'Find your hat or I won't take you.' Off he goes, running hither and thither, but the hat is not found. 'Well, I'm not taking you without your hat. Let it

---

*In French in the original—*Tr.*

be a lesson to you, you're always losing things.' He's almost in
tears. I ride off with Ilya and watch to see whether he will express any sympathy for his brother. None whatsoever. He
beams happily and chatters about the horse. My wife finds
Seryozha in tears, looks for the hat, but it is nowhere to be
found. It occurs to her that her brother,[1] who had gone fishing
earlier in the morning, had taken Seryozha's hat. She writes me
a note saying that Seryozha is probably not to blame for losing
the hat and sends him to me wearing a peaked cap. (She had
guessed right.) I hear hurried footsteps on the bathhouse
bridge as Seryozha comes running to me. (He had lost the note
on the way.) He begins to sob, Ilya follows suit, and even I
cry a little.

"Tanya is eight years old. Everyone says she resembles
Sonya, and I agree—not just because I like to think so but because it is obvious. Had she been Adam's firstborn, and had
there been no others after her, she would have been an unhappy little girl. Her greatest pleasure is looking after the
younger ones. She evidently derives a physical pleasure from
holding and touching a little body. Her dream, which by now
is quite conscious, is to have children. The other day I took her
to Tula to be photographed. She begged me to buy a little
knife for Seryozha, and something for this one, something for
that one. She knows just what will give each of them the greatest pleasure. I bought nothing for her, but not for a moment did
she think of herself. As we were driving home I said, 'Tanya,
are you asleep?' 'No.' 'What are you thinking about?' 'I was
thinking how when we get home I'll ask *maman* whether Lyolya has been good, and how I'll give him his present, and give
the others theirs, and how Seryozha will pretend he's not
pleased, but will be very pleased.' She's not very clever, and
doesn't enjoy using her mind, but she has good mental equip-
ment. She'll be a fine woman if God gives her a husband. I'm
prepared to pay a handsome premium to the man who makes
her 'a new woman.'

"The fourth, Lev. Dexterous, good memory, graceful. Whatever he wears looks as if it had been made for him. Everything

the others do he does too, and does it well and very skillfully. I still can't quite *understand* it.

"The fifth, Masha, at whose birth Sonya nearly died, is two years old. A weak, sickly child. Body white as milk, curly flaxen hair, strange large blue eyes, serious expression. Very intelligent and ugly. This will be one of the riddles. She will suffer, seek and not find, yet constantly seek what is most unattainable.

"The sixth is Pyotr, a giant. He's a huge, charming baby in a cap, who wriggles his elbows striving to go somewhere. My wife is thrown into an ecstasy of agitation when she holds him, but I understand nothing of all this. I know that he has a great fund of physical energy, but whether this energy will serve any purpose, I do not know. That's why I don't care for children under the age of two or three. I don't understand them."[2]

This letter was written in 1872, when I was six years old. Although my memories date from approximately that time, I can remember several things that happened even earlier.

By the time I was four there were four of us children: Seryozha, Tanya, Lev, and I.* I remember when Lev (we called him Lyolya) was vaccinated against smallpox; he was in the corner room upstairs and howled furiously when they hurt him.

Then I remember *papa* standing by the little old mahogany table in the balcony room, arguing with someone about the Franco-Prussian War.[3] He was on the side of the French and believed they would win. I was about four at the time.

I also remember that Seryozha and I once got hold of some tin caps from wine bottles and cut coins out of them downstairs outside the vaulted room. Seryozha, who was three years older than I, already knew how to write and scratched 1870 on them.

In the beginning we children had the corner room upstairs, where *maman* and *papa* also had their bedroom. *Papa*'s study was downstairs off the big terrace, next to the room occupied by Tatyana Aleksandrovna and Natalya Petrovna.[4]

Maman had no room of her own. In one corner of the drawing room stood a little desk where she wrote the dinner menus

---

*Pyotr died in 1873.—*I.T.*

and shopping lists and did her "copying." It was a long time before I knew what it was she was copying. I only knew that this was something very serious and important.

Papa used to go into his study during the day to "work," and we were not supposed to make any noise. Of course, no one ever dared to go into the room. We had no notion of what he was working at in there, but from earliest childhood we were accustomed to respect and fear him.

It was quite another matter with *maman*. She belonged to us, and she too was afraid of *papa*. She did everything for us: saw to our meals, made our shirts, mended our stockings and underclothes, scolded us when we got our shoes wet with dew, and "copied"—everything. No matter what happened, it was: "I'll tell *maman*." "*Maman*, Tanya's teasing me." "Tell her to come here. Tanya, don't tease Ilyusha, he's little." "Where's *maman*?" In the kitchen, in the nursery, sewing, copying. Her light quick step could be heard as she went from room to room, doing everything, always looking after everyone. I did not know then that she often sat over her "copying" till three or four o'clock in the morning, and that she copied *War and Peace*[5] by hand eight times. She probably made even more copies of *Anna Karenina* and the *ABC Book*.[6]

It never occurred to any of us that *maman* might sometimes be tired, or out of sorts, or wanting anything herself. She lived for me, for Seryozha, for Tanya, for Lyolya, for all of us, and there neither could nor should be any other life for her.

Remembering her now, when I am seventy, I often think: what an extraordinarily good woman, what an extraordinary wife and mother! It was not her fault that her husband ultimately became a giant and rose to heights unattainable by ordinary mortals. It was not her fault that his pace was such that she was inevitably left far behind him; or that in the mideighties, when he wanted to change his life and leave her, she could not bear to be separated from him and persuaded him to remain. Nor was it her fault that she had eight children to care for at the time, one of them an infant in arms.

Father was thirty-five when he married my mother, and she

was only eighteen. She was almost a child to him, little Sonya Behrs, and she remained so for a long time. The difference in age was never surmounted. When I was fifty and my mother seventy, to her I was still the same Ilyusha I had been as a child, and this was true in my parents' relations to each other. Her youth, her expansive nature, femininity, and remarkable selflessness gave him twenty years of unclouded family happiness. He could not have wished for a better wife. He educated her in his own way, instilled in her those views which at the time seemed right to him, and idealized her in his novels— partly in Natasha, partly in Dolly. Could he have known that the time would come when he would renounce his former ideals and evolve others, more exalted and more spiritual?

And would he have married her or have been happy those first twenty years of his married life had Sonechka Behrs been suddenly transformed from a Natasha Rostova into an advocate of pure Christianity, simplicity, and Platonic marriage—he, who at that time dreamed of increasing his wealth, was buying cheap land from the Samara Bashkirs, and making her bear thirteen children? How remote all that was from what Father later attained!

I remember him sometimes going to Moscow on business. In those days he still wore a frock coat on such occasions, one made to order for him by the best French tailor. And I recall how once on his return he delightedly told *maman* about his visit to the Governor-General, Prince Vladimir Andreyevich Dolgorukov, who had said to him that when Tanya (who was then seven or eight) grew up, he would give a ball for her. How strange that seems now! Strange too that Dolgorukov kept his word and Tanya did attend a ball given by him, but that was after Father had undergone his spiritual conversion and had renounced irrevocably going to balls or into society.

I say this not in judgment of anyone, but only to refute criticism of either my father or my mother. *Tout comprendre, c'est tout pardonner.* How many times have I heard those words from Father's lips!

Until the family moved to Moscow in 1881, my childhood was spent almost without interruption at Yasnaya Polyana. When we were growing up *maman* was the principal person in the house for us. Everything depended on her. She gave orders to Nikolai the cook, sent us out for our walks, bustled about the house all day, and was forever nursing one or another infant. We could be naughty with her, but there were times when she grew angry and punished us. She knew everything better than anyone else. She knew that one must wash every day, that one must have soup for dinner, learn to talk French, and not crawl about on all fours or put one's elbows on the table; and if she said we couldn't go out for a walk because it was going to rain, she was sure to be right and we did well to obey her.

Whenever I coughed she would give me licorice or "King of Denmark drops," and consequently I was very fond of coughing. If she went upstairs to play duets with *papa* after putting me to bed, it was a long time before I could fall asleep. I resented being left alone, and would start coughing and keep it up till Nurse went to fetch her, and if she was slow in coming I became very cross. On no account would I go to sleep till she came running to measure out exactly ten drops in a wine glass and give them to me.

Papa was the cleverest man in the whole world. He too knew everything, but it was impossible to be naughty with him. Later, when I had learned how to read, I found out that he was a "writer." I happened to like some lines of poetry I had read and asked *maman* who had written them. She told me they were by Pushkin, and that he was a great writer. I felt disconsolate that my father wasn't a writer. And when she told me that he was a famous writer too it made me very happy.

Papa sat across from *maman* at the dinner table and had his own round silver spoon. When old Natalya Petrovna, who lived downstairs with Tatyana Aleksandrovna, poured herself a glass of kvas, he used to pick it up, drain the glass, and say, "Oh, excuse me, Natalya Petrovna, I made a mistake." We all laughed with delight and found it strange that *papa* was not in the least afraid of Natalya Petrovna. Whenever we had jelly pudding for dessert he would tell us it was good for gluing boxes. This made *maman* very cross, but he wasn't afraid of her either.

Sometimes we had great fun with him. He rode a horse better than anyone, ran faster than anyone, and was stronger than anyone in the world. He hardly ever punished us, but when he looked into my eyes he knew everything I thought, and this scared me. We could fib to *maman,* but not to *papa,* because he saw through it at once, so no one ever lied to him. And he also knew all our secrets. When we played house under the lilac bushes we had three great secrets, which nobody but Seryozha, Tanya, and I knew. Suddenly one day *papa* told us that he knew all three of our secrets and that they all began with B, which was quite true. The first was that *maman* would soon have another baby, the second that Seryozha was in love with a baroness, and the third I no longer remember.

Besides *papa* and *maman,* there was Aunt Tatyana Aleksandrovna Ergolskaya. She lived in the corner room downstairs with Natalya Petrovna and had a big icon in a silver case. Aunt Tatyana always stayed in bed, and when we visited her she treated us to jam out of a green bowl. She was Seryozha's godmother and loved him more than any of us. When she died we were taken to her room, where we saw her lying in her coffin looking as if she were made of wax. There were candles burning all around her and in front of the icon, and it was very, very frightening. *Maman* told us not to be afraid, that she and *papa* weren't afraid; nevertheless, we huddled together and kept close to her.

Just outside the window of this low-ceilinged room was a deep well, which was also terrifying. *Maman* always told us not to go near it lest we fall in and drown. Once a bucket was dropped into it and they had a hard time getting it out.

I cannot remember exactly when the Englishwoman Hannah Tarsey [7] came to us. It was probably when I was still quite small. She was part governess, part nursemaid, and remained with us a long time, ten years perhaps. I passed directly from the care of my nurse Maria Afanasyevna into her charge. Kind, serene, and always cheerful, Hannah remains a bright memory in my life. We loved and obeyed her. I have no recollection of learning English, but it seems to me that I began speaking it at the same time as Russian. "Wash your hands, breakfast is ready," and other nursery phrases came quite naturally to me without my ever having to learn them.

At Christmastime we had a tree and she always made a plum pudding for us. Rum was poured over it and lit, and it was brought flaming to the table. When we walked in the garden with her, we always behaved properly and did not soil our clothes on the grass, but once when they sent Dunyasha out with us, we ran away from her and into the shrubs. She called after us, "Stay on the path, stay on the path!" So we nicknamed her "Dunyasha-stay-on-the-path." There was another Dunyasha, a housemaid who never remembered anything, so we called her "Dunyasha-forgot." A third Dunyasha was the wife of the steward, Aleksei Stepanovich, and we called her "Dunyasha-*maman*-has-come-on-business." She lived on the ground floor of the annex and always kept the door locked. When we went with *maman* to see her, we would knock on the door and shout, "Dunyasha, *maman* has come on business," and she would open the door and let us in. We enjoyed drinking tea with jam in it when we went to visit her. She used to give us the jam in a saucer, but had only one silver spoon, which was small, thin, and chewed out of shape. We knew the reason why: one day the pig had found it in the washtub and proceeded to chew it up.

When I reached the age of five and was no longer considered a baby, *maman* began teaching me to read and write. At first I did my lessons in Russian, but later in English and French. It was *papa* who taught me arithmetic, and having heard about how he taught Seryozha and Tanya, I dreaded these lessons, because when Seryozha failed to understand something, *papa* said he was doing it on purpose. At such times Seryozha's eyes took on a peculiar look and he began to cry. Sometimes I too failed to understand, and *papa* got angry at me. At the beginning of the lesson he was always kind and even made jokes, but when

it became difficult and he had to explain something to me, I was
so scared I couldn't understand a word.

I remember that by the time I was six *papa* had begun to
teach the village children.[8] They had their lessons in "the
other house," as we called the annex where Aleksei Stepanovich
lived, and occasionally on the ground floor of our house.

A great many of these children came to us, and when they
were in the house the front hall smelled of sheepskin jackets.
They were taught all together by *papa*, Seryozha, Tanya, and
Uncle Kostya.[9] Lesson time was very gay and lively. The
children did exactly as they pleased, sat wherever they liked,
ran about from place to place, and answered questions simultaneously, interrupting in their eagerness to help one another
remember what had been read. If one of them left something
out, another promptly sprang up with an answer, then a second,
and a third, and the story or the sum was reconstructed by
their joint efforts. *Papa* particularly valued the colorful and
original language of his pupils. He never required a literal
repetition of bookish expressions, and made a point of encouraging them to say everything in their own way. I remember
his once stopping a boy who was running into the next room.

"Where are you off to?"

"To Uncle, to bite off a piece of chalk."

"Well, run along, run along. It's not for us to teach them, but
for them to teach us," he remarked to someone when the boy
had gone. "Which of us would have expressed himself in that
way? You see, he didn't say 'to get' or 'to break off,' but very
accurately 'to bite off,' because that's exactly what they do—
bite the chalk off the lump, not break it off."

One day *papa* set me to teaching the alphabet to one of the
boys. I tried my best, but he understood absolutely nothing. I
lost my temper and began hitting him; we fought and both began to cry. *Papa* came and told me that I could never teach
again because I didn't know how. Naturally, I was mortified
and went to *maman* and told her it was not my fault, that
Seryozha and Tanya had been given good pupils, but mine was
stupid and bad.

III

Childhood Impressions

Childhood! Why are those impressions so fresh, so vivid? I am now over seventy, living in a foreign country far from all that is native to me, yet I clearly see them, sense their fragrance—and not only figuratively but literally. The five senses play a primary role in the life of a child, and, after sight, the sense of smell is, of course, predominant. If I wish to be transported to the past, nothing makes me experience it more vividly than recalling a particular scent.

At the beginning of May, when *maman* used to take our summer clothes out of the trunk and try our linen jackets and trousers on us, the whole house smelled of camphor. We have outgrown them; seams have to be let out, some of Seryozha's clothes are made over for Ilyusha, some of Ilyusha's for Lyo-

19

lya. The storm windows are taken out, the rooms become lighter and smell of summer.

Dressed in our summer clothes we run out to the little meadow in front of the house and pick flowers—fragrant yellow buttercups. In the avenues where the rills have only just dried up, the snow still lies in the gutters. The snail-clover is in flower. Another day or two and the violets will come out, dark fragrant violets that grow only in one place—under the lilac bushes in front of the house. We have forgotten that we are not supposed to dirty our knees, and scramble about in the meadow gathering bunches of tiny flowers that grow in the grass. When we take them into the house the fragrance is so strong that *maman* says we are not to keep them in our room at night.

Someone said the morels had appeared. In the afternoon the horses are put to the wagonette and we all drive to the woods. The ground is still soft and in places the wheels sink deep into the earth. We cannot drive up to the edge of the forest; there is still snow on the ground. We jump down and race into the woods. There is a smell of rotting leaves. We hallo to one another. Someone has found a morel and calls to the others. We cluster together, burrow among the leaves, clamber over a huge tree stump covered with dry twigs, over snail-clover ard wood violets, paying no attention to them now, oblivious to everything but those little morels that have sprung up on their long legs. They seem to be hiding from us, covering themselves with leaves and moss, burying themselves under the brushwood; and what joy, what triumph, when at last we find one and put it in the basket. It smells like the leaves, like the forest, and like my blackened fingers.

Summer! Early in the morning we spring out of bed, dress, and run to the stable. There it smells of horses and hay. The coachman, Filip Rodivonovich, is already saddling the horses, the white, pink-eyed Kolpik for me, the little Kirghiz, Sharik, for Seryozha, and the huge English thoroughbred mare, Frou-Frou, for *Papa*.[1] We mount our horses and ride off.

Papa is waiting for us at the porch. We set out to bathe in the Voronka, riding along forest paths instead of on the road. The branches, wet with morning dew, lash our faces. Holding our hats with one hand we lean over the horses' forelocks. At the bathhouse we tie the horses to birch trees, scamper along the footbridge, and undress as quickly as possible. The bathhouse is divided into two sections, a small one for the children and a larger one for the grownups. First a quick plunge. The water has that special river smell peculiar to Russian rivers. It is said that the water smells of fish. Not so! A fish may sometimes smell of water, only less pleasant, but water has its own smell, fresh and clean.

Papa is already swimming out into the river. Seryozha too. "Ilyusha, swim over here!" I muster my courage and swim out, making for the bank, my eyes bulging from the effort, my mouth and nostrils filling with water, but once the goal has been reached, it is less terrifying to swim back.

We dress, *papa* lifts me onto the horse, and we gallop up the hill. Halfway between the house and the bathhouse is a forest glade. In summer it is covered with forget-me-nots and at times completely blue. In one corner, on the side near the house, there is a clump of oak trees. The soil under these trees is curiously black, consisting of metallic particles of coal. The same sort of soil is found in other parts of the glade. Probably at one time ore had been smelted here.

The path along which we rode to bathe passed directly through this clump of oaks, and here and there was intersected by sinuous roots that projected above ground. How many times, riding among these trees, I bruised my knees on their trunks! And how remote from Father's thoughts at the time, that forty years hence on a cold November day, the Yasenki peasants would come with spades and crowbars to dig up the black earth, and an immense crowd would accompany his body there to be lowered into its grave.[2]

Had he found at last the "sacred stick," and did he know the magic words inscribed on it? I like to believe that he had. But I will not digress. Back to childhood.

I was given a butterfly net. Nikolai Nikolayevich Strakhov gave me a wonderful book, *The Butterfly Atlas,* in which every

butterfly was illustrated in color, with its Latin name, and he
taught me how to dry them and start a collection. From morning till night I ran through woods and fields catching butterflies. And Seryozha with me; he had a book on beetles and we
caught them too. Summer was at its height and we ran waist-
high in the tall grass. No, not grass, it was almost all flowers—
yellow, pink, red, blue, white—what beauty, what fragrance!
The mowing had begun, and here and there the village women
and girls in their colorful *sarafans* and red kerchiefs tossed and
stacked the hay. We take a running jump and dive into a hay-
stack. It crackles and gives off a soporific smell. Then we climb
onto the wagon and ride to the barn.

Lord, how many delightful memories are associated with the
smell of hay! There was the haymaking with Father, even then
in the eighties, nights spent in haystacks on the edge of the
marsh or in village haylofts during a hunt, and that same fragrance of hay in the nursery, where our crackling mattresses
smelled of it too, especially on the days they were freshly filled,
as they were once a month.[3]

In summer barefooted village girls brought small plates and
wooden bowls filled with white mushrooms and wild strawberries. They silently line up at the porch, touching, pitiful.
"Sofya Andreyevna, we've brought some berries." *Maman*
comes out and begins to bargain with them. "Ten kopecks for
you, your plate has less. Seven for you, and five for you."

The kerchiefs in which the plates were wrapped are untied
and all the berries are poured out onto a big platter and carried
to the icehouse. More fragrances, more enchanting perfumes!
Oh, how they smelled, those damp white mushrooms and
brown-cap boletes! And the saffron milk-caps! And the honey
agarics!

Maman makes jam in the garden under the linden trees.
There is a smell of coal from the burning brazier. The jam bub-
bles thickly and rises in a pink foam. Buzzing bees and wasps
swarm around it, and like them we inhale the sweet smell and
wait impatiently for the "skim."

"The skim is for tea," says *maman* sternly, "you may not have any before dinner, it will spoil your appetite."

"*Maman,* only a little, just a taste."

"You may not," we are told.

But we know that "may not"—it means nothing. In the end we get not only the "skim" but a little jam besides.

Autumn draws near. In August the apples begin to ripen and we start searching for the best trees and gathering windfalls. The orchard is over a hundred acres in area with several strips of *arkad* and sweet-apple trees. The yellow *arkads,* which *papa* loves, are in the big orchard by the barn and in the young orchard. We gather some for him too. Each of us has his own "storehouse" in some secluded nook. The main hut is in the big orchard, and there the gardeners stay. The whole farmstead smells of apples and straw. The bathing season is over, but the mushroom season is at its height. Who will gather the most?

There was not a single corner within a five-verst circumference of Yasnaya Polyana that would not be explored by me again and again in my pursuit of butterflies and mushrooms during early childhood and later when I hunted with gun and hounds. Put a few brown apples in a basket, and the world is forgotten for that day—you rejoice. Over what? Then I did not know, but now I understand that joy. It was the joy of life, your own and that of those about you. Pure, potent, unclouded joy of childhood.

IV

**The Household. Nikolai the Cook. Aleksei
Stepanovich. Agafya Mikhailovna. Maria
Afanasyevna. Sergei Petrovich**

I came into the world at a time when all the servants in our house were former serfs. None of them is living now, but I should like to say something about them.

The image of my nurse, Maria Afanasyevna Arbuzova, is inextricably bound up with my earliest memories. She was a former serf of the Voeikovs. I knew nothing about this family except that after the death of Grandfather Nikolai Ilyich, one of the Voeikovs had custody of Yasnaya Polyana, subsequent to which much of its wealth disappeared. Nikolai the cook used to say that in the old days we possessed untold pounds of silver plate, but after Voeikov none of it was left. Later, another mad Voeikov lived at Yasnaya Polyana, but that was during *maman*'s time. All I know of him is that he once dragged a rabid dog out of the house without being bitten.

Maria Afanasyevna was the typical nurse. A round little woman in a black cap, she was kind, colorless, and occasionally grumpy. She was nurse to the five eldest of us children. For some reason I always remember her sitting by a table on which there was a burning candle, her hands folded in her lap. When the candle began to smoke she would take a pair of snuffers and snuff it out. Sometimes she put it out with her fingers, wetting them with saliva first, snuffing out the candle, and wetting her fingers again.

"Nurse, milk!"

"Come now, Ilyusha, none of that! Lie down and go to sleep."

"Mi-i-lk!" Louder and with tears this time.

Fearing that I might wake Tanechka, Nurse gives me a glass of milk.

Maman has told me that I always used to throw the glass on the floor when I had finished drinking. I did it so suddenly and slyly that it was impossible for them to anticipate my action. Finally they bought me a silver mug. For years *maman* kept it on the chiffonier, all battered and bent from being thrown on the floor. Why I did this I cannot recall.

Maria Afanasyevna had the keys to the storeroom and we delighted in running to her and begging for "waisins 'n' almonds." Her son, Sergei Petrovich Arbuzov, was our footman for many years, and later, in 1881, used to accompany Father on his trips to Optina Pustyn.[1] He was a carpenter by trade, with bright red whiskers and a penchant for drinking. Her second son, Pavel, was a shoemaker. He lived in the village and was Father's first instructor when he became interested in shoemaking.

Another important person at Yasnaya Polyana in my childhood was the old cook, Nikolai Mikhailovich Rumyantsev. At one time, twenty years before I was born, he had been a flute player in Prince Nikolai Sergeyevich Volkonsky's serf orchestra. In those days the orchestra played in the linden avenue in the evenings, and when *maman* came to Yasnaya Polyana after her marriage, the musicians' benches still stood in the garden. But when Nikolai lost his front teeth, he lost his *embouchure,*[2] so they made him a cook. I have often thought of poor Nikolai's mental anguish when, sitting in his dark damp kitchen on a summer day, he caught the strains of a waltz. Hearing the familiar flute melody played by someone more fortunate, deep lines of bitterness creased the corners of his mouth.

By the time Father married and brought his inexperienced young bride to Yasnaya Polyana, Nikolai was established as cook. His salary had been five rubles a month up to that time, but *maman* raised it to six, and he continued at that rate to the end of his days, that is, till sometime in the late eighties. Nikolai was the typical serf with all the serf's merits and shortcomings. He was unmindful of the changes brought about by the Emancipation, and there were times, such as when *maman* reprimanded him for being so drunk that his wife had to come and do the cooking for him, when he became indignant and cursed his "freedom."

"We weren't in bondage then, but now we are. You take one drink, and right away they holler 'drunk!' We were better off in those days. They kept a firm hand on us, we had to mind our p's and q's, but they looked after us well. In those days you knew you'd never have to starve. But now if they turn me out and I have to leave my masters, where will I go?"

He feared and respected his masters to the point of groveling. He was one of those men, and I have seen many of them, who in no way rejoiced over their freedom.

We children were forever running to the kitchen to beg him for something: a carrot, a piece of apple, a little hot pie. He invariably grumbled but gave it to us. His *levashniks* were specially delicious. Like little pies, they were made of rolled dough and filled with jam. To prevent their "settling," Nikolai blew into them from one corner—not through a straw but simply with his lips. This was known as *les soupirs de Nicolas*.

One of our French tutors, Monsier Nief, once killed a viper in the garden, cut off its head, and to prove to us children that it wasn't poisonous, decided to fry and eat it. We all followed him to the kitchen where he showed Nikolai Mikhailovich the viper dangling from his hand and in his broken Russian asked him for a frying pan.

We hid behind the door and waited to see what would happen. At first Nikolai Mikhailovich could not make out what the Frenchman was saying, but when it finally dawned on him he picked up the frying pan and brandishing it over the Frenchman's head shouted, "Get out of here, you heathen! I'll teach you to defile the master's pots—away with you! Last time it was a squirrel he brought in here to fry, and now, of all things, a viper! Get out!"

"Qu'est-ce qu'il dit, qu'est-ce qu'il dit?" asked Monsieur Nief, backing away in confusion.

We were delighted and ran off in high glee to tell *maman* all about it.

Dear, simplehearted old man, how little I appreciated your boundless devotion, your hard, joyless work, your participation in the life of our whole family!

Nikolai Mikhailovich was succeeded in the kitchen by his son, Semyon Nikolayevich, an upright lovable man who was my mother's godson and my playfellow. Under *maman*'s supervision he used to prepare Father's vegetarian dishes with zealous care, and but for him, who knows, perhaps Father would not have lived to such an advanced age. During his last years, Father felt well only at Yasnaya Polyana, and whenever he went anywhere else and was obliged to submit to an unfamiliar diet, suffered from gastric disorders.

Another of our domestic servants, Aleksei Stepanovich Orekhov, was also a former serf. When Father went to Sevastopol he took him along as his orderly.[3]

I remember my father telling me that during the siege of Sevastopol he was quartered with a fellow officer in the 4th Bastion who also had an orderly. The man was a dreadful coward, and whenever they sent him to the soldiers' mess to fetch their dinner he crouched and skulked in the most comic way trying to dodge flying shells and bullets, whereas Aleksei Stepanovich walked out boldly and fearlessly. As a consequence, they gave up sending Aleksei to run their errands and always sent the coward instead. The officers would all turn out to watch him cowering and slinking and throwing himself to the ground at every step.

In my time Aleksei Stepanovich was the steward at Yasnaya Polyana. He and Dunyasha lived in "the other house." He was a sober, steady man and we had great respect for him and wondered at *papa*'s addressing him with the familiar "thou." Later I will have something to say about his death.

Agafya Mikhailovna was an old woman who had first served in the kitchen and later became one of our yard servants. Tall and thin, with large expressive eyes and the straight graying hair of a witch, she was rather terrifying, but more than that, she was odd. Long, long ago she had been a housemaid to my great-grandmother, Countess Pelageya Nikolayevna Tolstaya, and was fond of talking about her youth.

"I was a beauty. When gentlefolk came to the big house, the Countess used to send for me. She was strict, the mistress was, but she loved me, may her soul rest in peace. 'Gashette,' she would say to me, *'femme de chambre, apportez-moi un mouchoir.'* And I'd reply, *'Toute de suite, madame la comtesse.'* They couldn't take their eyes off me. And when I went back to the annex, they'd be lying in wait for me, hoping to catch me on the path. Many a time I tricked them. I would run around the other way and jump over the ditch. Even then I didn't like that sort of thing. A maid I was and a maid I remained."

After my grandmother died, for some reason Agafya Mikhailovna was sent out to tend the sheep. She grew so fond of them that she never again ate mutton. Then she grew fond of dogs, and it is that period in her life that I remember. Dogs were everything to her, and we called her "the dog governess." She lived in the kennel with them, in the most horrible filth and stench, and devoted herself to them heart and soul. We always kept setters, harriers, and borzois in those days, and this kennel, which at times was quite numerous, was entirely in her charge, with only one boy, generally a stupid backward one, to help her.

I have many interesting memories connected with this clever and original old woman, most of them associated in my mind with the stories my father told me about her. He could always catch and highlight any interesting psychological trait, and these traits, which were mentioned quite casually, stuck in my mind. He used to tell, for instance, how Agafya Mikhailovna complained to him of sleeplessness.

"For as long as I can remember her she's been suffering from 'a birch tree growing up inside me from my stomach and pressing against my chest, so I can't breathe for that birch tree.' " Complaining of sleeplessness and the birch tree she once said, "I lie there alone, all is still but the ticking of the clock on the wall, 'Who are you, what are you, who are you, what are you?' And I start thinking, 'Who am I, what am I?' and spend the whole night thinking about it."

"Just imagine, this is *gnothi seauton*—know thyself—why, this is Socrates!" said Lev Nikolayevich, recounting it with delight.

My mother's brother, Styopa, who was studying at the school of jurisprudence at the time, used to come and stay with us in the summer, and when Father and I took the borzois and went hunting in the autumn he would join us. Because of this Agafya Mikhailovna grew fond of him. When Styopa had his examinations in the spring, she would anxiously wait to hear whether he had passed them or not. Once, she lit a candle before the icon and was praying for him, when suddenly she remembered that her borzois had got out and had not returned. "Good Lord, they'll run off somewhere, rush at the cattle, do some mischief. Oh, Nikolai-the-Wonder-Worker, let my candle burn for the speedy return of the dogs, and I'll buy another one for Stepan Andreyevich. . . . And the thought had no sooner come to me than I heard the clanking of the dogs' collars in the porch. They'd come back, thank God! That's what prayer can do."

Another of her favorites was Misha Stakhovich, a young man who was a frequent visitor at the house.

"Now see what you've gone and done to me, little Countess," she said reproachfully to my sister Tanya. "You've introduced me to Mikhail Aleksandrovich, and I've fallen in love with him in my old age, sinner that I am."

On the fifth of February, her name-day, Agafya Mikhailovna received a telegram of congratulation from Stakhovich. It was delivered by messenger from Kozlovka. When *papa* learned of it, he jokingly said to her, "Aren't you ashamed that a man had to trudge three versts in the frost at night because of a telegram for you?"

"Trudge, trudge! Angels bore him on their wings, he didn't trudge. You get three telegrams from some Jewish woman who's coming to see you, and telegrams every day about Golokhvastova—that's not trudging! But when I receive congratulations, then it's trudging!" she grumbled, and one could not help feeling that she was right. That telegram, the only one in the year addressed to the kennel, was certainly, by virtue of the pleasure it gave her, more important than any news about a ball given in Moscow in honor of a Jewish banker's daughter, or about Olga Andreyevna Golokhvastova's arrival at Yasnaya.

When Aleksei Stepanovich lay ill and dying all alone in his room, Agafya Mikhailovna used to sit with him by the hour, nursing him and diverting him with conversation. He was sick for a long time, suffering from cancer of the stomach, I believe. His wife, "Dunyasha-*maman*-has-come-on-business," had died several years earlier. On one of those long winter evenings when Agafya Mikhailovna sat at his bedside giving him tea, they got into a conversation about death and agreed that whichever of them died first would let the other know whether it was good to die. When Aleksei Stepanovich grew so weak that it was obvious the end was near, Agafya Mikhailovna recalled their conversation and asked him how it was with him.

"Just fine, Agafya Mikhailovna," he replied, and those were probably his last words. (That was in 1882.)

She was fond of repeating this story, but I heard it also from Father. He was always intensely interested in the sensations of the dying and whenever possible tried to find out the most minute details about what they had experienced at that moment. In his heart he associated this story with the memory of his elder brother Dmitry, with whom he had made a pact that whichever of them should die first would come back after death and tell the other about the life "beyond." But though Dmitry Nikolayevich died fifty years before my father, he never appeared to him after death.

Agafya Mikhailovna loved not only dogs but a pet mouse that used to come out and eat the bread crumbs on the table while she was drinking tea. Once when we children had gathered a lot of wild strawberries we got together sixty kopecks to buy a pound of sugar and make a pot of jam for her. She was very pleased and grateful.

"But suddenly when I was about to have my tea," she told us, "I reached for the jam pot, and there was the mouse in it! I took it out and washed it in warm water—I had quite a time getting it clean—and let it go on the table again."

"What about the jam?"

"I threw the jam out—after all, a mouse is a heathen, I wouldn't eat anything it had touched."

Agafya Mikhailovna died at the beginning of the nineties. By that time there were no longer any hunting dogs at Yasnaya, but she continued to shelter all sorts of mongrels, which she tended and fed to the end of her days.

V

The Yasnaya Polyana House. Ancestral Portraits. Father's Study

I still remember the Yasnaya Polyana house as it was in the first years after Father's marriage. In 1871, when I was five years old, the salon and study were added to the house. I remember the masons working, remember the laying of the cornerstone, when they placed a tin box containing silver coins under the foundation, and how a wall was broken through to make a doorway to the old house. But I remember most vividly the laying of the parquet floors. I enjoyed sitting on the floor and watching the carpenters fit the oak blocks, plane them, smear them with a thin, strong-smelling glue, and then hammer them into the mortises. When they had finished the parqueting and the floor was waxed, it was so slippery we were afraid to walk on it. And after it had begun to dry, we were sometimes startled by a loud sound like the report of a gun, and if I happened to be alone in the room I was so frightened that I instantly ran out.

33

The walls of the salon were hung with old ancestral portraits. They were rather awesome and I was afraid of them too at first, but later we got used to them and I even grew fond of one of them, that of my great-grandfather Ilya Andreyevich Tolstoy, because I was told that I resembled him. He had lived in the village of Glukhie Polyany, also in the Province of Tula. He had a plump, good-natured face. *Papa* told us that he was said to have sent his linen to Holland twice a year to be laundered and had a special cart for the purpose. He drank only French wines and only from Bohemian crystal. Generous, jovial, and lavishly hospitable, he wined and dined everyone in the district till at last he had run through his wife's immense fortune. He was the prototype of old Count Rostov in *War and Peace*, though probably somewhat more colorful than Father portrayed him.

Next to his portrait hung that of my other great-grandfather, my grandmother's father, Prince Nikolai Sergeyevich Volkonsky, with his bushy black eyebrows, gray wig, and crimson caftan. It was this Volkonsky who had erected all the buildings at Yasnaya Polyana. He was a model landowner, intelligent and proud, and enjoyed the respect of the entire district.

On another wall, in the space between two doors, hung a large portrait of the blind old Prince Gorchakov, father of my great-grandmother Pelageya Nikolayevna Tolstaya, Ilya Andreyevich's wife. He was depicted with eyelids lowered, seated at a semicircular table on which lay several of the handkerchiefs he always used to wipe his watering eyes. He was said to have been very rich and very avaricious, and took such pleasure in counting his money that he used to spend whole days counting and recounting piles of banknotes. After he lost his sight he would have one of his retainers, the only person he trusted, bring him his cherished mahogany casket, and after unlocking it with his own key would sit fingering the old crumpled notes over and over again. While he was thus engaged the trusted retainer was slyly stealing the banknotes and replacing them with pieces of newspaper, and the old man, still thinking he was counting his money, went on handling these bits of paper with his thin quavering fingers.

Further along hung the portrait of a nun with a rosary, Gorchakov's mother, née Princess Mordkin (born in 1705); then came Nikolai Volkonsky's wife, née Princess Trubetskaya; then another portrait of Volkonsky's father, who had laid out the park, "prospects," and linden avenues at Yasnaya Polyana.

Papa had arranged a study for himself under the salon, on the ground floor off the entrance hall. There he had a semicircular niche made in one wall to hold the marble bust of his favorite brother Nikolai. He told us that it was an excellent likeness, having been made from a death mask by a good sculptor and under his personal supervision.[1] It was a kind, rather pitiful face, with the hair brushed smooth like a child's and parted on one side. There was neither beard nor mustache, and it was all white and very very clean.

Papa's study was divided into two sections by a partition of big bookshelves that contained a great number of books of all sorts. The shelves were connected by large beams to keep them from collapsing. A thin birchwood door was made between them, behind which stood his desk and an old-fashioned round-backed armchair. One of those beams is still there, and to this day I would shrink from looking at it, knowing that at one time *papa* wanted to hang himself from it.[2] But I will speak of this later, it does not belong here.

The walls of the study were adorned with antlers that he had brought back from the Caucasus, and a stuffed stag's head on which he used to hang his hat and towel. There were also photographs of Dickens, Schopenhauer, Fet as a young man, and of the famous group of the *Sovremennik* circle in 1856.[3]

In the morning *papa* used to come out of his bedroom, a corner room upstairs, in his dressing gown, his beard uncombed and in a tangle, and go downstairs to dress. He would soon emerge from his study in a gray smock, fresh and vigorous, and come to the salon where we were all assembled for breakfast. When there were no visitors he did not remain long but took his tea to his study; if there were visitors, however, or if we had friends staying with us, he would begin talking, and once he had warmed to his subject was unable to tear himself away.

With one hand thrust into his leather belt and the other holding
a full tumbler of tea in a silver glass-holder, he would stop at
the door and sometimes remain standing in the same spot for
as long as half an hour, talking and talking, not noticing that his
tea was growing cold. And somehow it was always precisely at
that moment that the discussion became specially lively and
interesting. We all knew that spot by the threshold, knew very
well that when *papa* walked resolutely toward the door, tea in
hand, he was sure to pause there to make his concluding remark
—and that was when the most interesting part would begin.

At last he would leave and go to his study to work. In winter
we children dispersed to our various classrooms, in summer to
the garden or croquet lawn, while *maman* sat in the salon making clothes for the babies or copying something she had not
finished the night before, and silence reigned in the house till
three or four o'clock in the afternoon.

Later *papa* would come out of his study and set off, sometimes to go hunting with his dog and gun, sometimes to ride
horseback, and sometimes simply to walk to the Crown forest.
At five the bell that hung on the broken bough of the old elm
tree in front of the house was rung, and we all ran to wash our
hands and get ready for dinner. Occasionally *papa* was late and
we waited for him. At such times he came in looking somewhat
abashed and apologized to *maman* before pouring a little herb
brandy into a silver wineglass and sitting down at the table.

He was hungry as a rule and ate ravenously whatever was in
front of him. *Maman* would try to restrain him, telling him not
to fill up on kasha because there were chops and vegetables to
come. "Your liver will give you trouble again," she would say,
but he paid no heed and repeatedly asked for more till he had
eaten his fill. Then he would tell us about his walk: where he
had put up a covey of black grouse, what new paths he had discovered in the forest beyond the "Kudeyarov Well," how the
young horse he was breaking in was beginning to understand
the reins and the pressure of his leg, and all in the most vivid
and interesting way, so that dinner was a very gay and lively
occasion.

"*Maman*, what's the dessert today?" asks Tanya, always daring and independent.

"Ilyusha's favorite, pancakes with jam," *maman* answers quite seriously, not catching the note of mischief all too frequently heard in Tanya's voice.

Sitting beside *papa*, I am afraid to take more than two pancakes. But it's quite safe to take lots of jam, because one can quickly cover it over with the second pancake and roll it all up so it won't be noticed. I no sooner have it ready to eat than *papa* suddenly puts out his hand and takes away my plate saying, "Come, you've had enough now." I don't know whether to laugh or cry. Fortunately he sees the look in my eyes and bursts out laughing, otherwise I would have started to bawl.

After dinner he would go to his room and read. Tea was at eight o'clock in the evening, and then came the best hours of the day, when everyone was assembled in the salon and the grown-ups talked, read aloud, or played the piano, and we either listened or devised some amusement of our own, constantly dreading to hear the click and wheeze of the old English clock on the landing as it slowly and clearly began to chime ten. Is it possible that *maman* won't notice? She is sitting in the drawing room copying something.

"Time for bed. Say good night."

"Just five little minutes, *maman!*"

"Run along, run along, or tomorrow there'll be no getting you up for lessons."

After a lingering good night and attempting to find an excuse for delay, we go downstairs to our room under the vault. We resent being little and having to go to bed when the grown-ups can stay up as long as they like. What are they doing up there without us? Probably now, just when we've gone, they're beginning to have fun. No wonder *papa* always likes to say, "When I grow up." He's only joking, of course, because he's already grown up and has everything—everything that I long to have! He has three guns, several daggers, dogs, a saddle horse, and never has to do lessons, while I'll still be little for a long time and have to sleep in this dark nursery with Maria Afanasyevna, who has already blown out the candle and told me to stop tossing and turning in my bed. Shall I cry? No, I mustn't. Better to bury my head under the covers and go to sleep. And no sooner have I shut my eyes and dozed off than it's morning—bright and joyous.

So many pleasures lie before me: first to get dressed and dash into the garden where Tanya and I have dug a cellar storeroom in the earth; then to run about catching butterflies in the tall grass near the thicket—I simply must catch a Machaon butterfly as Seryozha has one and I haven't—then lessons, but that's nothing, mustn't even think about that, then breakfast, and a swim, and dinner. . . .

How delightful life is! How brightly the sun shines! How lustily the nightingales sing under my window! What a lot of pleasures lie ahead. . . .

VI

Papa. Religion

My father was a true aristocrat by birth, education, and manner. Despite the workman's smock he always wore and his disdain for all patrician prejudices, he was a nobleman and remained one to the end of his days.

Literary critics are pleased to see self-portraits in Pierre Bezukhov and Levin. How it annoyed him to be asked whether in Levin he had described himself! His answer was that an author creates a character out of any number of persons, and therefore it never can and never should be the portrait of a specific person.

In 1865, replying to a lady who had written to ask him who Prince Bolkonsky was, he wrote, "Andrei Bolkonsky, like any character described by a novelist, in contradistinction to a biographer or a writer of memoirs, is no one. I would be ashamed to publish my work if it consisted in nothing but observing, remembering, and producing a likeness." [1]

39

If many of my father's characteristics can be found in Bezu-khov and in Levin, he resembles Prince Andrei and his father, old Prince Bolkonsky, even more. There was the same aristo-cratic pride, almost arrogance, the same outer severity and touching shyness at any display of tenderness or love.

In all my life my father never once caressed me. This does not mean that he did not love me; on the contrary, I know that he did love me, and there were times when we were very close, but he never expressed his love in any overt, spontaneous way and always seemed to be ashamed of such demonstrations of affection. In our childhood every expression of affection was called "sloppy sentimentality."

I must add that toward the end of his life Father softened perceptibly. He was tender with my youngest brother, Va-nechka, and with his daughters, especially with my sister Ma-sha who died. Sometimes she could go to him quite simply, as to a beloved elderly father, and stroke his hand or caress him, and he accepted this affection and returned it with like sim-plicity.

For some reason it was not the same with us, his sons. Our mutual love was understood but never expressed. When we hurt ourselves as children it was, "Don't cry! . . . Your feet are chilly? Hop out and run behind the carriage. . . . You've got a stomachache? Here, take some kvas with salt, you'll get over it." He never sympathized, never expressed affection. If we wanted sympathy or felt like "bawling," we ran to *maman*. She applied a compress, then petted and consoled us.

Later, when my father was old and ailing, how I sometimes longed to caress and comfort him as my sister Masha had done, but I always had misgivings, feeling it might seem unnatural.

Earlier I mentioned Father's pride and nobility. I fear this might be misunderstood and should like to explain what I mean. By nobility I mean a certain refinement of manner, an outward neatness, and, above all, a scrupulous sense of honor. The word "noble" is somewhat outdated now. It has been re-placed by the word "cultured," but in my father's youth the

word defined a specific notion and meant something good. It
was what is so aptly expressed in the saying, "A king can be
recognized even in sackcloth."

When our footman, Sergei Petrovich, announced a visitor to
my father, he would say, "Lev Nikolayevich, someone is asking
for you downstairs." "Who is it?" "A nobleman," or, "A peasant," or, "Some man."

Sergei Petrovich made these distinctions by the outer aspect
of the man, but I apply "nobleman" to my father in the full
sense of the word.

And Father's pride also was purely aristocratic. This pride
was the cause of much suffering in his life. When in his youth
he could not keep up with the gambling and carousing of rich
young noblemen for want of money; when he challenged Turgenev [2] to a duel just at the time he was embarking on his literary career; when the police made a search of Yasnaya Polyana [3] and he was so outraged that he was ready to leave
Russia and live abroad for the rest of his life; when the Governor-General of Moscow, Prince Dolgorukov, sent his adjutant to
him demanding information about the sectarian Syutayev who
was living in his house at the time; when his enemies reviled
him for continuing to live in luxury at Yasnaya Polyana while
preaching freedom from possessions; when both government
and church heaped calumny on him and called him godless—
all this and a great deal more exacerbated his pride and gave
rise to suffering and reflection. Yet it was perhaps this very
pride, noble and spiritual, that contributed significantly to his
developing into the man he became in the second half of his
life. To be sure, I am describing him now as he was at the age
of forty-five, and it is quite understandable that he was not then
what the world knows him to have been.

I remember Father as looking more or less like Kramskoy's [4]
portrait of him up to the time he began to write *Anna Karenina*.
His beard was short, dark, and curly at the ends, and his movements were brisk and self-assured. He was a very powerful, agile
man and taught us children gymnastics, and how to swim,

skate, and ride. It was on these occasions that his severity was
apt to manifest itself. The words "tired" and "I can't" did not
exist for him.

"Swim!" And he would push me into a deep part of the river,
watching to see that I didn't drown, of course, giving me no
help, but encouraging me if I managed to reach the opposite
bank, my eyes bulging out of my head with fear and gasping
for breath. Or we might be out riding and suddenly he would
put the horse to a brisk trot. . . . I try to keep up with him, feel
that I'm losing my balance, grow more and more frantic with
every jolt. I know I am lost, yet must try to go on. After a few
more spasmodic unavailing movements, I find myself on the
ground. Father reins in his horse. "You're not hurt?" "No," I
answer, trying to keep my voice steady. "Mount your horse."
And again he sets off at a brisk trot as if nothing has happened.

Our religious training was in no way different from that of
other children of our day. Neither *papa* nor *maman* believed
very strongly in the religion of the church, but neither did they
deny it. They went to church and said their prayers because
these were things that everyone did, and because everyone else
gave their children religious instruction we were given it too.

The pillar of Orthodoxy at Yasnaya Polyana in my early
youth was Auntie Tatyana Aleksandrovna, then a decrepit old
woman who had once been Father's governess. Near the window in one corner of her room were several enormous old icons,
grown black with age, before which burned an icon lamp, and
whenever I went into that room I was filled with a mystical
feeling of awe and reverence. When she died we were taken to
"say good-bye to her," and seeing the coffin standing in front of
those icons, my feeling of awe became even more intense.

Later, another aunt, Pelageya Ilyinichna, who was also very
devout and kept an icon lamp burning, died and was laid out
in that same room, and although the room was subsequently
occupied by maidservants, I never got over the eerie feeling I
had about it. Even now, just thinking about it, I can see those

frightening icons and corpses and smell the suffocating odor of incense.

Maman made us say our prayers every night and mention every member of the family in them: "*papa* and *maman* and our brothers and sisters and all good Christians." On the eve of a religious holiday, a priest always came to the house to hold a vesper service, and at Shrovetide we ate pancakes followed by cabbage, baked potatoes with savory lenten oil, and coffee and tea with almond milk.

We painted eggs for Easter and went to church on Easter Eve. This was a very gay and festive occasion. Most years Easter fell at the beginning of the spring thaw, but when it came early we drove to church in a big broad sledge. The snow would be half melted and mounds of brown horse dung lay on the road. Here and there the snow was discolored, the runners slid over the mud, and rivulets flowed from the water-filled hollows. The horses' tails were bound up short. We shivered in the dark, sleepless night. At last the lights of the church appeared. Empty carts were drawn up around it, and in the porch stood the beggars and the blind.

Making our way through the crowd we enter the church and go down the left side to the front. Our neighbor Aleksandr Nikolayevich Bibikov and his son Nikolai are already there, standing in the choir. The peasants come in their long overcoats over clean unbleached linen shirts, their hair combed and oiled, and the women wear bright-colored dresses with beads around their necks. There is a smell of candle wax, incense, and tanned leather coats. It is a solemn service. From time to time a candle is passed up to the iconostasis. A man in the back of the church taps his neighbor on the shoulder with a thin penny candle, "For Nikolai-the-Wonder-Worker." His neighbor takes the candle and taps the man in front of him in turn, and on it goes till the candle reaches the iconostasis and is placed among the countless candles burning in candlesticks thick with dripping wax.

"Mother of God . . . Our Savior . . . Wonder-Worker . . ."

Midnight approaches. All, with lighted candles in their hands, join in the procession around the church, passing the ancient overgrown graves. In front of the church the priest, in a nasal voice, proclaims, "Christ is risen!" And again everyone crowds into the church and the long exhausting service begins. When at last it is over, we go to the priest, exchange kisses in commemoration of Christ's resurrection, and congratulate one another on the advent of Easter. After repeating this ritual with several of the peasants, we joyfully set out for home.

Dawn is breaking. The horses gallop briskly homeward. The rushing rivulets no longer scare us. Everyone's mood is so festive and gay that all thought of sleep or fatigue has vanished; our only fear now is that *maman* will suddenly decide to send us to bed too soon. So many delights lie ahead—to break our fast, roll the eggs, exchange kisses with everyone, and then, a whole week without lessons!

My understanding of God was always rather vague and confused. First, of course, He was an old man with a long white beard, and very cross. I could never forgive Him for his harsh treatment of Adam and Eve. Just because they had eaten an apple from some special kind of tree of the knowledge of good and evil, He had banished them from Paradise and condemned them to suffer and toil "in the sweat of their brow." In my opinion, this was far too cruel. Then there was the Flood, when everyone except Noah was drowned. And His command to Abraham to kill his only son. Fortunately He had showed him the ram in the thicket just in time, otherwise it would have been awful.

And then I never understood why God was so fond of Solomon, who had done so many horrid things and had such a multitude of wives. And I felt sorry for Lot's wife, and for Hagar, the poor slave who had borne Abraham a fine son and then was driven out and replaced by old Sarah.

The more I learned of the Scriptures, the more incomprehensible they seemed. In the beginning I tried to believe and understand, and I asked all sorts of questions of *maman* and the

priest who came to give me religious instruction, but their explanations did not satisfy me, and I became more and more
confused. By the time I came to Filaret's catechism and the
church service, I was completely baffled.

"Faith is the substance of things hoped for, the evidence of
things not seen." I gave up trying to understand these statements and resigned myself to learning them by heart. I was unable to understand "the symbol of faith," the Holy Trinity, why
I should believe that the communion bread and wine were
turned into the body and blood of Christ, and why I had to eat
that bread and drink that wine. In short, my mind was in a
hopeless muddle where these matters were concerned, and all I
could do was try to believe in that muddle because *papa* and
maman, Nurse and Nikolai the cook, and everyone else believed
in it.

My notions of Jesus Christ were also rather dim. He was the
son of the old god, who did to him what Abraham had almost
done to his son—sacrificed him for our sins, the sins of mankind. Again that cruelty and heartlessness of a god I could not
understand.

And why was it necessary to sacrifice His beloved son?
Wasn't it possible for God, who could do everything, to arrange
things differently? It was very important that Christ was bap-
tized by John the Baptist, and still more important were his
miracles, but most important of all of course was the resurrection, when he rose from the grave and went up to heaven again.

As to what Christ taught—that was not important. After all,
he was the Son of God, and he had his own relation to his father,
just like ours to our father. No one dared to treat our *papa* the
way His children treated him. And Christ treated God like a
father, but we had no right to treat God that way. He would
punish us after death, send us to hell, where there were only
devils, and make us lick red-hot frying pans and walk on burning coals.

Here my childish imagination inevitably transported me to
the kitchen, where huge black frying pans hung by the stove

and where I had seen Nikolai the cook take up a hot coal and toss it in his hand several times before lighting his homemade cigar from it. I always wondered how he could do this without burning his hand, and it was of considerable comfort to me— evidently burning coals weren't so dreadful after all. But to lick a red-hot frying pan, that must be really awful!

VII

Study. Childhood Games. "It's the Architect's Fault." Prokhor. Anke Cake

I T is understandable that having been brought up in the traditions of the old-fashioned nobility my father should have wanted his children to have the same upbringing. He thought it necessary to give them a knowledge of as many languages as possible, to teach them good manners, and to protect them as far as possible from all outside, extraneous influences. Since the *gymnasia* of the period were considered worthless, children had to be taught at home until it was time for them to go to the university. Father pursued this educational program to the end with my brother Seryozha and my sister Tanya, but with me, unfortunately, only to the fifth grade.

In the beginning we had all our lessons with *papa* and *maman*. *Papa* taught us arithmetic, Latin, and Greek, and *maman* taught us French and Russian. The differences between them were apparent in the lessons as in everything else: with *maman* it was sometimes possible to gaze out the window, ask

47

irrelevant questions, or even fail to understand and simply look blank; but with *papa* one had to exert oneself to the utmost and not allow oneself to be distracted for an instant. He was a wonderful teacher and made everything clear and interesting, but as with the horseback riding, he always proceeded at a brisk trot and one had to struggle to keep up with him. It was probably due to the good start he gave me that I made excellent progress in mathematics and always enjoyed it, though in general I was a poor student.

Meanwhile, our family continued to increase: Masha was born, then Petya, then Nikolenka. There were times when *maman* did not feel well and was completely exhausted from overwork. Soon they had to engage tutors and governesses for us.

Our first tutor, Fyodor Fyodorovich Kaufmann, was a German, a simple, primitive, and somewhat coarse man. His teaching methods, based on discipline and punishment, were decidedly German. Without Father's knowledge, he sometimes took a ruler to us, or made Seryozha and me remain for hours at a time on our knees in a corner. It was he who first instilled in me my aversion for study, an aversion I was never to overcome. Fyodor Fyodorovich was with us for about three years and was followed by Monsieur Rey, a ruddy-faced young Swiss. He too was rather coarse and obtuse and was given to drinking wine, which he kept in his room.

I can never forgive him for his method of punishment: *"Une page à copier; deux pages à copier,"* and so on, till by Sunday it amounted to an entire notebook to be filled. And it was always hopeless; although my whole Sunday was wasted in copying, while my brothers and sisters were running about playing croquet, or swimming, or hunting for mushrooms, I was never able to finish it. Monsieur Rey only succeeded in nourishing the seeds sown by Fyodor Fyodorovich and making me a confirmed enemy of learning.

Besides our tutors, there were always French governesses for my sisters, and for several years a Russian teacher lived in the house while helping to prepare Seryozha for his school certificate examination and teaching Tanya, Masha, Lev, and me at the same time. A music teacher came once a week from Tula, and when Tanya was no longer a child she had a drawing teacher too. Thus a private university was gradually organized in our home. Lessons were scheduled by the hour, and during the school term, in winter, that is, we spent most of the day at our studies, going from one teacher to another. In the intervals we took walks, went ice skating, skiing, or devised various games to be played in the house.

One of my parents' main concerns during these early years was to shield us from outside influences. The world was divided into two parts: one composed of ourselves and the other of everyone else. We were special people, and the others were not our equals. "We" included *papa* and *maman,* the Kuzminskys, Uncle Seryozha and his children, the rare visitors we saw at that time—and no one else. The others were inferior beings fit only to serve and work for us, whom we must hold ourselves aloof from and, above all, never imitate. Village boys might pick their noses, but we—never. They might have dirty hands and torn trousers, nibble sunflower seeds and spit the shells on the floor, fight and use bad language, but such behavior would be *shocking* * in us. It was mostly *maman,* of course, who was guilty of entertaining such notions, but *papa,* too, jealously guarded us from association with the village children. He was responsible to a considerable degree for the groundless arrogance and self-esteem that such an upbringing inculcated in us, and from which I found it so hard to free myself.

"The more toys children are given the more meaningless their games; ready-made toys destroy originality and inventiveness." And so our stock of toys was replenished only once a year, at Christmas time. Most of them were brought to us by the Dyakovs—Dmitry Alekseyevich, Father's boyhood friend and my godfather, his grown daughter, and the governess Sofyesha—and they were always the best ones.

Christmas was a yearly festival. A month before the holidays,

---

*In English in the original.—*Tr.*

maman would go to Tula and come back with a whole boxful of wooden dolls, "little skeletons," as we called them. Throughout the year she had accumulated remnants of cloth, scraps of ribbon, velvet, and chintz for the purpose, and triumphantly brought her big black bundle to the salon where we all sat down at the round table, needle in hand, and began making all sorts of little petticoats, shirts, caps, and trousers, and trimming them with gold lace and ribbon. We were delighted when the naked dolls, with their silly painted faces, were transformed into handsome, well-dressed little boys and girls, and it seemed to us that once they were dressed their faces looked more intelligent and acquired individual and quite interesting expressions.

We usually dressed thirty or forty of these dolls, which were meant for the village children, and when we had finished, set to work gilding nuts and tying little ribbons on all sorts of cardboard cutouts, fancy gingerbread, Crimean apples, and other sweets for them. We never knew what our own gifts would be.

On Christmas Eve the priests came for a vesper service. We wore our best clothes all day on Christmas, and when we went to the salon, there, where the dining table usually stood, was a huge, luxuriant tree that filled the whole room with the scent of fir needles. We always rushed through dinner, anxious to finish as quickly as possible and run back to our own rooms. It was then that the doors to the salon were locked and the grownups trimmed the tree and set out our gifts on little tables. Our excitement was such that we were unable to sit still and ran to the door at least twenty times to ask whether they would soon be ready and to peek through the keyhole. The time seemed to drag endlessly.

After dinner a group of village children in sheepskin coats and little caftans, together with some peasant women and a few of the men, all crowded into the entrance hall. They smelled of tanned leather and sweat.

At last everything was ready. The doors of the salon were unlocked and the peasant children squeezed through one door as we rushed in from the drawing room. The immense tree, glittering with gold ornaments and burning candles, reached the ceiling and filled the room with a fragrance of resin and fir needles. Our presents were laid out on little tables along the wall: colored letter paper, sealing wax, a pencil box, things that were generally given to everyone. Then came the Dyakovs' gifts. There was a big doll that shut its eyes and said "mamma" and "papa" when you laid it down and pulled two strings with little blue beads on the ends which were attached between its legs; a miniature kitchen with plates, forks, pots, and pans; a bear on wheels that nodded its head and growled; wind-up toys, horses with riders, toy mice, steam engines—and what all didn't they give us! Seryozha received a gun that fired a cork and a tin watch on a chain.

Meanwhile the grown-ups had distributed the dolls and sweets to the village children, who had come in by another door and stood in a group apart on the right of the Christmas tree, never crossing to our side of the room.

"Give me a doll too, Auntie, you gave Vanka one. There wasn't one left for me."

We proudly showed our gifts to the village children, never dreaming that they might be envious of us. We were special people, so it was quite natural that we should be given real presents and that they should get only those "little skeletons." They ought to be glad to get even those.

Sometimes a mummer with an accordian came from the village, and then there was dancing. And once *papa* himself dressed up and led a performing bear around the room—the bear being Nikolai the cook disguised in a raccoon coat.[1] "Come along, Misha, give us a dance. Show us how the peasant women steal peas from the kitchen garden. . . . Show us how grandpa falls off the stove, and how the village girls paint their faces red and white. . . . Come on now, let's fight!" And the bear danced, crawled about looking for peas, fell down on the floor, fought, and did all the tricks customarily performed by trained bears.

How we loved those "Mishkas" whenever they appeared at our home! I was sorry later when a law was passed prohibiting the exhibition of trained bears. *Maman* used to tell how on All Saints' Sunday, May 22, 1886, she had returned from Mass with *papa* to find a performing bear and his trainer on the grounds, and that same day toward evening I was born. Can this have been the cause of my fondness for bears?

Our delight with our new toys was of short duration. They only provoked unpleasant feelings of personal ownership and envy, and soon were either broken or destroyed. The only toys that ever lasted very long were the Russian and Turkish soldiers that Dyakov gave to Seryozha and me, and which we used to play with all winter. We would line them up in regiments at opposite ends of the big salon, and lying on our stomachs roll buckshot at the opposing army and demolish it. Is it possible, the reader will ask, that Lev Nikolayevich allowed his children to play at war? Yes, he saw nothing wrong in it at the time, and never thought of stopping us.

Another interesting game, devised by Tanya, was called "Ulverston." She had read some silly novel translated from English and decided to make a play of it for a paper-doll theater.[2] The actors were cut out of the colored pages of a fashion magazine. From an arm or a neck of the fashion model we cut bits of paper about an inch in size to make heads and faces, and from a colored sleeve or a skirt we made the bodies. It was easy to distinguish the characters because they were all of different colors. The hero of the story was Ulverston. Exactly what his adventures were I no longer remember, but the most important scene in the play was when he said to the heroine, "I am a bachelor and lonely," and asked her to be his wife. Tanya always spoke these words with particular feeling, and being very much in sympathy with poor Ulverston's hopeless love, we waited for them with bated breath.

Once *papa* found us at this game. Lying on the floor on our stomachs with our heads toward the theater, we formed a star as we moved the figures about. When he saw what we were doing, he took one of the old fashion magazines and went to the drawing room. A few minutes later he returned with the figure of a little boy which he had cut out of the bosom and shoulder of a lady in décolleté. It was all a rosy flesh color and completely naked.

"Who's that, *papa?*" we asked in perplexity.

"That can be Adolfik."

There was no such person in the novel, but of course we immediately devised a role for him, and soon Adolfik became our favorite character, supplanting Ulverston himself.

Childhood—a succession of delights! I don't know whether this is true for others, but for me it was unquestionably so. But only childhood, not all of life? I shall have more to say of this.

The first Christmas tree I remember was in the balcony room that later became Father's study. The second, when I was five years old, was in the new unfinished salon. That year I was given a big porcelain teacup and saucer; *maman* knew that I had been longing to have one and decided to give it to me for Christmas. When I saw the teacup on my little table, I snatched it up in both hands, and without even glancing at my other presents ran to show it to the others. Crossing the threshold to the drawing room I tripped and fell, and the teacup was smashed to pieces. Naturally I set up a howl and pretended to be hurt more than I was. *Maman* came running to comfort me, then told me it was my own fault for being careless. When *papa* heard her he laughed and said, "It's the architect's fault, it's the architect's fault!" And I was even more upset and couldn't forgive him for making fun of me.

From that time "It's the architect's fault" became a family saying, and *papa* was fond of repeating it whenever one of us tried to shift the blame for anything onto someone else. When I fell off my horse "because he stumbled" or "because the coachman didn't tie the saddlecloth properly"; when I did a lesson poorly "because my tutor didn't explain it well"; or when I blamed my drinking during my military service on army life—in all such instances Father would say, "Yes, yes, I know, it's the architect's fault," and one always had to leave off and admit to being in the wrong.

Papa had many of these sayings taken from life; "for Prokhor" was another. I believe that somewhere, possibly in one of his letters, he himself has spoken of the origin of this phrase. As a child I was given piano lessons, but being frightfully lazy I always played indifferently; it was enough for me to rattle off an hour's practice and run out to play. One day *papa* heard the most brilliant roulades being executed in the salon and couldn't believe it was Ilyusha playing. When he came in he saw that it really was me at the piano, but he also saw Prokhor the carpenter putting in the winter window frames. Only then did he understand why I was outdoing myself: I was playing "for Prokhor." This "Prokhor" became rather prominent in my life, and Father often found occasion to reproach me with him.

Another expression he enjoyed using was "Anke cake." My mother's parents had a friend, a university professor by the name of Dr. Anke, who had given my grandmother, Lyubov Aleksandrovna Behrs, the recipe for an exceedingly delicious name-day cake. When *maman* married and came to Yasnaya Polyana, she passed the recipe on to Nikolai the cook, and ever since I can remember "Anke cake" was served on every festive occasion, every name-day or important holiday. No dinner party or celebration would have been complete without it. What sort of name-day would it have been without krendels sprinkled with almonds for breakfast and "Anke cake" in the evening? It would have been like Christmas without a Christmas tree, Easter without rolling eggs, a wet-nurse without her headdress, or kvas without raisins—the occasion would not have been properly consecrated.

All of our family traditions—and *maman* had innovated a great many of them—eventually came to be known as "Anke cake." *Papa* sometimes used the term in a mildly ironic way to allude to *maman's* precepts as a whole. At that remote period of my childhood, however, he could not have failed to value them, for it was thanks to those steadfast principles of hers that we enjoyed an absolutely ideal family life, one that was the envy of all who were familiar with it.[3]

Who could have known then that the time would come when "Anke cake" would be unendurable to Father, an oppressive yoke that he would dream of casting off at any cost?[4]

VIII

Aunt Tanya. Uncle Kostya. The Dyakovs. Urusov

My mother's younger sister, Tatyana Andreyevna Kuzmin-skaya—Aunt Tanya—played a very active role in the life of our family. She died not long ago, having spent the last years of her life with one of her grandchildren at Yasnaya Polyana, which by then was quite deserted. Dear Auntie, I fondly evoke your memory to adorn my story; without you it would not be complete.

Aunt Tanya spent almost every summer with us at Yasnaya Polyana, bringing her whole family and installing them in the annex. The family consisted of herself and her husband, Aleksandr Mikhailovich, her daughters Dasha (who died young in the Caucasus), Masha, and Vera, with whom we were great friends, and four sons. Masha and Vera were our playmates and virtually members of the family; the little boys were much younger and had no part in my life as a child.

I have never known a more captivating woman than Aunt Tanya. She was not beautiful in the usual sense of the word; her mouth was too large, she had a slightly receding chin, and she was just the least bit squint-eyed, but all this only accentuated her extraordinary femininity and allure. She was what the French called *charmante*.

Aunt Tanya was a second mother to us. When she and *maman* both had nursing infants, they sometimes took each other's children to the breast. I cannot think of my past without her. *Maman* loved us—Aunt Tanya adored us; *maman* was always there—Aunt Tanya was with us only in the summer; *maman* scolded us and made us study—Aunt Tanya gave us nothing but pleasure; *maman* was everyday—Aunt Tanya was a holiday.

When we were still children we heard that there had been some sort of "romance" between Aunt Tanya and Uncle Sergei (Sergei Nikolayevich Tolstoy). The particulars of this interesting story are not known to me; all I know is the following. First I shall go back to the late forties, when my father and Uncle Sergei were young men of twenty and twenty-two, respectively. As the youngest son, Lev had inherited Yasnaya Polyana, the ancestral home, and Sergei the Pirogovo estate in the black-earth district of Krapivensky, thirty-five versts from Yasnaya Polyana and fifty from Tula.

Sergei Nikolayevich was a handsome former Imperial Rifleman who was fascinated by gypsies and used to spend whole days and nights in their company. He even introduced his younger brother to these pleasures, the favorite pastime of the gilded youth of the period. Champagne (never vodka—Heaven preserve them from the drink of porters) flowed like water. They went mad over songs such as "Not the Evening," "Once Again I Hear Thee," "The Blue Kerchief," and other popular ballads of the day.

The gypsy chorus of Tula rivaled those of Moscow and Petersburg. Inveterate enthusiasts used to come from Moscow just to hear the singing of some "Fesha" or "Masha." Only in Tula did they know how to sing the authentic gypsy songs. Chopin, Mozart, Beethoven—artificial, trumped up, boring; the only music in the world worth listening to was those gypsy songs. So thought Uncle Sergei in those days, and it is doubtful whether he ever changed his opinion in the matter. Finally he fell in love with a gypsy girl, Maria Mikhailovna Shishkina, and they lived together in a common-law marriage for many years.

Meanwhile my father had gone to the Caucasus, where he took part in the Sevastopol campaign. Afterward he went abroad for a time, was an Arbiter for the Emancipation in 1861, and in 1862 married and brought his young bride to Yasnaya Polyana.

All during this time, Sergei Nikolayevich had been living at Pirogovo. He had not married Maria Mikhailovna, but they had had several children, and if he put off marriage it was only because he did not believe in it, considered it an empty formality, which in any case could be performed at any time. He had given up the dissipations of his youth and devoted himself to his superb stud farm, to hunting, and to cultivating his land. Being an extraordinarily proud man, he was ashamed of his gypsy consort and led a secluded domestic life; he neither visited his neighbors nor invited them to his home. The only place he ever went, and always alone, was to Yasnaya Polyana. And it was there that he met Tatyana Andreyevna, then an unmarried girl of eighteen. They fell madly in love from the first moment. It was as if they were caught up in the vortex of a hurricane that swept everything from its path; it was an elemental force, the "one and only" love that never comes again, is never over or forgotten.

They decided to marry and the wedding day was set. Sergei Nikolayevich went to Tula to make arrangements to terminate his relations with Maria Mikhailovna, give her money, provide for their children, and return her to the gypsy camp. She had resigned herself to her fate, and he was prepared to recompense her generously. In his heart he knew of course that what he was doing was wrong, but as always in such cases, he dismissed

58   TOLSTOY, MY FATHER

these thoughts and tried to persuade himself that there was no other solution, that he had no right to sacrifice his own and Tatyana Andreyevna's happiness.

When he drove up to the house before dawn, all was dark and silent within. He entered cautiously and glanced into Maria Mikhailovna's room. In the flickering light of the icon lamp he saw her on her knees in prayer before the holy image. That same night he sent a letter to Tatyana Andreyevna telling her that the gypsy woman was in despair, and that he could not break with her all at once. Not long afterward he married Maria Mikhailovna and legitimized their children. Aunt Tanya took poison, was gravely ill, but recovered and later married her cousin, Aleksandr Mikhailovich Kuzminsky.

Would Sergei Nikolayevich have been happier had he not happened to look into Maria Mikhailovna's room that night and found her praying? Would he have been happier if he had married Aunt Tanya? I do not believe that the feeling they had for each other ever died. When he used to come to Yasnaya Polyana, I always saw that special look in their eyes when they looked at each other, a look that can never be disguised. They had perhaps succeeded in smothering the flames of the fire, but it was not within their power to extinguish the last sparks.

How could anyone help loving Aunt Tanya? Always gay, beautiful, clever, imaginative, and original, she was all woman. We could play croquet with her the whole day, go hunting or fishing, vie with her in searching for mushrooms—everything. She was not only a beloved aunt, she was our best friend. We considered it the greatest happiness to be invited to dine with her at "the other house."

And how she sang! I realize now that her voice was neither big nor absolutely steady, but if anyone had told me then that it was possible for anyone to surpass her, I would never have believed him. *Papa* often accompanied her on the piano. I can see him now, bent over the keyboard, his back tense with exertion, and hear her pure voice as she stood near him, with eyebrows raised and an ardent expression on her face.

When Ivan Sergeyevich Turgenev used to visit us and listen

to her sing, I was sure he would say she had the finest voice he had ever heard (I did not know then that he was a friend of the celebrated Viardot). I was surprised when he was sparing of his praise and ascribed it to a lack of understanding.

I have heard many excellent singers since then, but none that ever affected me as she did, and particularly at the time of my early adolescence. My God, what she did to me then! Even without that my soul was seething with vague seductive emotions and I went around like a charged battery, not knowing how to expend those secret feelings; even without that my daydreams were filled with alluring images—and to crown it all, her singing! There was "The Murmuring Forest," "A Wonderful Moment," "When in an Hour of Gaiety," and Glinka's mazurka. . . .[1]

On summer evenings the windows of the salon were thrown open and we all assembled there to hear her sing. *Papa* sat down at the piano to accompany her, and suddenly Aunt Tanya's eyes began to glow. We held our breath as *papa* bent over the keyboard and struck the opening chord—it was beginning!

How many times, unable to restrain my tears, I rushed out to the balcony! The moon in a starry sky, deep shadows of the linden trees falling on the meadows, nightingales calling in the lilac bushes. . . . Everything combined to heighten the electrifying tension within me. What could I do? Where could I go? And that pure silvery voice continued to rise in song . . . "divinity, and inspiration, and life, and love, and tears. . . ." [2]

I felt that somewhere that divinity existed, somewhere there was inspiration, and life, and love, and tears, but thus far they were all unknown to me. And I longed for them—painfully, sweetly, and above all fearfully, for I knew that there neither was nor could there be any solution. Those blissful years, when one's inner powers have not yet been squandered, when one's soul is still unsullied—how beautiful, how alluring then the unknown future!

My father was thirty-four years old when he married my mother, and Aunt Tanya was still a young girl, almost a child. Although with time the difference in age became less pro-

nounced, one always felt that *papa* had a rather protective
attitude toward Aunt Tanya, as to a much younger person, and
that she loved and respected him as her elder. So their relations
were on a very good and firm foundation and remained so to
the end. *Papa* always responded to her unexpected outbursts,
which were usually provoked by some minor household annoyance, with good-natured humor, or a jest that never failed to
induce a smile, a rather sulky one at first which gradually
broadened till in the end she was laughing with him. Unlike
maman, she understood a joke and knew how to respond to it.

Later, when I was a grown man, I often asked myself
whether *papa* was in love with Aunt Tanya. I believe now that
he was. But lest the reader misunderstand me, I wish to make
clear at once that I do not mean love in the vulgar sense of a
desire to possess a woman—naturally my father could not have
had such a feeling for Aunt Tanya—I mean the inspirational
feeling of rapture that is accessible only to the pure soul of the
poet. For that kind of feeling the image of a woman is only the
shell, which he himself invests with magic, endowing it with
colors and qualities drawn from the treasure house of his own
soul. Dreams are intangible, and as long as they remain so are
beautiful. Touch a dream and it vanishes. Such wondrous
dreams would dissolve in an instant on awakening.

The feeling my father had for Aunt Tanya, it seems to me,
was what the French call *amitié amoureuse*, though it is regret-
table that they often vulgarize it and give it an unnatural pi-
quancy. I believe that in Father this feeling was so pure that he
himself was unaware of it. He idealized his marriage and family
life to such a degree that for him even the possibility of another
love was inconceivable. He loved my mother with all the
strength of his passionate nature, and was never unfaithful to
her even in thought, but could he purge his soul of dreams?

"I made a mixture of Sofya Andreyevna and Tatyana Andreyevna, stirred it up, and got Natasha," he jokingly remarked.[3]
There is no doubt that Natasha more closely resembles Aunt
Tanya than my mother. Reading *War and Peace* I see her with
her sisters, at the hunt, hear her singing to the accompaniment
of Uncle's guitar—yes, that is Aunt Tanya; everything Natasha

does is exactly as she would have done it. And I ask myself: could an artist have created such a wonderful image without being in love with it? Of course not; one would have to be in love with such a dream, and therein lies the whole mystery.

And there is something else that has often given me pause for thought. Whatever suggested to Father the idea of *The Kreutzer Sonata*? Certainly there is much in it that comes straight out of his own married life. But my mother never gave him cause for overt jealousy, never betrayed him by so much as a touch of the hand. But who was that violinist she accompanied and for whom Pozdnyshev killed his wife?

A long, long time ago, probably in the late seventies, a violinist by the name of Ippolit Nagornov, the brother-in-law of my cousin Varya (Maria Nikolayevna Tolstaya's daughter), came to Yasnaya Polyana. It is hardly necessary to describe him here, as he has been portrayed with stunning accuracy in *The Kreutzer Sonata*. He had received the gold medal from the Paris Conservatory, possessed a marvelous Stradivarius, combed his hair in a bang over his forehead, wore gawdy Parisian neckties, wiggled his hips like a woman when he walked, and had a common, sensual face. But he played absolutely divinely. I have never been as impressed by a violinist as I was by Zipa, as we called him. More often than not it was *papa* who accompanied him, and he occasionally accompanied Aunt Tanya on the violin. And, may she forgive me for this, I seem to remember that my dear Auntie flirted a bit with him. Nagornov spent several days at Yasnaya Polyana, then vanished from our lives, never suspecting that he was destined to inspire one of Tolstoy's masterpieces. It happened that he died not long after this visit, while still a young man.

Was my father jealous of Aunt Tanya at the time? Yes, if one can be jealous of a dream. Outwardly his relation to her was purely brotherly; they were always dear friends and remained so to the end. The dream faded but was never shattered.

I remember Uncle Kostya from my earliest childhood. He was my mother's uncle and my father's boyhood friend. Only much later did I learn that he was the illegitimate son of my

great-grandfather, Aleksandr Mikhailovich Islenyev, and that
his whole life was ruined by his having neither property nor
social position.

Uncle Kostya always turned up unexpectedly and loved taking us by surprise. Returning from a walk we would hear someone playing the piano very brilliantly in the salon, and *papa*
always guessed at once who it was. "It's Kotenka!" he would
say, running upstairs to greet him. By the time we entered the
room the music had stopped and there was Uncle Kostya standing on his head in the corner; or, we might come into the salon
for breakfast one morning and find him sitting at the table solemnly reading a newspaper. No one ever knew when he had
arrived or how he had had time to wash and to part his handsome blond beard so meticulously.

To us children Uncle Kostya was the epitome of elegance and
good breeding. No one could speak French as well as he; no one
could bow as beautifully and say just the right word of greeting; and no one could be so unfailingly amiable. Even when
finding fault with our manners, he always expressed himself so
mildly that it never left an unpleasant impression.

He used to come to us for Christmas and other family holidays, and always remained for some time. When our family
moved to Moscow, Uncle Kostya helped *maman* furnish the
house, gave her advice when she began to go into society, and
was helpful to her in many other ways. He was delighted to act
as master of ceremonies,[4] and was also fond of us children. He
used to tell me that I resembled both of my grandfathers, in
character as well as physique.

Uncle Kostya was a musician of outstanding talent. Nikolai
Rubenstein, with whom he was very friendly at one time, had
predicted a brilliant musical career for him, but unfortunately
Uncle Kostya did not follow that path and remained unsuccessful, solitary, and in straitened circumstances to the end of his
life. Through Katkov *papa* obtained a place for him on the edi-
torial staff of the *Moscow Gazette,* and he worked there for
some time. Later he was superintendent of the Sheremetyev
Hospital, where he died in 1903.

He left absolutely nothing when he died, not even much personal linen. It seems that he had always given whatever he had to the poor. Neither his close friends nor the acquaintances who were accustomed to seeing him elegantly dressed whenever they met him in fashionable drawing rooms ever suspected that this handsome urbane old gentleman had nothing but the clothes on his back and that everything else had been given away to those as unfortunate as himself.

Of all of our visitors during that early period of my childhood, the Dyakovs were our favorites. Like Uncle Kostya, Dmitry Alekseyevich was one of Father's oldest friends. We could hardly believe him when he told us that he could remember Dyakov as a very thin young man, for he was the stoutest man we had ever seen, and had such a round, resilient paunch that with one jerk of his stomach muscles he could bounce a person off it like a rubber ball.

The moment he arrived the entire household was enlivened by his high spirits, and life was gayer than at any other time. We sat listening to him, eagerly awaiting the jokes that made us all roar with laughter—and *papa* loudest of all. Once our footman Yegor, who had put on a red waistcoat for dinner in honor of the visitors, heard one of these jokes while he was serving the blancmange and was seized with such a fit of laughter that to our great amusement he had to set down the plate and rush from the room.

Sometimes Dmitry Alekseyevich sang Glinka duets with Aunt Tanya, and that was always very beautiful. "What a splendid fellow Dyakov is! And how he can sing!" We were all so delighted that we would beg him to sing again and again.

Besides being great personal friends, he and *papa* had a common interest in the management of their estates. The Dyakovs had a large and admirably organized property in the Novosil district, which Dmitry Alekseyevich managed like a model landowner. In those days *papa* too was interested in his property and devoted a great deal of time to it. I can remember his planting a huge apple orchard at Yasnaya and several hundred acres of birch and pine forest, and he was also interested in buying land cheap in Samara for the purpose of breeding steppe horses and sheep.

Although he was in sympathy with my father, Dyakov was never in accord with his convictions; his practical mind, together with his capacity for seeing the comic rather than the tragic side of life, prevented him from sharing Father's new world-view. I believe that their steadfast friendship can be explained by their having been close as youths. *Papa* valued his old friends and always had a warm and sincere affection for them.

I also remember Prince Sergei Semyonovich Urusov from this period of my life. He was an odd and very original man and almost a giant in stature. He had commanded a regiment during the Sevastopol campaign and was said to have distinguished himself by his extraordinary bravery. He used to leave the trenches and walk about under a shower of bullets and shells dressed entirely in white.

The story is told—I recall his having told it to me himself—that after the harrowing siege of Sevastopol he had to turn his regiment over to another general, a pedantic German, who when reviewing the troops berated a soldier for a missing button on his uniform. Urusov shouted an order to the soldier: "Fire on him!" The man obeyed the command, taking care not to hit the general, of course. Urusov narrowly escaped being discharged from the army, but in the end was pardoned.

During the siege he made a proposal to the Allies that the conflict be settled by a game of chess, thereby avoiding further bloodshed. He himself was an excellent chess player and could easily beat my father even after giving him a knight.

We children were rather intimidated by him because of his enormous size, his deep bass voice, and the St. George Cross he wore in his buttonhole. In spite of his great height, he always wore big heels on his shoes, and even reproached me for not wearing them. "How can you disfigure yourself so?" he once said to me, pointing to my shoes. "The beauty of a man is in his stature—everyone ought to wear heels."

By some means, higher mathematics perhaps, he used to calculate everyone's life span, and assured my parents that he knew exactly when they would die. He kept this information to himself, however, and never told anyone.

He was a strict Orthodox believer and a mystic. I do not know whether or not he influenced my father to turn first to the church at the beginning of his religious quest, but it seems quite possible that Urusov may have had something to do with it.

IX

Journey to Samara

I still have rather vivid, if somewhat fragmentary and inconsequent, memories of our three summer excursions to the Samara steppes. *Papa* had gone there in 1862, before his marriage, and later on the advice of Dr. Zakharin, who was treating him. He took the kumiss cure in 1871 and '72, and in 1873 the whole family accompanied him. He had bought several hundred acres of land in the Buzuluk district, and we lived at a farm on our new property.

I recall with particular clarity, for some reason, our first journey. We went by way of Moscow and Nizhny Novgorod, and down the Volga to Samara on a wonderful steamer that belonged to the Caucasus and Mercury Company. The captain, a charming, amiable man, turned out to have been at Sevastopol with my father in the Crimean campaign.

We touched at Kazan in the daytime, and when the boat docked, *papa*, Seryozha, and I roamed about the outskirts of the town. *Papa* wanted to have a look, even if from a distance, at the city where he had once lived as a university student. We were so engrossed in conversation that we were unaware of the passage of time and walked too far. When we got back we found that the steamer had left sometime before and was a mere speck on the horizon.

Papa exclaimed loudly and began making inquiries about other steamers going in the same direction, but it seemed that those of the other companies had all departed earlier and we would have to wait in Kazan till the next day. *Papa* groaned, having no money with him, and I of course bellowed like a calf. *Maman*, Aunt Tanya, and the rest of the family had gone off and left us all alone! A crowd of sympathetic onlookers gathered round and tried to comfort me.

All at once someone noticed that the little speck we had been watching on the horizon was growing bigger and bigger, and it soon became apparent that the boat had turned around and was coming back. A few minutes later it reached the pier and we were taken on board and continued our journey.

Papa was terribly embarrassed by the captain's kindness in acceding to *maman's* request and coming back for us; he could not thank him enough and even wanted to pay for the extra wood that had been burned. Now that the steamer had returned for him, his groans were even louder than they had been when it was disappearing into the distance, and he was exceedingly mortified.

From Samara we traveled a hundred and twenty versts in several two-horse wicker chaises and a huge *dormeuse* carriage drawn by six horses and with a postillion. *Maman,* who was nursing my little brother Petya at the time (he died in the autumn of that year), rode in the *dormeuse* with the younger children Lyolya and Masha, while Seryozha, Tanya, and I changed about, riding either in *papa's* chaise, or on the box of the *dormeuse*, or in the two-seated dickey attached to the back of it.

In Samara we lived in a ramshackle wooden house at the farm, and not far from us in the steppe were pitched two felt nomad tents where our Bashkir, Muhammadshah Romanych, lived with his wives. Morning and evening the mares were tied up outside these tents and milked by veiled women, who then concealed themselves from the sight of men behind a motley calico curtain inside the tent and made the kumiss.

The kumiss was sour and unsavory, but *papa* and Uncle Styopa liked it immensely and drank quantities of it every day. They would go into the tent, where Muhammadshah Romanych greeted them cordially with his toothless smile, and sit cross-legged on cushions ranged in a semicircle on a Persian rug. From behind the curtain the hand of an unseen woman held out a leather drinking pouch filled with kumiss. The Bashkir beat it up with a special stirrer, then took a ladle of Karelian birchwood and ceremoniously filled the cups with the foaming white liquid. The cups too were of birchwood and of various sizes, some large and shallow, others narrow and deep. *Papa* always took the biggest cup, and holding it in both hands drained it at one draught. Romanych filled it again and again, and Father often drank eight cups or more at a sitting.

"Why don't you drink some, Ilya? Try it, it's delicious!" he said, offering me a brimming cup. "You have only to drink it straight off and you'll ask for more." I forced myself to take a mouthful or two, and although *papa* and Styopa drank it three times a day, I found the taste and smell so revolting that I rushed from the tent and spat it out.

My father was very much interested in farming and horse breeding at that time. We had droves of mares roving the steppe, each drove with its stallion. The horses were of several different breeds: English racehorses, stud horses of the old-fashioned Rostopchin breeds, trotters, Bashkirs, and Argamaks. Eventually our stud farm comprised four hundred head, but in the eighties, after the famine years in which many perished, the whole enterprise somehow dissolved. A few of the Samara horses were brought to Yasnaya Polyana. They were excellent saddle horses and we rode them for many years. Several of their stock are still living.

That summer *papa* organized horse races. A ring of five versts was measured and marked with a plow furrow, and word was sent to all the neighboring Bashkirs and Kirghizes that there were to be races with prizes for the winners. The prizes were a gun, a silver watch, and a silk Tatar robe.

I should perhaps mention that on our second visit to Samara, in 1875, we also had horse races, and it is possible that I have confused the two and am recounting what happened the second time. This is of no importance, however.[1]

The Bashkirs began to arrive a day or two before the appointed time, bringing with them their tents, horses, and wives. In the steppe, alongside Muhammadshah Romanych's tent, a whole village of *kibitkas* sprang up, each with its own horse ties and earthen stove for cooking. The steppe came to life. Veiled women glided in and out of the tents; portly, dignified Bashkirs were seen strolling about; and the horses training for the race flew by with their wildly whooping riders.

Two days were spent in feasting and preparing for the race. Vast quantities of kumiss were consumed, along with fifteen sheep, a horse, and a legless English colt that had been fattened specially for the occasion. In the evenings, after the heat of the day had abated, the men in their distinctive varicolored robes and embroidered skullcaps gathered for bouts of wrestling. *Papa* was stronger than any of them, and when two men sat on the ground and had a tug-of-war with a stick, he could always pull his opponent to his feet. The only man he was unable to defeat was a Russian village elder who weighed over three hundred pounds. He would pull with all his might, lift him halfway off the ground, and just when it looked as if he would have him on his feet, the elder suddenly flopped back onto the ground with his full weight, and *papa,* raised to his feet, stood before him smiling and shrugging his shoulders.

One of the Bashkirs was very good at "playing on the throat," and *papa* always made him perform. This is a very curious art. The performer lies down on his back, and it is as if a little organ were playing deep in his throat and emitting pure, delicate, and rather metallic tones. It is hard for the listener to understand where these sweet, melodious, and unaccountable sounds come from. There are no longer many practitioners of the art, and even at that time it was said to be dying out among the Bashkirs.

On the day of the races everyone went to the course, the women in covered carriages and the men on horseback. A great many horses ran, and one of ours took second prize. A distance of twenty-five versts was run in thirty-nine minutes. Afterward *papa* took us to Karalyk to pay a visit to the Bashkirs, and we were given mutton soup. The host took pieces of mutton in his hands and distributed them to his guests, and when one of the Bashkirs refused what was offered to him, the host wiped his face with the greasy lump of mutton as with a sponge, till the visitor gave in and ate it.

Later we walked out into the steppe to look at the Bashkir's herds. *Papa* expressed his admiration for a certain light bay horse, and when we were getting ready to go home we found it tied to the shaft of our cart. *Papa* was embarrassed, but to have refused the gift would have offended our host, Nikita Andreyevich, so we were obliged to accept it, and my father had to make him a substantial present of gold pieces in return.

Another Bashkir, Mikhail Ivanovich, visited us several times. *Papa* enjoyed playing checkers with him. During the game Mikhail Ivanovich kept repeating, "Have to think. A bi-i-g think." But he often lost the game in spite of his "big think," as *papa* usually blocked his men and he was unable to move. This always delighted us children and made us laugh uproariously.

We boys lived with our German tutor, Fyodor Fyodorovich, in an empty barn in which rats ran about squeaking at night. Flocks of beautiful *dudaks*, or bustards, roved the steppe near the house, while huge golden eagles soared high in the clouds. Sometimes *papa*, Styopa, and Fyodor Fyodorovich tried to shoot the bustards, but they were cautious birds and it was almost impossible to get within range of them. Once Fyodor Fyodorovich managed to creep up on one from behind a flock of sheep and wounded it. When the bird was brought home alive, held by the wings from either side, we all rushed out to see it. This was such a momentous event that I still remember it, and many years later, when he was old and paralytic, Fyodor Fyodorovich came to see me and he too recalled the occasion.

Papa left the farm several times to go to buy horses at the Buzuluk and Orenburg fairs. I remember the first time a drove of wild steppe horses were driven into the enclosure. When the men tried to catch them with a stick-lasso, several of the horses made a run for the earthen-brick wall, jumped over it, and galloped off into the steppe. Our Bashkir, Lutai, galloped after them on our swiftest horse and drove them back into the enclosure late that night.

This same Bashkir could break in the most refractory of wild horses. Once the horse had been lassoed and bridled, two men held it by the bit and the ears, and Lutai jumped onto its back and shouted, "Let go!" He gave the horse rein and they disappeared into the steppe. Hours later he brought it in at a walk, and although in a lather, the horse was as docile as if it had been ridden for years.

Once Father brought back from Orenburg a wonderful white Bokhara Argamak, and a pair of young donkeys that we took back to Yasnaya Polyana and rode for many years. *Papa* named them Bismarck and MacMahon.

On our second visit to Samara, in 1875, he rode into Buzuluk to see an old hermit who had lived in a cave for twenty-five years.[2] He had heard of this man from the local peasants, who revered him as a saint. I begged to be taken along, but because my eyes were very bad at the time he refused to take me. I don't believe that the hermit had anything particularly interesting to say, however, since I have no recollection of our being told about him.

The first year we were at the farm there was a serious crop failure in the province of Samara, and I remember my father riding through the villages and going from door to door to make a register of the condition of the peasants' property.[3] The first question he asked at every house was whether the owners were Orthodox or Molokans, and he was particularly interested in discussing religious questions with the dissenters.

The peasant he liked best to converse with was a dignified, intelligent old man, Vasily Nikitich, who lived in Gavrilovka, the nearest village to us. Whenever he went to the village, *papa* stopped at his house and had a long talk with him. I cannot recall what they discussed, since I was quite small at the time and neither famines nor religious questions were of much interest to me. I only remember that Vasily Nikitich kept repeating the word "reely" [4] and that he "found sustenance in tea," which he always served to us with the most wonderful clear white honey.

X

Games. Father's Jokes. Books and Lessons

Eᴠᴇʀ since I can remember, we children were divided into "the big ones" and "the little ones." * The big ones were Seryozha, Tanya, and I, and the little ones were Lyolya and Masha, who was called "little Masha" * to distinguish her from our cousin "big Masha" * Kuzminskaya. We older children always kept apart and never admitted the younger ones into our company, since they were incapable of understanding anything and only spoiled our games. It was on their account that we had to be in the house early—they might catch cold; on their account that we were not allowed to make any noise—they had to have their naps; and if one of them cried or complained to *maman* about anything, it was always we who were scolded and punished.

---

*In English in the original.—*Tr.*

I got along best with my sister Tanya, who was closest to me in age and temperament. She was a year and a half older than I, black-eyed, vivacious, and imaginative. We always had fun together and understood each other without words. She and I knew things that no one else could understand.

We loved running around the dining table in the salon. I would hit her on the shoulder and run off as fast as my legs would carry me. "Last tag! Last tag!" Then she would run after me, give me a slap, and dash off again. "Last tag! Last tag!" Once I caught up with her and was just about to "tag" her when she suddenly turned around and began jumping up and down in front of me, flapping her arms and crying, "This is an owl! This is an owl!" Naturally, I realized at once that if "this" was an owl, it was out of the question to touch it. And from then on whenever anyone said, "This is an owl," he couldn't be touched.

Seryozha, of course, would never have understood this. He would have begun by asking a lot of questions and arguing about why an owl couldn't be touched, and in the end would have decided that the whole thing was pointless. But I immediately saw that it was very clever. Tanya knew that I would understand her and that was why she had done it.

Papa was the only person who really understood Tanya and me—but not always. He had some very good tricks of his own, and taught us a few. For instance, there was his "Numidian cavalry." We would all be sitting in the salon, rather subdued after the departure of boring visitors, when suddenly he would jump up, raise one arm, and prance full speed around the table. We all flew after him, skipping and waving our arms as he did. After racing around the room several times, our mood changed and we sat down again in a different frame of mind, breathless, but invigorated and cheerful. There were many times when the "Numidian cavalry" had a very salutary effect: quarrels and hurt feelings were forgotten, and tears dried up with remarkable celerity.

Also effective for such purposes were the humorous verses Father used to recite to us. I don't know where he got them, I only know that they amused us enormously. One of them went like this:

> Die angenehme Winterzeit
> Ist fery nice indeet,
> Beweilen wird's ein wenig kalt,
> Unless it turns to heat.
> Auch wenn man noch nach Hause kommt,
> Da steht der Punsch bereit,
> Ist das nicht fery fery nice
> An kalter Winterzeit!

Another of these verses, which was also recited in broken German, was:

> Toctor, Toctor Hüppenthal,
> Take pity on me please!
> I'm dying of starvation
> And tobacco deprivation,
> Enough! Enough! Enough!

Such verses were turned to good account on many an occasion when, for no particular reason, one of us seemed to have "swimming eyes."

At this period of our childhood, we were deeply engrossed in reading Jules Verne. *Papa* had brought the books from Moscow, and every evening read aloud to us from *The Children of Captain Grant, Twenty Thousand Leagues Under the Sea, From the Earth to the Moon, Three Russians and Three Englishmen*, and *Around the World in Eighty Days*. The last of these had no illustrations, and *papa* decided to illustrate it for us himself. Each day he prepared the appropriate pen and ink drawings for the evening, and the pictures were so fascinating that we preferred them to those in the other books. I can still see one of his drawings, which represented a fantastic frightening Indian goddess with several heads adorned with snakes.

Father really didn't know how to draw; nevertheless the pictures all turned out well and we were enormously pleased. We could hardly wait for evening to come, and when he reached the place he had illustrated and interrupted his reading to take the drawing out from under the book, we all crawled across the table to see it.[1]

Jules Verne was followed by Dumas's *The Three Musketeers*, which our tutor, Monsieur Nief, read to us, but only after *papa* had crossed out the passages we were not supposed to hear. We were terribly curious about those forbidden pages, which described the love affairs of the heroes, and were eager to read them in secret, but we could never quite bring ourselves to do it.

Earlier I spoke of our beloved nurse, Hannah. After her came young red-cheeked Dora, then Emily, then Carrie, and the last of our English nurses departed when my youngest brothers, Andrei and Mikhail, were grown. As I have said, we boys always had tutors after a certain age, the first of whom was Fyodor Fyodorovich Kaufmann. I can't say that we were particularly fond of him; his only redeeming feature was perhaps that of being an ardent hunter. He had a habit of pulling the blankets off us in the morning and shouting, *"Auf, Kinder, auf!"* and then tormenting us during the day with German calligraphy.

He had thick dark hair, which was always smoothly combed. I once woke up at night and, still half-asleep, saw him sitting in front of the mirror shaving himself, his head as bald as an egg. I was very frightened, and he ordered me to turn over and go back to sleep. In the morning I didn't know whether what I had seen was real or a dream. It turned out that Fyodor Fyodorovich wore a wig, a fact he had always taken great pains to conceal.

Our next tutor was a Swiss, Monsieur Rey, who was with us for several years, and he was followed by the French communard, Monsieur Nief—the one who took a squirrel and a viper to the kitchen to be roasted. In Russian we called them simply Gray and Blue, because one always dressed in gray and the other in blue. When the Amnesty was proclaimed in France, Monsieur Nief departed for Algeria, and it was only then that we learned that his real name was Vicomte de Montels.

Speaking of Monsieur Nief, I should like to relate an amusing incident that illustrates his character. Once when we were sitting at tea in the evening, *papa* was looking through the *Moscow Gazette,* which had just come by post. It reported an attempt on the life of Emperor Aleksandr II.[2] Reading it aloud to us, *papa* translated it into French for the benefit of Monsieur Nief. When he reached the place where it said, "But God preserved His anointed one," he read, *"Mais le bon Dieu a conservé son—son—"* and hesitated, evidently searching for the French word for "anointed one." *"Son sang-froid?"* suggested Monsieur Nief, quite seriously. We all roared with laughter, and that ended the newspaper reading.

I have already mentioned how *papa* taught me arithmetic when I was a small boy. Later, when I was about thirteen, he taught me Greek. I remember when he himself began studying it; he applied himself with such zeal and perseverance that in six weeks he was able to read and translate Herodotus and Xenophon. It was on Xenophon that he started us. He explained the alphabet to me and immediately set me to work on the *Anabasis.* It was hard at first; I used to sit glassy-eyed, sometimes even cried, but realizing that it had to be done, I learned it.

I also studied Latin. When I took the entrance examination at Polivanov's Classical School in 1881, I surprised the teachers by reading and translating the classics far better than was required, though I was completely ignorant of the grammar. In this I see a proof that my father's original method of teaching was the right one.

Later he studied Hebrew in exactly the same way and got to know it so well that he had no difficulty reading any passage he wanted to in the Old Testament, and frequently submitted his own interpretations of certain texts to Rabbi Minor, his teacher.

XI

Horseback Riding. "The Green Stick." Skating

THE predominant passion of my childhood was horseback riding. I remember the time described by my father in a letter quoted earlier in these memoirs, when he used to put me in front of him on his horse and we rode off to bathe in the Voronka.

I remember how I was jounced up and down when he trotted, how my hat used to fall off in the forest, and Seryozha or Styopa had to dismount and pick it up. But above all I remember the smell of the horse when I approached it and the footman Sergei Petrovich took me by the leg and hoisted me into the saddle. I clung to the horse's withers as to a life preserver and held on for dear life.

When we reached the bathing place, we would tie the horses to birch trees and run down the little footbridge. *Papa* and Styopa always dove into the river headfirst, but we splashed about in the shallow water of the bathhouse and watched the

little fish and the swift long-legged spiders that skittered over
the surface of the water and for some reason never seemed to
drown. *Papa* taught us to swim, and when we were at last able
to leave the confines of the bathhouse and swim out into the
river, we boasted about it to everyone and felt that it showed
great courage.

Our first horses were Kolpik and Kashirsky. Fyodor Fyodorovich used to call them *"der Kolpinka und der Kassaschirsky."*
My first ride alone was on the white horse, Kolpik, and from
then on I was able to ride without help.

Papa sometimes took us riding with him, and then we rode
a long way. I shall never forget the torment I was subjected to
on one occasion. Hearing that he was going out I begged to be
taken along. He was riding a sturdy English mare, and they
gave me a Samara bay—the one that had taken second prize in
the race—with only a saddlecloth and no stirrups. It was an
easy horse to ride, but its back was thin and bony. We set off,
and the moment we reached a level place *papa* put his horse to
a brisk trot and I jogged along behind him. We rode on and on
till we were about five versts from home. I was so exhausted I
could hardly endure it, but he kept going farther and farther.
He would glance back now and then and say, "Not tired, are
you?" to which I of course replied, "No!" and on we went.

We rode all over the forest reserve, following footpaths and
ravines to beyond Grumont, and when at last we reached home
I could hardly get off the horse. For three days I went around
like a cripple, and everyone laughed at me and called me "John
Gilpin," after the hero of an amusing English poem.[1] Gilpin's
horse ran away with him and, unable to stop it, he galloped on
for a dreadfully long time, having all sorts of adventures. When
he was finally taken off the horse he was bowlegged. We were
very fond of the pictures in this book, one of which was of John
Gilpin a-gallop, his wig flying through the air, and another
after he had dismounted, bald and bowlegged.

I have several other interesting recollections connected with
our rides to the bathhouse. First among them is the story of the

"Green Stick." At the top of the ravine, to the right of the "bath-house road," is a place which I have described earlier, where the path leads through a clump of oaks with peculiarly artificial soil beneath them. It was just here, according to *papa*, that his brother Nikolai buried the mysterious green stick with which he associated a naive and childlike legend of his own devising. "If one of the ant-brothers finds this stick, he will enjoy great happiness, and by the power of love bring happiness to all mankind." [2] *Papa* liked to tell us this story whenever we rode past the spot, and he always related it with special tenderness. I remember asking him one day what the stick looked like, and was prepared to take a spade and go in search of it.

Another recollection from that same period is of a day when we were on our way to the river to bathe, and out of a clear sky he turned to me and said, "Do you know, Ilyusha, I'm very pleased with myself today. For three days now I've been tormented by her and couldn't get her to go into that house. I just couldn't do it, that's all. It wouldn't come out right. But today it suddenly occurred to me that every entrance hall has a mirror and every lady wears a hat. And as soon as I had thought of that, she went right where I wanted her to go and did everything she was supposed to do. Now, you may think that a hat is a mere trifle, but it all worked out because of that hat."

Recalling this conversation now, I realize that Father must have been talking about the scene in *Anna Karenina* where Anna goes to see her son. Although in its final form there is nothing in this scene about either a hat or a mirror—only a thick black veil is mentioned—I presume that when he was working on this section of the novel he must have had Anna go to a mirror either to arrange her hat or to take it off.

When I think of the vivacity with which he told me this, I find it curious that he should have shared such a subtle creative experience with a boy of seven who was hardly capable of sympathizing with his feeling at the time. This sort of thing was not unusual with him, however.

I once heard him give a very interesting definition of what a writer needs for his work. "You can't imagine how important your mood is," he said. "Sometimes you get up in the morning, fresh, vigorous, clearheaded; you begin to write and it's all sound and coherent—and next day you read it over and have to throw everything out because, although it's good, the chief thing is lacking. There's no imagination, no artistry, it lacks 'that certain something,' that special nuance, without which all your cleverness is worth nothing.[3] Another day you get up having slept badly, your nerves strained, and you think—now, today I'll write well. And, in fact, you write beautifully, graphically, with all the imagination you could wish for. You look it over—again it's worthless, because it's written stupidly. The color is there, but it lacks intellect. Only when intelligence and imagination are in balance can writing be good. As soon as one overpowers the other—you can throw it out and make a fresh start."

And, indeed, there was no end to his rewriting. His capacity for such work was truly astonishing.

Besides riding and hunting, we were terribly enthusiastic about croquet and skating. As soon as the pond froze over, we got out our skates and spent all our free time on the ice. We could hardly sit still at our lessons and kept gazing at the windows covered with hoarfrost in delicate patterns of lace, fern fronds, and little stars. The morning sun appeared bright red behind these patterns. It was cold outside, but in the house fires crackled in the stoves and Semyon, who tended them, brought in extra bundles of frozen birch logs and dumped them on the floor with a clatter.

Time for lunch at last! *"Lavez vos mains,"* and we run upstairs. *Maman* sits in front of the samovar drinking coffee; she never ate lunch. We sit down at the table, bolt our food, and race downstairs to put on sheepskin coats, boots, and caps with earlaps, then pick up our skates and run down to the pond.

Monsieur Nief, in a short black sheepskin coat, hunched over with cold and rubbing his hands, keeps repeating, *"Oh, les russes sont frileux!"* Why, when he himself was freezing, he should blame the Russians for feeling cold, is incomprehensible, but of no interest to us.

We put on our skates and begin to run races. The paths to the pond have all been cleared, but we ourselves make little lanes, and labyrinths, and blind alleys and run around in them. *Papa* and *maman* come out and put on skates too. Though my feet are chilled and my fingers numb, not a word do I say for fear of being sent home to get warm. Everyone has a wonderful time. Even when it is past time to go home, we plead for just a few more minutes. The village children come and marvel at our skill. This flatters our vanity and we begin doing all sorts of tricks, showing off till we all but fall on our faces.

"Time to go home!"

When we reach home it turns out that in spite of my earlaps my ears have turned white. *Papa* takes some snow and rubs them with it unmercifully. Oh, how it hurts! But I must endure it without a whimper, or next day I'll be left at home.

At the beginning of winter, when the ice was not yet firm, we were not allowed to skate on the Big Pond, but had to go to the Lower Pond, which was smaller and, what was more important, shallower. *Papa* told us a story about this Lower Pond. Once, when he was a child, a boy called Volodenka Ogarev, a conceited, self-important boy who was scornful of everything, came to visit them. The Tolstoy children took him out to show him the park, and when he saw the pond he very pompously and contemptuously said, "And what's that?" "A pond." "That —a pond?" he said, "I could jump over it." "Go ahead, jump!" the children cried, egging him on. Volodenka took a running start from the top of the knoll and jumped. Of course he landed right in the middle of the pond and would probably have drowned if some women who were haymaking nearby had not pulled him out with their rakes. That took him down a peg or two.

I once played an awfully dirty trick at the pond, for which I payed dearly afterward. We had gone there to skate and five or six village boys of about my own age joined us. The ice was thin and we kept hearing loud, splintering metallic reports here and there. I took it into my head to test the soundness of the ice, and gathering the boys together told them that at the count of three they were to jump with all their might. I myself stood off to one side. The boys jumped, the ice gave way under them, and they all fell to the bottom of the pond in a heap. Fortunately it was at the shallow end, and no harm was done. The children were taken into the house, dried, and given hot tea. And I was punished.

A wooden tobogganing hill was built for us on the Big Pond, and all winter long tracks were cleared on it. Seryozha was the swiftest among us, but once he failed to get out of our way at a crossing and Tanya and I collided with him going full speed. We all fell in a heap, Seryozha on the bottom, and when we got up we saw that his face was blue and his legs were twitching. He was helped to his feet and taken home at once. Though he walked briskly and carried his own skates, he didn't seem to realize or remember anything. When we asked him what day it was he said he didn't know; he was even unaware that it was Sunday and that we had no lessons. They sent to Tula for a doctor at once, applied leeches to his ears, and he slept for twenty-four hours. The next day he was completely well.

Another time, my brother Lyolya, who was eight at the time, saw a big hole covered with a thin layer of ice and skated right over it. Fortunately the ice did not crack till he reached the far side, where he could catch hold of the embankment. Some women who were rinsing linen at another ice hole saw that he was drowning and pulled him out. They carried him home in his wet sheepskin coat and he was rubbed with alcohol. There was much oh-ing and ah-ing over him: it seems that the place where he had fallen in was deep and he might very well have drowned.

XII

Hunting

W E were ardent hunters from earliest child-
hood. I remember Father's favorite dog, an Irish setter named
Dora, as well as I remember myself. And I remember too the
cart drawn by a docile horse in which we drove to the marsh,
either to Degatna or Malakhovo. *Papa* sat on the seat, sometimes with *maman* or the coachman beside him, and I sat on the
floor with Dora. When we reached the marsh, *papa* got out,
stood his gun on the ground, and holding it in his left hand began to load it. First he poured powder into both barrels, then
inserted wads of felt which he tamped down with a ramrod.
The ramrod struck the wad and bounced up again with a metallic sound, and *papa* went on tamping it till it sprang right out
of the muzzle. Then he poured in shot and tamped that down
too. Dora meanwhile was restlessly trotting about, whining
with impatience and wagging her bushy tail in broad sweeps.

When *papa* went into the marsh, we drove around the bank
not far behind him and breathlessly followed the ranging of the

dog, the flushing of snipe, and the shooting. *Papa* sometimes shot well, but he often got excited and missed badly.

In spring we enjoyed going tracking with him. Sometimes we took our stand in the forest reserve near the "Green Stick," but our favorite place was on the other side of the Voronka, where there had been an apiary years before. Our one-eyed beekeeper still lived there in a low smoke-blackened hut.

Papa was very keen on hunting in the autumn when the woodcocks flew over, and a rivalry sprang up between him and our tutor. Fyodor Fyodorovich usually went *zur Eisenbahn* to where the railway crossed the forest reserve, while *papa's* favorite spot was beyond the Voronka. Returning at dinnertime, they traded stories, each boasting of his bag. When Fyodor Fyodorovich came back with fewer birds than *papa,* he always said it was because *papa* had the advantage of a dog. Once the opposite proved true, however. *Papa* had decided not to go hunting that day and let Fyodor Fyodorovich take Dora. But when he had gone *papa* couldn't resist, and taking his gun went off to the woods without saying a word to anyone. When they came back at dinner time, he brought in a brace more than Fyodor Fyodorovich. According to him, the woodcocks flew lower when there was no dog there and were therefore easier to hit. So Fyodor Fyodorovich was shown up, and we children were delighted.

There was a short period in my youth, two or three years perhaps, when I used to go hunting with *papa.* At that time he had his black spotted Bulka and I had an extraordinarily intelligent and independent pointer called Malysh. Even after Father had given up hunting, Malysh used to accompany him on his walks, and he grew so fond of the dog that he never went out without him. He used to tell us how Malysh came to his study to invite him to go for a walk. The door would open at the accustomed hour, and in came Malysh. If he saw that my father was working at his desk, he looked at him timidly out of the corner of his eye and quietly crept in on his pads with his claws drawn in. When *papa* glanced up at him, he responded with an almost imperceptible movement of the tail and lay down under the table. "Just as if he knew I was busy and mustn't be disturbed," Father said, amazed at the dog's sensitivity.

Our favorite sport was coursing with wolfhounds. How happy we were when the footman Sergei Petrovich came to our room, candle in hand, and woke us up before dawn! We leaped out of bed, full of energy and joy, and, shivering in the cold morning air, hastily dressed and ran to the salon, where the samovar was boiling and *papa* was waiting for us. Sometimes *maman* came out in her dressing gown and made us put on sweaters and mittens and an extra pair of woollen stockings. "What are you going to wear, Lyovochka?" she would say to *papa*. "It's very cold today and there's a wind. Again only the Kuzminsky coat? * You must put on something more underneath—please do it for me." *Papa* always made a face, but in the end gave in, then belted the short gray overcoat and went out.

Day was just breaking as the horses were brought around to the house. We mounted and rode first to "the other house," or to the kennel to get the dogs. Agafya Mikhailovna would be anxiously waiting for us, the dog collars in her gnarled bony hands, coatless in spite of the cold and her black jacket open and revealing her dirty withered old bosom flecked with snuff.

"Have you gone and fed them again?" asked *papa* sternly, looking at the dogs' distended bellies.

"Fed them? Not at all, I only gave them each a crust of bread."

"Then why are they licking their chops?"

"There was a bit of yesterday's oatmeal left."

"You see! Now the hares will all get away again! You are simply impossible. What do you do it for—just to spite me?"

"Well, Lev Nikolayevich, the dogs can't be running all day

---

*This was my father's favorite overcoat. He had bought it years before from A. M. Kuzminsky. It was a light gray coat that had the special virtue of fitting everyone. It was twice turned within my memory.—*I.T.*

on an empty stomach, you know," she snapped as she angrily began to put on their collars. "This one for Krylatka, this one for Sultan, and this for Milka . . ."

In a corner under a blanket lay the smoke-colored Tuman, who wagged his tail and growled as she approached. When I stroked his short silky coat he stiffened all over and growled in an affectionate, comical way. "Tumasha, Tumasha . . ." "Grrr . . . grrr . . . grrr . . ." "Tumasha, Tumasha . . ." "Grrr . . . grrr . . . grrr . . ." like a cat purring.

At last the dogs were ready, some on leashes, others running free, and we rode at a brisk footpace past the Bitter Well and the grove, out into open country.

"Line out!" *papa* ordered, indicating the directions we were to take, and we spread out over the stubble fields and meadows, whistling, winding in and out of the steep balks, beating the bushes with our hunting crops, and peering sharply at every little mark or spot on the ground.

Something white appears ahead. I peer intently at it, take up the reins, examine the leash, and can scarcely believe my good luck in having come upon a hare at last. I ride closer and closer, my eyes glued to it. It turns out not to be a hare at all, but a horse's skull. What a pity! I glance back at *papa* and Seryozha. "I wonder whether they saw that I mistook a bone for a hare?"

Papa, looking alert, sits on his English saddle with the wooden stirrups smoking a cigarette, while Seryozha appears to be having difficulty trying to disentangle a leash. "No, thank Heaven, nobody saw me, otherwise how ashamed I should have felt!"

We ride on. The horse's even gait begins to lull me to sleep; it's boring not getting anything up. Then suddenly, just when I least expect it, a hare springs up only twenty paces in front of me. The dogs have already seen it and are in full pursuit. "Halloo! Halloo!" I cry frantically, and whipping my horse with all my might fly after them.

The dogs come up with the hare but miss it, then miss it a second time; the young and mettlesome Sultan and Milka scud past it, come up with it again, and again fly past it. At last the old experienced Krylatka, who has been galloping alongside, seizes the moment, makes a spurt, the hare gives a helpless cry like a baby, and the dogs surround it, sinking their fangs into it and pulling it in all directions. "Let go! Let go!" We gallop up, finish off the hare, and give the dogs the pads, tearing them off toe by toe and tossing them to our favorites, who catch them midair. *Papa* teaches us how to strap the hare to the saddle and we ride on.[1]

We are in high spirits after the coursing and go on to better places near Yasenki and Retinki. More hares are put up, and before long we all have quarry strapped to our saddles and begin to dream of a fox. But foxes rarely turned up, and when they did it was generally the old and selective Tumashka who distinguished himself. He was no longer interested in hares and made no effort to pursue them, but would go after a fox for all he was worth, and almost always caught it.

Sometimes it was late, after dark, by the time we got home. We unstrapped the hares and laid them out on the floor in the entrance hall. *Maman* came downstairs with the younger children and grumbled over the bloodstains on the floor, but *papa* was on our side, and we didn't care in the least about the floor. What did a few stains matter, when we had run down eight hares and a fox! And besides, we were tired.

Once when we were hunting, *papa* and Styopa had a quarrel. We were about twenty versts from home, near Yagodnoe, and Styopa was riding through a sparse wood when a hare jumped out right under him. He let his dogs go and we ran the hare down. *Papa* came galloping up and hotly rebuked him for coursing a hare in the woods. "You'll kill the dogs, running them into the trees like that! How can you do such a thing?" Styopa made some retort and they both lost their tempers. After a caustic exchange, Styopa handed his dogs over to Seryozha and set off for home without another word.

We spread out over the field and rode off in another direction. Suddenly we saw a hare spring up in front of Styopa. He started, spurred his horse, and shouted, "Halloo!" He was about to go after it when the thought of his quarrel with "Lyovochka" evidently made him change his mind, and reining in his horse (he was riding Frou-Frou), he rode on at a footpace without looking back.

The hare turned in our direction and we let the dogs go and ran it down. After it had been strapped up, *papa* remembered Styopa and felt ashamed of having been so harsh with him. "Oh, how wrong that was, how disagreeable!" he said, looking toward the retreating figure in the distance. "We must go after him. Seryozha, go and tell him that I beg him not to be angry with me and to come back. And tell him we ran the hare down," he shouted after Seryozha, who had put spurs to his horse and galloped off, delighted for Styopa's sake.

Styopa was soon back with us and we continued hunting till evening, in high spirits and without further mishap.

Still more interesting was the coursing over new snow. The excitement began the night before. Would the weather settle? Would the snow cease falling in the night? Would there be a blizzard?

Early in the morning we ran out to the salon half-dressed and scanned the horizon. If the horizon line was clearly defined, it meant the weather had settled and we could go, but if it melted into the sky, it meant that the snow was still drifting over the fields, covering the tracks made during the night. We waited for *papa,* sometimes venturing to send someone to wake him, and then we all got ready and set out.

This kind of hunting is specially interesting because you can follow the hare's entire nocturnal life by his tracks. You see where he got up and went in search of food, where he tore at the snow-covered vegetation, broke down the wormwood, sat down, gamboled about, and at last, having eaten his fill and grown tired of running, turned to find a den for the day. And it is here that his cunning begins. He doubles, covers his tracks, doubles again, and even triples to cover them. When he is finally convinced that they are sufficiently obscured, he digs himself a hole under the warm lee side of a balk and lies down on it.

Whoever discovered his track had to hold up his hunting crop and give a long mysterious whistle. The rest of the hunters rode up, *papa* went ahead to make out the track, and we cautiously followed, holding our breath with excitement. Once when coursing in new snow we ran down twelve hares and two foxes in a single day.

I do not recall exactly when my father gave up hunting. I believe it was in the mid-eighties, at the time he became a vegetarian.[2]

On October 28, 1884, he wrote to my mother from Yasnaya Polyana, "Went riding, the dogs at my heels. Agafya Mikhailovna said they would attack the cattle if they were not on a leash and sent Vaska with me. Felt like testing my old hunting instinct. After a habit of forty years' standing, it's pleasant to ride out in search of game. But when a hare sprang up, I merely wished it well. Mainly it's the shame of it. . . ."

Even later, the passion for hunting was not entirely extinguished in him. Whenever he went out walking in the spring and heard the wheeple and hork of the woodcock, he would break off a conversation, raise his head, and excitedly seizing his companion's arm say, "Listen, listen, there's a woodcock!" [3]

In the nineties, when he was staying at my estate in the Chern district while setting up soup kitchens for the starving, he had a disturbing and rather touching experience. He enjoyed riding through the forest on my Kirghiz hunter, and was often accompanied by the greyhound Don, who was used to the horse. One day he was riding through a field when he heard some village children cry, "A hare, a hare!" "I looked up," he told me later, "and saw a hare running toward the forest. It was a long way off and there was no question of running it down, but I wanted to see Don run and couldn't resist showing him the hare. He darted off, and imagine my horror when I saw him overtaking it! I began to pray, 'Get away, for God's sake, get away!' I looked up and saw Don turning him again and again. What could I do? Fortunately, the hare was quite close to the edge of the forest and darted into a bush and escaped. But if Don had caught it, I should have been in despair."

Not wishing to grieve my father, I did not tell him that Don had come back an hour after his return, covered with blood and his belly distended like a barrel. He had obviously caught the hare in the bushes and had eaten it then and there. But *papa* never knew about it, thank Heaven. That was the only secret I ever managed to keep from him in my entire life.

XIII

Anna Karenina

I can just barely remember the horrifying case of the suicide of a woman living in our district, which Father later used in describing Anna Karenina's death. It occurred in January 1872.

Aleksandr Nikolayevich Bibikov, father of the half-witted Nikolenka who used to come to see our tree at Christmastime, had a housekeeper named Anna Stepanovna Sykova.[1] Out of jealousy of the governess, she threw herself under a moving train in the Yasenki station and was crushed to death. I remember someone coming to Yasnaya to inform Father of what had happened. He left at once, going first to Bibikov's, then to Yasenki, and was present at the post-mortem examination.

I even have a dim recollection of Anna Stepanova's round, genial, and rather foolish face. I liked her for her kindheartedness and was very sorry when I heard of her death. I could not understand how Aleksandr Nikolayevich could have given up such a fine woman for someone else.

Although I remember Father writing his *ABC Book* and *Reader* in 1871 and 1872, I have absolutely no recollection of his beginning *Anna Karenina*. I probably knew nothing about it at the time: what did it matter to a seven-year-old boy what his father was writing? It was only later, when I kept hearing the name, and when bundles of proof sheets were received and dispatched almost daily, that I realized that *Anna Karenina* was the title of a novel on which both *papa* and *maman* were at work.

To us it seemed that *maman*'s work was even harder than *papa*'s, not just because she worked where we could see her, but because she worked so much longer than he did. Every free moment was spent writing. She used to sit at her little table in the drawing room, bent over the manuscript trying to decipher Father's scrawl with her nearsighted eyes, often working long after everyone else had gone to bed.

Occasionally, when something was quite illegible, she took it to *papa* to ask him about it, but this she did rarely, since she was reluctant to disturb him. At such times he would take the manuscript in his hands and in a tone of annoyance say, "What is it you don't understand?" and begin reading aloud. But when he came to the troublesome passage, he faltered and had a hard time himself making out, or rather guessing, what he had written. His handwriting was very poor, and he had a deplorable way of inserting whole sentences between lines, in corners, or even right across the page. Sometimes *maman* discovered flagrant grammatical errors, which she corrected and pointed out to him.

When *Anna Karenina* began to appear in the *Russian Herald*, long galley proofs were sent to Father, which he corrected and revised. At first only proofreader's marks, punctuation marks, and letters omitted were written in the margins, but little by little words were changed, then sentences, lines were crossed out and others added, till the proof sheets were so blotched and blackened that it was impossible to send them back in that state; no one but *maman* could decipher the black web of signs, transpositions, and deletions.

She would sit up all night making a fresh copy of the whole thing. In the morning the new pages, covered with her small clear handwriting, would be neatly piled on her table, ready to be sent back by post "when Lyovochka gets up." But first *papa* had to take them to his study to look over them "for the last time," and by evening it was the same thing all over again: everything had been rewritten and scribbled over.

"Sonya, darling, forgive me. I've spoiled all your work again. This is the last time," he would say, shamefacedly showing her the places he had changed. "Tomorrow we'll send it off without fail." But the repetition of that "tomorrow" sometimes went on for weeks and even months. Or, to relieve his mind, "There's just one little place I want to look at again," and then, carried away, he ended by rewriting the whole thing. There were even times when he thought of words he wanted changed after the proofs had been sent back, and the corrections had to be telegraphed. Publication of the novel in the *Russian Herald* was held up more than once because of this rewriting, and sometimes months passed before the next installment appeared.[2]

At the time he was working on part 8 of *Anna Karenina,* the Russo-Turkish War was being fought in Russia.[3] It was presaged by the extraordinarily beautiful comet of 1876 and a whole series of aurorae boreales, which we delighted in watching throughout the winter. There was something elemental and ominous in that effulgent comet tail and in the fiery nocturnal glow.

The whole family, including the children, took a great interest in the war. When the newspapers arrived from Tula, the entire household assembled to listen to one of the grown-ups read them aloud. We not only knew the names and patronymics of all the generals but were familiar with their faces, which were reproduced in cheap prints, on calendars, and even on chocolate candies. The Dyakovs had given us regiments of Russian and Turkish toy soldiers for Christmas and we spent long hours playing at war.

One day we heard that a party of Turkish prisoners had been brought to Tula, and we drove over with *papa* to look at them.

I remember our going into a big yard surrounded by a stone wall, where there were a number of stalwart, good-looking men in wide blue trousers and red fezzes. *Papa* boldly approached them and started a conversation. Several of the men spoke Russian and asked him for cigarettes, which he gave them along with some money. Then he asked them how they were getting on, and before long had made friends with them. He persuaded two of the biggest men to give a demonstration of Turkish wrestling. Afterward one of the Turks wrestled with a Russian soldier.

"What charming, gentle, handsome men they are," *papa* remarked as we drove away, and it seemed strange to me that he should be so friendly with those terrible Turks, whom we were supposed to fear as our enemies because they were fighting our soldiers and massacring Bulgarians.

In the last part of *Anna Karenina,* where he described the end of Vronsky's career, Father dealt with the volunteer movement and the Pan-Slavist committees in a depreciating way, and this led to a misunderstanding with Katkov. I remember how angry he was when Katkov refused to publish these chapters as they stood, and asked him either to delete certain passages or to qualify them. He finally returned the manuscript to Father and printed a brief notice in his journal stating that the novel, properly speaking, ended with the death of the heroine, but that later there was to be an epilogue of a couple of pages in which, according to the author's plan, such and such facts would be recounted, and that the author "will perhaps develop these chapters for a special edition of the book." [4] As a result of this incident Father quarreled with Katkov and never saw him again.

In this connection I am reminded of one of my father's characteristic definitions. He used to say that as a general rule those who are masters of the literary form do not talk well, whereas those who are eloquent are incapable of writing, and cited Katkov as an example of the former, saying that he mumbled and stammered and could not put two words together, and mentioned F. N. Plevako and several other well-known orators as examples of the latter.

In concluding this chapter, I should like to say a few words about how my father himself felt about *Anna Karenina.*

In 1877, in a letter to N. N. Strakhov, he wrote, "I confess that the success of the last installment of *Anna Karenina* also delighted me. I was quite unprepared for it, and was really amazed that people should like anything so ordinary and *insignificant.*" [5]

In 1875 he wrote to Fet, "It's two months now since I have defiled my hands with ink or my heart with thoughts, but I am now setting to work again on my *tedious, vulgar Karenina,* with only one wish, to get it out of the way as soon as possible and have the leisure for other occupations—not pedagogical, however, which I love but intend to give up. It takes too much time." [6]

In 1876, again to N. N. Strakhov, he wrote, "I feel with dread that my usual summer mood is upon me: I am revolted by what I have written, and now have to face the proof sheets of the April installment and am afraid I won't be up to correcting them. *Everything* in it is *execrable,* and the whole thing ought to be rewritten—all that has been published too—scratched out, thrown away, repudiated; I ought to say: 'I'm sorry, I won't do it anymore,' and try to write something fresh instead of this incoherent, neither-fish-nor-fowl sort of stuff." [7]

That was how my father felt about his novel while writing it. Later I heard him speak even more scathingly of it.

"What's so difficult in writing about an officer falling in love with a married woman?" he used to say. "There's nothing difficult in that, and, what's more, nothing good either. It's bad and it serves no purpose!"

I am fully convinced that if it had been possible to do so, Father would have destroyed this novel, which he never liked and toward which he always had a negative attitude.

XIV

The Postbox

I n the summer when the two families, ours and the Kuzminskys, were living at Yasnaya and both houses were filled with relatives and guests, the Postbox was installed. It originated a long time ago when I was still a small boy and had only just learned to write, and continued till the middle of the eighties.[1]

This box was hung next to the grandfather clock on the landing at the top of the stairs, and during the week everyone dropped into it whatever he had written—verses, articles, and stories—on current topics. On Sundays we all assembled around the big table in the salon, the box was ceremoniously opened, and one of the grown-ups, often *papa* himself, read the contents aloud. Nothing was ever signed and it was a point of honor not to peek at the handwriting, but we could almost always guess who the author was by his style, his self-conscious air, or the forced indifference of his expression.*

The first time I wrote some French verses for the Postbox as a small boy, I was so abashed when they were read that I hid under the table and remained there for the rest of the evening, and they finally had to drag me out by force. I wrote nothing more for a long time, preferring to listen to the compositions of others rather than my own.

All the "events" of our Yasnaya Polyana life found their way into the Postbox, and no one was spared, not even the grown-ups. There all our secrets, our love affairs, all the little incidents of our complex family life, were exposed and made good-natured fun of by ourselves and our friends.

Most of these compositions have unfortunately been lost, but here are a few of the more interesting ones from that period (the eighties).

¶ "The old fogey" continues to ask questions. Why, when a woman or an older man enters the room does every well-bred person not only ask him to sit down, but offer him his own seat?

Why, when Ushakov or some Serbian officer comes to pay a visit, is he not permitted to leave without tea or dinner?

Why is it considered incorrect to allow an older man or woman to help you on with your coat, and so on?

And why are all these excellent precepts considered obligatory for others, when there are people who come here every day who are not asked to sit down, to stay for dinner, or to spend the night, and to whom we not only render no service but would think it the height of impropriety to do so?

Where do we draw the line between those to whom we owe such courtesies and those to whom we do not?

How do we distinguish the one from the other?

And are not all these rules of courtesy bad if they do not apply to everyone? Is not what we call courtesy a delusion— and a very bad one?

Lev Tolstoy

---

*The items from the "Postbox" were indeed unsigned; the signatures here appended represent the inferences of the author.—*Tr.*

¶ Question: Which is more dreadful, a case of cattle plague for a farmer, or the ablative case for a schoolboy?

L. Tolstoy

¶ At what age should a man or woman marry? [2] At an age when they are no longer apt to fall in love with someone else.[3]

L. Tolstoy

¶ An answer is requested to the following question for next time. Why are Ustyusha, Masha, Alyona, Pyotr, etc.,[4] obliged to cook, bake, sweep, empty slops, wait at table, while the masters eat, gorge themselves, quarrel, produce waste matter, and eat again?

L. Tolstoy

¶ From the April issue of *Russian Antiquity* in the year 2085. According to the wealth of material that has come down to us from the year 1885, we are able to reconstruct the life of the inhabitants of Russia at that time more or less as follows. Let us take, for example, the district of Yasnaya Polyana, where there now stands a meeting house. In 1885, this region was inhabited by seventy families, noble tillers of the soil who, despite the onerous conditions of that period, lived a life of true enlightenment—practicing the science of communal life and work, the arts of cultivating the land and raising livestock—and two families of completely uncivilized people who had lost all consciousness not only of love for their fellow man, but of a sense of justice and the essential collaboration among men. The seventy enlightened families lived in a narrow street, where young and old worked from morning to night, ate nothing but bread and onions, had only three or four hours of sleep out of the twenty-four, yet fulfilled all that was demanded of them. Although the two families who accepted all this work from them fed and housed strangers and passers-by, they sent those who were sick among the workers elsewhere and, when it was required, sent the best of the men into the army, that is, into slavery. And those two barbarian families lived apart from the others, in two immense houses surrounded by extensive shady gardens that were the size of fifteen of the dwellings of those enlightened inhabitants, and were taken care of by forty people who did nothing but feed, wash, dress, and pamper them. The occupations of these two barbarian families consisted for the most part of eating, conversing, putting on and taking off their clothes, playing instruments that produced strange sounds, reading love stories, learning the most inane and useless rules, and sometimes studying very blasphemous works known as sacred histories and catechisms. The amazing thing is that the people of these two barbarian families called their most profligate forms of idleness work and often considered them burdensome, yet were always proud of their ignorance and idleness. The life of these barbarian families consisted in . . .[5]

L. Tolstoy

¶ A lady once got into a cab and, it being hot, was at a loss as to where to put her coat. The driver noticed this and said, "You can give it to me if you like, madam." "Where will you put it?" "Under my _____." All those present were embarrassed. Yet wearing bustles did not embarrass ladies in 1885.

¶ A certain landowner took one of the villagers and put him into footman's livery to accompany his daughters when they went out for a drive. Coming out of a shop with their escort one day, the young ladies did not see their footman. After looking around and waiting for a while, they saw him emerge from behind a gate. "Where have you been?" asked one of the girls. "Had to answer a call of nature." The young ladies nearly died of embarrassment. Yet women and girls of the gentry, both married and single, make other people clean their rooms for them, with all that this implies—but that does not embarrass them.

L. Tolstoy

¶ Why is a sanitary barrel like a society lady? Both are taken out at night.

L. Tolstoy

¶ What would be the difference if, instead of Ilya chasing foxes and wolves, the foxes and wolves ran of their own accord and Ilya simply ran along the path from the house to the annex? None at all, except for the peace and comfort of the horses.

L. Tolstoy

When Aunt Tanya was in a bad temper because the coffee had been spilt, or because she had been beaten at croquet, she was in the habit of sending everyone to the devil. My father wrote a little story about this, which he called *Susoichik*.

¶ The devil—not the chief devil, but one of the rank and file who was entrusted with the management of social affairs, Susoichik by name—was greatly harassed on the sixth of August 1884. Since early morning, people sent to him by Tatyana Andreyevna Kuzminskaya had been arriving all day long. The first to appear was Aleksandr Mikhailovich Kuzminsky; the second was Misha Islavin; the third was Vyacheslav; the fourth was Seryozha Tolstoy; and the last, accompanied by Prince Urusov, was Lev Tolstoy senior. The first visitor, Aleksandr Mikhailovich, caused Susoichik no surprise, as he often turned up at his wife's request.

"What, has your wife sent you here again?"

"Yes, again," replied the Presiding Judge of the District Court bashfully, not knowing exactly how to explain why he had been sent this time.

"You come here rather often. What do you want?"

"Nothing special; she asked me to bring you her greetings," mumbled Aleksandr Mikhailovich, deviating from the truth only with difficulty.

"Well, all right, you're always welcome; she's one of my best workers."

Before Susoichik had time to show the Judge out, the children appeared, laughing and shoving and hiding behind one another.

"Well, did my Tanechka send you youngsters? That's all right, no harm in coming. My compliments to Tanya, and tell

her I'm always at her service. Come whenever you like, Susoichik might be of some use to you."

No sooner had the youngsters taken their leave than old Lev
Tolstoy arrived with Prince Urusov.

"Ah-ha! The old man! Thanks to Tanya. It's a long time since
I've seen you, old fellow. Still hale and hearty? What can I do
for you?"

Lev Tolstoy shuffled about somewhat abashed. Prince Urusov, recalling the etiquette of diplomatic receptions, stepped
forward and explained Tolstoy's appearance by saying that he
wished to make the acquaintance of Tatyana Andreyevna's
oldest and most faithful friend.

"Les amis de nos amis sont nos amis."

"Quite so, ha! ha! ha!" said Susoichik. "I must reward her for
today's work. Be so kind, Prince, as to convey this token of my
esteem to her."

And he handed him a morocco leather case containing the
insignia of the Order. It was necklace of imps' tails and two
toads, one to be worn on the bosom and the other on the bustle.

                                        Lev Tolstoy (the elder)

¶ Ideals at Yasnaya Polyana

Lev Nikolayevich	1. Poverty, peace, and concord.
	2. To burn everything he worshipped, to worship everything he burned.
Sofya Andreyevna	1. Seneca.
	2. To have a hundred and fifty babies who would never grow up.
Tatyana Andreyevna	1. Eternal youth.
	2. The emancipation of women.
Ilya	To guard against showing that he has a heart, and to look as though he had killed a hundred wolves.
*Big Masha**	A communal family, founded on the principles of grace and watered with the tears of sensibility.

*Masha Kuzminskaya.–I.T.

Madame Seuron	Elegance.
Vera	Uncle Lyolya.†
Prince Urusov	To settle croquet scores and forget everything terrestrial.
The little ones	To stuff themselves all day with all sorts of rubbish and, for the sake of variety, to shriek their heads off from time to time.
Tanya	Bobbed hair. Spiritual refinement and new shoes every day.
Lyolya	To be editor of the *News*.
Princess Obolenskaya	Universal happiness and family bliss.
Little Masha‡	The sound of guitar strumming.
Trifonovna	Their marriage.

¶ To Aunt Tanya

When the sun was shining daily
Everyone was living gaily
At Yasnaya.
Suddenly it struck Tatyana
That at Yasnaya Polyana
Childhood has to end and schooling
Has to take the place of fooling.
For the girls to become smart,
Education has to start.
Look for instance at Mamzelle,
Who knows everything so well.
Notebooks, pens, and books were bought,
More than you'd have ever thought,
And the girls, ah, what a sight,
Turned into students over night,
With no problems whatsoever!
When Bible study came however,
Trouble started. "It's not for me,"
Our Masha said, "This cannot be!"

---

†Lev Nikolayevich Tolstoy.–*I.T.*
‡Masha Tolstaya.–*I.T.*

And Vera, "Now that's quite enough,
No more of that old sacred stuff!"
Never could she take that sorry
Paradise expulsion story.
How could anyone believe
God would banish Adam and Eve?
What had they done? A stupid thought,
Things like that should not be taught.
Madame's answer was to say,
"Punished for *curiosité*."
"Knowing too much is always forbidden,
And real truth must needs be hidden."
Mother simply did not know
What to say and let it go.
We only knew that Vassily
No more could shake the apple tree.
What sort of paradise is this,
Where one can't eat one's fill in bliss?

Lev Tolstoy

¶ What is stronger than death or fate?
Our ambrosial Anke cake.

L. Tolstoy

¶ Aunt Sonya and Aunt Tanya
and Generally Speaking
What Aunt Sonya Likes and What Aunt Tanya Likes

Aunt Sonya likes making underclothes, doing *broderie anglaise* and various kinds of fine needlework. Aunt Tanya likes making dresses and knitting. Aunt Sonya likes flowers, and in early spring is seized with a passion for gardening. Her face takes on a preoccupied look, she digs in the flower beds, consults the gardener, and astonishes Aunt Tanya by using the Latin names of all the flowers. And Aunt Tanya thinks, "She really knows everything!" Aunt Tanya says she can't stand flowers, that it's not worth bothering with such rubbish but secretly delights in them.

Aunt Sonya wears a gray bathing costume, goes sedately down the bathhouse steps gasping with cold, then decorously dips into the water and swims off with smooth even strokes. Aunt Tanya puts on a tattered oilcloth cap tied under the chin with pink chintz ribbons, and with a desperate plunge sinks to the bottom where she momentarily lies flat on her back.

Aunt Sonya is afraid when the children jump into the water. Aunt Tanya shames them when they are afraid to jump in.

Aunt Sonya puts on her spectacles, collects the children, and walks resolutely to the plantation saying, "Mind you keep close to me, my little dears," and likes to walk slowly about the forest gathering birch mushrooms, not even spurning the *agaricus torminosus*, and says, "Children, be sure to pick the brown-cap boletes, your *papa* is very fond of them pickled, and by spring what we have will all be eaten." When Aunt Tanya goes for a walk she's always afraid that someone will interfere with her or tag along after her, and if the children do attach themselves to her, she sternly says, "Run along, but keep out of my sight, and if you get lost don't bawl!" She dashes all about the woods and hollows, likes to gather aspen mushrooms, and always carries gingerbread in her pocket.

When things are difficult, Aunt Sonya always thinks, "Who needs me most? To whom can I be the most useful?" Aunt Tanya always thinks, "Who will be most useful to me today? Whom can I send on an errand?"

Aunt Sonya washes in cold water. Aunt Tanya is afraid of cold water.

Aunt Sonya likes reading philosophy, holding serious conversations, and astounding Aunt Tanya with big words—and fully succeeds in this aim. Aunt Tanya likes reading novels and talking about love.

Aunt Sonya can't stand pouring tea. And neither can Aunt Tanya.

Aunt Sonya doesn't like hangers-on and God's fools. Aunt Tanya loves them.

When playing croquet, Aunt Sonya always finds some useful activity for the idle moments, such as sprinkling sand on the stony places or mending the mallets, and says that she is too active to sit and do nothing. Aunt Tanya follows the game with furious concentration, hating her opponent and oblivious to everything else.

Aunt Sonya is nearsighted and sees neither cobwebs in the corners nor dust on the furniture. Aunt Tanya sees all such things and has them removed.

Aunt Sonya adores children. Aunt Tanya is far from adoring them.

When the children hurt themselves, Aunt Sonya caresses them and says, "Never mind, my pet, my darling, just wait, we'll bump that old floor—there, take that, and that!" And both Aunt Sonya and the child strike the floor violently. But Aunt Tanya rubs the hurt place furiously when they bump themselves and says, "What a nuisance—who needs this! And where are those nurses, devil take them! The least you can do is to get me some water, instead of standing there with your mouths open!"

When the children are sick, Aunt Sonya consults medical books with a gloomy air and administers opium. Aunt Tanya scolds them when they're sick and gives them castor oil.

Aunt Sonya likes dressing up from time to time and surprising everyone by appearing at Sunday dinner in something outlandish. Aunt Tanya also likes dressing up, but in something that makes her look younger.

Aunt Sonya sometimes likes doing her hair *à la* injured innocence, and then assumes the air of a woman oppressed by man and fate, and looks so meek and innocent with her braid hanging down her back and her hair combed smooth in front that you think, "Good Heavens, who could have hurt her, who is that scoundrel, and how could she have borne it?" And your eyes fill with tears at the mere thought. Aunt Tanya likes to wear her hair high on her head, revealing the nape of her neck, with little locks falling over her forehead; she imagines that this makes her eyes look bigger and keeps blinking them.

Aunt Tanya never lets you forget a quarrel. Aunt Sonya likes to start talking at once after a quarrel as if nothing had happened.

Aunt Sonya never eats anything for breakfast, and if she does boil herself a couple of eggs now and then, she surrenders them to anyone who wants them. When Aunt Tanya gets up she says to herself, "What would my lady fancy?" Aunt Sonya eats quickly, taking little bites with her head bent low over her plate, like a hen pecking. Aunt Tanya stuffs her mouth full, and if anyone looks at her while she is eating, she tries to look as if she is only eating because she is obliged to, and not at all because she enjoys it.

Aunt Sonya likes to sit at the piano playing and singing to the children in a singsong voice. "Hop, hop, hop! Hey, faster, gallop!" And the children frolic about. Aunt Tanya can't bear mixing children and music, but though she tries to hide it, she has no objection to her own children dancing when Aunt Sonya plays.

When Aunt Sonya makes clothes for her children she allows for fifteen years' growth. Aunt Tanya leaves no margin for growth, and the clothes have to be remade after the first washing.

Aunt Sonya does not mind prolonged visits. Aunt Tanya can't stand them.

Aunt Sonya is constantly worrying about someone, especially if he has gone away. Aunt Tanya, once she has said good-bye to anyone, tries to forget him and never worries.

When Aunt Sonya is enjoying any pleasure or festivity, she instantly mingles a feeling of melancholy with her enjoyment. Aunt Tanya gives herself wholly to the pleasure of the moment.

Aunt Sonya is very delicate where someone else's property is concerned, and so, when Aunt Tanya has a mushroom pie, says, "You're sure I'm not robbing you, Tanechka?" (In such instances she always says "you" instead of "thee.") And with these words takes only the crust. Aunt Tanya pleads desperately with her to take the middle, but in vain; no action is taken on her appeal.

When Aunt Tanya isn't given fresh bread for breakfast, she asks Aunt Sonya, "Haven't you got any fresh bread today?" and without waiting for an answer picks up the bread and smells it, smells the butter, pushes both to one side and cries, "The bread

is always sour, the butter always smells of the cow!" and then
proceeds to eat other people's bread and butter.

Who has the smaller foot, Aunt Tanya or Aunt Sonya, has yet
to be decided.

¶ What Men Live by at Yasnaya Polyana

Lev Nikolayevich lives as though he had found the solution to
the riddle of life.

Aleksandr Mikhailovich lives for the summer months of repose.

Sofya Andreyevna lives to be the wife of a famous man, and for
trifles such as wild strawberries on which she can expend
her energies.

Tatyana Andreyevna lives to please, amuse, and make herself
loved.

Tanya Tolstaya lives to be pretty and because there is such a
blessing as marriage.

Sergei Lvovich lives in the belief that sometime he will begin to
live a different life.

Ilya Lvovich lives in hope of family happiness.

Madame Seuron lives for her Alcidushka.

Big Masha lives to be the center of attention of the youth of
Yasnaya Polyana.

Little Masha lives because there is a Vanechka Meshchersky in
this world.

Vera Kuzminskaya lives because there are such things as *macé-
doine* and other sweets, and also for her little sister
Masha.

Alcide lives because his mother thinks and feels for him.

Lyolya lives for the sake of studying as little as possible.

A week later a reply to this article appeared.

¶ What Men Die from at Yasnaya Polyana

Lev Nikolayevich dies when he goes to Moscow and, taking a
walk there, is depressed by what he sees around him.

Sofya Andreyevna dies when the children are ill, and when Ilya
plays at knucklebones.

Aleksandr Mikhailovich dies when he leaves Yasnaya Polyana.
Tatyana Andreyevna dies when Aleksandr Mikhailovich leaves,
and when she loses a game of croquet.
Tanya dies when *maman* tries to marry her off to Fedya Samarin.
Seryozha dies when Alyona goes away.
Ilya dies when it's time for Greek grammar.
Lyolya dies when a hare escapes him, and when the Kuzminskys
leave.
Vera dies when she is questioned on religious studies and when
the gooseberries have all disappeared.
Little Masha dies because Vanechka Meshchersky lost his grand-
mother.

From time to time the half-mad religious fanatic Blokhin
used to appear at Yasnaya. He suffered from megalomania,
based on the conviction that he had "risen through all the ranks
of the nobility" and was the equal of Emperor Aleksandr II and
of God. Consequently he lived only "to have a good time," and
to have "an open bank account." He called himself a Prince and
Knight of all the Orders. When he was asked why he had no
money and begged for charity, he smiled ingenuously and without a trace of embarrassment replied that there had been some
delay in his remittance, but that he had "let them know" and
would receive it in a few days. My father equates many of the
"inmates" of Yasnaya Polyana, all of whom he considers dangerous and in need of radical treatment, with this Blokhin, who is
number twenty-two on the sick list that appears below; he com-
pares Blokhin himself, however, with the baby Sasha, and considers him the only one who can be certified as reasoning entirely consistently.

¶ Medical Bulletin of Inmates of
the Yasnaya Polyana Lunatic Asylum

No. 1. (Lev Nikolayevich) Sanguine temperament. Belongs
to harmless category. Patient is subject to mania called by
German psychiatrists *Weltverbesserungswahn.** The crux of his

---

*Mania for reforming the world.—*Tr.*

madness is that the patient considers it possible to change people's lives by words. General symptoms: dissatisfaction with the
existing orders of things, condemnation of everyone except
himself, an irritable garrulity irrespective of his audience, frequent transitions from fury and exasperation to an unnatural,
lachrymose sentimentality. Particular symptoms: busying himself with unsuitable and unnecessary occupations, such as
cleaning and making boots, mowing hay, etc. Treatment: complete indifference of those surrounding the patient to what he
says; occupations of a kind that will consume all the patient's
energy.

No. 2. (Sofya Andreyevna) Belongs to the harmless category,
but has to be shut up at times. Patient is subject to the mania:
Petulantihurryupica maxima. The madness is expressed in the
patient's belief that everyone demands everything of her and
that she cannot manage to get everything done. Symptoms:
solving problems which have not arisen, answering questions
before they are asked, justifying herself before she has been
accused, and satisfying demands which have not been made.
Patient suffers from Blokhin-bank mania. Treatment: strenuous
work. Regime: isolation from frivolous and worldly people.
Also effective in such cases is giving the patient "what for."

No. 3. (Aleksandr Mikhailovich Kuzminsky) Patient formerly suffered from advanced stage of mania *Senatorialis
ambitiosa magna* complicated by mania *emolumentum pecun-
iorum,* and is now in the process of being cured. Patient's malady at present time is expressed in a desire to unite the
functions of his yardman with those of the Presiding Judge of
the District Court. General symptoms: taciturnity, lack of self-
confidence. Particular symptoms: useless digging in the earth,
equally useless reading of newspaper articles, frequent moods
of despondency expressed in outbursts of temper. Cure: greater
penetration into the problems of life, greater conformity with
reality, more humility, and more confidence in those principles
which he considers valid.

No. 4. (Madame Seuron) Patient is suffering from *comme-
il-fautis simplex* complicated with vestiges of *sacracordia*

*catholica.** General symptoms: muddled view of life combined with firm and unwavering manner. Actions better than words. Special symptoms: conversation frivolous, way of life austere. Patient seriously infected with prevalent Blokhin-bank mania. Treatment: morality and love for son. Prognosis favorable.

No. 5. (Ekaterina Nikolayevna Kashevskaya) (?) Mania *seuronofilia maxima.* Exceedingly dangerous illness. Radical treatment: marriage.

No. 6. (Tatyana Andreyevna Kuzminskaya) Patient suffers from the mania known as mania *demoniaca complicata,** a rather rare malady offering little hope of cure. Patient belongs to the dangerous category. Origin of the disease: unwarranted success in youth and habit of gratified vanity with no moral principles of life. Symptoms of the disease: fear of imaginary personal devils and a particular predilection for their work and for every sort of temptation: sloth, luxury, malice. Concern for that life which does not exist, and indifference to that which does exist. Patient feels constantly in the snare of the devil, likes being in his snare and at the same time fears him. Patient suffers acutely from the epidemic mania of Blokhism. Prognosis doubtful because recovery from fear of devil and fear of future life is possible only by renunciation of his works. But patient's entire life is occupied by these works. Two forms of treatment possible: either complete devotion to the devil and his works to the point where patient is consumed with bitterness, or complete estrangement from these works. In the first instance, two large doses of compromising coquetry, two million rubles, two months of complete idleness, and a summons to appear before a Justice of the Peace for her contumely. In the second instance: three or four children to be nursed by the patient herself, a life wholly filled with activity and mental development. Regime: in the first case, truffles, champagne, lace dresses—three new ones daily. In the second: cabbage soup, kasha, with sweet curd tarts on Sundays, one dress of same cut and color for life.

---

*Catholic bigotry.—*Tr.*
*Mania of being in thrall to the devil.—*Tr.*

No. 7. (Brother Seryozha) Patient suffers from a mania called *universitelis libertatis palaver.* Belongs to the category of the entirely harmless. General symptoms: a desire to know whatever others know but what he does not need to know, and lack of desire to know what he should know. Particular symptoms: pride, self-assurance, and irritability. Case has not yet been fully investigated, but patient also suffers to a high degree from Prince Blokhin mania. Treatment: forced labor and, most important, service or love or both. Regime: less confidence in learning and more profound study of knowledge already acquired.

No. 8. (Ilya) Mania *Prochoris egoistica complicata.* Patient belongs to the dangerous category. The crux of his madness consists in thinking that the whole world is concentrated on him and that the more insignificant and absurd his activities, the more interested the world will be in them. General symptoms: patient cannot occupy himself with anything unless there is some Prokhor present to admire him. But since the higher the order of occupation the smaller the number of admiring Prokhors, patient continually descends to a lower level of activity. Particular symptoms: patient is excited to the point of rapture by every form of approval and without it sinks into apathy. Seriously infected by Blokhin epidemic. Dangerously ill, prognosis twofold: either the patient will become habituated to submitting to the judgment of inferior people—the Prokhors—and continually lower himself in proportion to the simplicity of their approval, or he may become disgusted with this and try to take an interest in activities which are gratifying and at the same time independent of the Prokhors. Treatment not possible. Regime: isolation from the society of those less cultivated than himself.

No. 9. (Prince L. D. Urusov) Patient suffers from a complicated malady called *mania metaphysica,* which is further complicated by demoralizing ambition, *vanitas diplomatica highlifica.* Also suffers from perpetual conflict between his habits and his philosophy of life. General symptoms: depression and a desire to appear lively and gay, love of solitude. Particular symptoms: reversion to old habits and dissatisfaction with himself, excessive irritability and excitement in the communication of his own ideas. Only treatment of undoubted efficacy is to retire from his present occupation and be united with his family.

No. 10. (Sister Tanya) Patient suffers from the mania known as *Kapnisto-Meshcherian simplex,* which consists in total suspension of every kind of mental and spiritual activity, of being in a state of rapt expectation of the doorbell ringing, or in thrall to the excitements of life because of vanity. General symptoms: lassitude, inattention to her surroundings or to any spiritual stimulation. Subjugation of her will to the will of those who are younger and less developed. Special symptoms: violent, spasmodic movement of feet at sound of music, accompanied with marked twitching of shoulders and torso. Patient acutely affected by Prince Blokhin epidemic. Treatment: early rising, physical exercise daily and to the point of sweating, regular fixed days for mental, artistic, and physical work, and submission to guidance. Regime: deprivation of dressing gown, mirror, and entertainment. With fulfillment of this regime, prognosis is favorable.

No. 11. (Masha Kuzminskaya) (?) Patient only recently arrived at Yasnaya Polyana, therefore has not yet been thoroughly examined, but present diagnosis is the following: *mania Kapnisto-Meshcherian Petersburgiana* complicated with *hypertrophia-modesticae.* General symptoms: inertia, languor, dreaming of cavaliers. Same convulsive movements of feet at sound of music, though without twitching of body. Subject to a high degree to *Blokhin simplex.* Radical treatment: a good dose of "what for," strong affection for a good man.

No. 12. (Brother Lev) Patient under observation. So far has manifested acute symptoms of mania known to Russian psychiatrists as *lascivia,* which it to say that the crux of his madness consists in thinking that what is needed is not the thing itself, the feeling itself, the knowledge itself, but something resembling the thing, the feeling, the knowledge. Special symptoms: a desire to appear omniscient and to be noticed by everyone.

Malady not very dangerous. Treatment, which has already
been undertaken: humbling.

No. 13. (Vera Shidlovskaya) (?) Patient under observation.
Belongs to category of completely harmless. Symptoms requir-
ing her to remain in the asylum are only the following: a passion for icon lamps, pointed toes, ribbons, bustles, etc., and being subject to Prince Blokhin epidemic. Medical treatment
unnecessary, only a regime of isolation from company of afflicted people, after which patient may perhaps be certified as
cured.

No. 14. (Vera Kuzminskaya) Dangerous. Patient suffers
from mania known to Portuguese psychiatrists as *mania blunt-
iana honesta maxima.* Crux of madness: preoccupation with her
own appearance and thinking everyone else is too. Symptoms:
shyness, silence, outbursts of rudeness. Acutely afflicted with
Prince Blokhin disease. Treatment: tenderness and love. Prognosis favorable.

No. 15. (Sister Masha) Patient suffers from mania known to
English psychiatrists as *mania anglica as-you-like-itude.* Crux
of the madness consists in thinking that one must do not what
one wants to do, but what others want one to do. Minor degree
of Prince Blokhin disease. Treatment: faith in what her conscience considers right and distrust of what others consider
right.

No. 16. (Misha Kuzminsky) Patient under observation. Crux
of madness: rubles and Uncle Lyalya. Belongs to category of
perfectly harmless. Only slightly infected with Blokhinism.
Recovery possible.

*No. 17.** Under observation. Buttoned up. Infected with
Blokhinism.

*Nos. 18, 19, 20.** Under observation. Only mildly infected
with Blokhinism.

No. 21. (Baby sister Sasha) Still in care of wet-nurse. Completely healthy and may be discharged without danger. In the

_____
*The younger children.—*I.T.*

Lev Nikolayevich Tolstoy (1828–1910).

The Tolstoy children, Ilya, Lev, Tatyana, Sergei.

Tolstoy and his wife, Sofya Andreyevna, 1887.

Tolstoy with his pupils.

Maria Afanasyevna and
Nikolai Mikhailovich,
nurse and cook in the
Tolstoy household.

Agafya Mikhailovna and Misha Stakhovich at Yasnaya Polyana.

Tatyana Andreyevna Kuzminskaya, Tolstoy's sister-in-law.

Dmitry Alekseyevich Dyakov.

Sofya Andreyevna
Tolstoy, Tolstoy's wife
and Ilya Tolstoy's
mother.

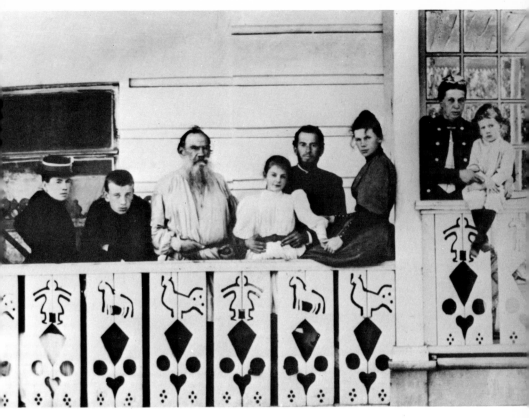

The Tolstoy family on the veranda of the Yasnaya Polyana house.

Sergei Nikolayevich Tolstoy,
Tolstoy's brother.

Ivan Sergeyevich Turgenev.

event of remaining at Yasnaya Polyana, unquestionably liable to infection, since she will soon realize that milk used by her is bought from the baby of her wet-nurse.

No. 22. (The idiot Blokhin) Prince Blokhin. A military Prince who has risen through all the ranks of the nobility and ended as a Knight of all the Orders of Blokhin. The cause of his madness consists only in this: that other people are obliged to work for him, and he has only to receive money, keep an open bank account, enjoy a home, carriages, clothing, and all the pleasures of life, living only to have a good time. Patient not dangerous and, like No. 21, can be cured. The fact that his, Prince Blokhin's, life can be spent in enjoying himself while everyone else's must be spent in toil is explained by him with perfect consistency as being the result of his having gone through all the ranks of the nobility, whereas no explanation whatever can be given for idleness in others.

No. 23. (Uncle Sergei Nikolayevich) Patient has been under observation before but has returned to Yasnaya Polyana Asylum. Not dangerous. Suffers from mania known to Spanish psychiatrists as *mania katkoviana antica nobilis Russica** and from chronic *Beethovenophobia.* General symptoms: after taking nourishment, patient experiences uncontrollable desire to have the *Moscow Gazette* read to him and is dangerous in the following respect: he may resort to violence in his insistence on having it read to him. After taking nourishment in the evening, again becomes dangerous when hearing *The Spinner* sung, stamping his feet, waving his arms, and uttering wild cries. Particular symptoms: unable to pick up all his cards at once, has to take them one by one. Once a month, for reasons unknown, drives to a town called Krapivna** where he spends his time in strange and unnatural activities. Preoccupied by female beauty. Treatment: friendship with men and with nihilists. Regime: no smoking, drinking, or going to the circus.

L. Tolstoy

---

*The reference is to Katkov's conservative publication.—*I.T.*

**Sergei Nikolayevich was District Marshal of the Nobility.—*I.T.*

¶ A Poem by My Father Dedicated to My Sister Tanya

In the morning pale and sour,
At dinner time a flower.
The metamorphosis was strange,
What could have made her change?
Something goes on in secrecy,
Kapnist perhaps? What else could it be?***

¶ Poem by V. V. Treskin

Intrepidly I undertook a critique for the Postbox.
Little did I find to praise, enough and more to condemn,
And dipping my pen into poison left none unscathed.
Yet, whence those dark and mystic fears,
Trammeling my thoughts and holding me in their thrall?
O gods, reveal to me the cause of my infirmity and distress!
Hark, the Thunderer's voice: Zeus speaks:
"Pitiful critic, know'st not that even now at Yasnaya
Nikolai Strakhov, king of critics dwells,
Ready to rush into battle and lay thee low,
Then to inscribe on thy tombstone a crushing epitaph,
Eternal warning to trespassers on his realm?"
The thunder had long since died away,
And earth had long been cloaked in shadow.
Yet I sat quaking in the dark, summoning courage
To brave my fate and lay my stumbling lines before you.

***Tanya paid frequent visits to Count Kapnist's house at the time.—*I.T.*

XV

Sergei Nikolayevich Tolstoy

I remember Uncle Seryozha from my earliest childhood. He lived at Pirogovo and used to visit us often. His facial features were very much like my father's, but he was altogether more delicate and patrician-looking. He had the same oval face, the same nose, the same expressive eyes beneath bushy, beetling eyebrows, but the difference between his face and my father's can be judged by the fact that in those remote days when Father cared about his personal appearance he was always tormented by his ugliness, while Uncle Seryozha was considered, and indeed was, a very handsome man.

In his fragmentary *Reminiscences,* Father said of him:

"Nikolenka I respected, Mitenka was my comrade, but Seryozha I admired and imitated; I *wished to be him.* I admired his handsome appearance, his singing—he was always singing —his drawing, his gaiety, and especially, strange to say, his forthrightness and egoism.

"I was always self-conscious, diffident, always sensing, rightly or wrongly, what people were thinking or feeling about me, and this destroyed my pleasure in life. That is probably the reason why I loved the opposite—spontaneity and egoism—in other people. And I particularly loved it in Seryozha—though the word 'loved' is wrong. I loved Nikolenka, but I admired Seryozha as something alien and incomprehensible. His was a human life that was beautiful but completely beyond my understanding—mysterious, and therefore specially attractive.

"He died a few days ago, and during his last illness, even while dying, he was just as unfathomable and just as dear to me as he had been in that remote period of our childhood.

"Lately, in our old age, he grew more fond of me, valued my attachment to him, was proud of me, and even tried, though without success, to accept my views. But he remained what he had always been, completely individual, unique, proud, aristocratic, handsome, and the most straightforward and sincere man I have ever known. He was what he was, never concealing anything and never trying to be what he was not. I enjoyed being with Nikolenka, talking and thinking with him, but when I was with Seryozha, I only wanted to imitate him, and this had its origin in early childhood. . . ." [1]

We were always delighted when his carriage, drawn by three magnificent horses with little silver bells on their harnesses, drove up to the house, and Uncle Seryozha stepped out looking very handsome and lordly in his broad-brimmed black felt hat and long black overcoat. *Papa* would come out of his study and shake hands with him, *maman* would joyfully run out to the entrance hall, ask about Maria Mikhailovna and the children, then hurry off to the kitchen to tell the cook to prepare some special dish "for our visitor."

Uncle Seryozha never showed any affection for us children; he seemed to put up with us rather than to like us, but we always treated him with great deference, which, as I now realize, was in part due to his aristocratic appearance, but mostly to the fact that he called *papa* "Lyovochka" and treated him the way *papa* treated us. He was not in the least afraid of him and even teased him and disputed with him as an older person does with a child.

For instance, everyone knew that there were no swifter dogs in the world than our black-spotted Milka and her daughter Krylatka. No hare could escape them. Yet Uncle Seryozha contended that the hares in our district were sluggish. A steppe hare, now—that would be another matter. Neither Milka nor Krylatka could get near a steppe hare. We listened and did not know whom to believe, Uncle Seryozha or *papa*.

One day Uncle Seryozha went hunting with us. We ran down a number of hares, not one got away, but he showed absolutely no surprise and said that it was only because they were a poor lot of hares. And we had no way of knowing whether he was right or wrong. Perhaps he was right; he was more of a hunter than *papa*. After all, he had run down countless wolves, and we had never known *papa* to get one. *Papa* only kept the dogs because he had Agafya Mikhailovna, but Uncle Seryozha had given up hunting because he had no one to take care of his dogs.

"Since the Emancipation of the peasants, hunting is out of the question," he said. "There are no huntsmen to be had, and the peasants turn out with sticks and run the sportsmen off the fields. What is there left to do nowadays? Country life has become impossible."

In the summer, sometimes the whole family went to Pirogovo to visit Uncle Seryozha. It was a journey of about thirty versts over open country. We passed Yasenki on the way and Kolpna; it was somewhere near there, *maman* told us, that *papa* had once defended a soldier on trial for insulting an officer.[2] The man was condemned, however, and immediately taken out into a field and shot. Just to think of it was awful. It might have been according to law, but it was incomprehensible to us children.

Farther on, the road led past Ozerka and the mysterious bottomless lake, then dropped down and passed Cow's Tail and Sorochinka. At last, where a solitary shrine stood in a meadow, we turned left off the main road and saw in the distance a lovely church and a park in the depths of which was an interesting-looking two-winged stone house of an unusual architectural style.

Driving up to it, one became aware of a distinctly seignorial atmosphere peculiar to Pirogovo and quite different from what we were accustomed to at Yasnaya. This atmosphere could be felt in the village, where the peasants stopped and bowed obsequiously, the women and children followed us with their eyes as we drove by, and the kitchen boy rushed headlong to the house to announce the arrival of visitors, as well as in the whole aspect of the estate, with its neatly trimmed hedges and well-swept drive freshly sprinkled with sand.

From the entrance hall one went into the winter garden, where lemon trees grew in big tubs. In the salon stood a huge stuffed bear, and behind a sofa on some sort of stand lay a fox curled up asleep, looking exactly as if it were alive.

We were warmly welcomed by the charming Maria Mikhailovna and her three daughters, Vera, who was Tanya's age, and Varya and Masha, who were younger. Hearing the commotion, Uncle Seryozha came out of his room near the salon. In this room he not only slept but spent most of the day going over accounts, reckoning the income from his property by means of a complicated, laborious system of bookkeeping understood by no one but himself. One was required to enter the room very quickly and slam the door shut as fast as possible to keep the flies from getting in. It was on their account that the winter window frames were never taken out and no one except Uncle himself was ever permitted to go in and tidy the room.

Our hosts were always delighted to see us and gave us a hearty welcome. Uncle Seryozha would immediately begin telling "Lyovochka" about his latest frustrations in managing the estate.

"It's all very well for you, you're free as a bird and neither sow nor reap. You dash off a novel or buy up some property in Samara, but you should try this for a while. I've had to dismiss my steward again; he was robbing me right and left. Now Vasily is running things again, so I'm without a coachman."

Papa would smile and turn the conversation to another topic, and we children felt that the situation was quite normal, for Vasily, who had been Uncle Seryozha's coachman for many years, was almost always replacing one or another dishonest steward and was very rarely seen on the coach box.

It is astounding to what a degree certain of Uncle Seryozha's characteristics make one think of old Prince Bolkonsky in *War and Peace*, though he was certainly not the model for this character, having been a young man at the time the novel was written. I discussed this question with his eldest daughter, Vera Sergeyevna, and we were both struck by the prophetic insight of my father who, in describing the old Prince's relations with his beloved daughter Princess Marya, gave an exact picture of Uncle Seryozha's relations with Vera. There were the same mathematics lessons, the same shy, tender affection masked by indifference and outward cruelty, the same deep understanding of her nature, and the same indomitable, aristocratic pride that raised an impregnable wall between them and the rest of the world. A more perfect incarnation of the old Prince I cannot imagine.

Being a man of exemplary honesty and integrity, Uncle Seryozha never sought to conceal any aspect of his nature, with the exception of one: his tenderheartedness, which he hid out of shyness. And if he occasionally revealed his feelings, it was only in unusual circumstances and against his will. This inordinate restraint, the masking of feelings of affection with indifference or unwonted harshness, was a family trait, and while particularly marked in Uncle Seryozha, also was somewhat characteristic of my father.

When it came to wit or sarcasm, however, Uncle Seryozha was patently original. Once when he and his daughter had attended a historic concert [3] by Anton Rubenstein, they came to have tea with us afterward in Khamovniky Street. When Father asked Uncle Seryozha how he had enjoyed the concert, he said, "Do you remember Lieutenant Himbut, Lyovochka, a forester not far from Yasnaya? I once asked him what was the happiest moment of his life, and do you know what he replied?

'When I was a cadet, they used to take down my breeches, lay me across a bench, and flog me; when they finally stopped beating me, that was the happiest moment of my life.' Well, when Rubenstein finally stopped playing and there was an intermission, that was the happiest moment for me."

Even Father was not spared. Once when I was out hunting near Pirogovo, I stopped at Uncle Seryozha's for the night. At tea that evening, we happened to speak of Father, and in what connection I no longer remember, he began talking about "Lyovochka's pride."

"He's always preaching humility and nonresistance, but he himself is proud. Maria's sister had a footman called Foma who used to crawl under the staircase and curl up there whenever he got drunk. If he was told that the Countess was calling for him, he'd say, 'Let her come herself is she wants me.' And Lyovochka is just like that. When Dolgorukov sent his adjutant Istomin to ask him to come and discuss the sectarian Syutayev [4] with him, do you know what his answer was? 'Let him come himself.' Isn't that exactly like Foma? Yes, Lyovochka is very proud, nothing would have induced him to go. And he was absolutely right, but that has nothing to do with humility."

During the last years of Sergei Nikolayevich's life, he and Father were much closer, and Father enjoyed sharing his thoughts with him. Once he gave him one of his philosophical works and asked him to read it and tell him what he thought of it. Uncle Seryozha read the whole book through conscientiously, and when he returned it said, "Do you remember what it was like, Lyovochka, in the days when we traveled by post? The mud was frozen into hummocks in the autumn and you'd bounce along in a tarantass being bumped in the back, bumped on the sides, till you felt as if you couldn't stand another minute of it, and then suddenly you'd come out onto a smooth stretch of road and they'd give you a fine Viennese calash drawn by four splendid horses. Well, when I was reading your book, there was only one place where I felt as though I had got into the calash, and that was the passage—just a page—where you quote Herzen. All the rest, your stuff, was like bumping along in the tarantass." [5]

When he said such things, Uncle Seryozha knew of course that Father would not be offended but would laugh whole-heartedly with him. One could hardly have arrived at a more unexpected conclusion, and it goes without saying that no one but Uncle Seryozha would have ventured to say such a thing to my father. He once told us about an encounter on a railway journey with an unknown lady, one of those "buttonholing bores" who, when she learned that she was traveling in the same carriage with Count Tolstoy, brother of the celebrated writer, began pestering him with questions about what Lev Nikolayevich was writing at the time, and whether he himself also wrote.

"What my brother is writing, I do not know, but as for my-self, madam, I write only telegrams," he replied curtly, hoping to shut her up.

"Oh, what a pity!" she replied sympathetically. "It so often happens in life that one brother has all the gifts and the other has none." And she lapsed into silence.

The question put to Sergei Nikolayevich by the lady in the railway carriage is one that inevitably arose in the minds of those who were intimately acquainted with this remarkably clever and original man. As a writer he might have gone far; he was certainly not without material. Sitting alone in his room year after year, he spent a great deal of time thinking and living his own inner life, and if he sometimes uttered loud groans and exclamations for no apparent reason, it never alarmed his fam-ily when they heard him from several rooms away, for they knew it only meant that a thought had just occurred to him.

It was only very rarely, when someone he felt close to hap-pened to be present, that he let himself go and conversed brilliantly, enlarging on his thoughts and observations, which were always explicit, original, and deeply considered. Like the self-sufficient egoist described by my father in the fragment from his *Reminiscences* quoted earlier, Uncle Seryozha never felt a need to share his thoughts and impressions with others, and this was his great misfortune. He was deprived of that feeling of satisfaction that the writer experiences in pouring out his feelings on paper, and for want of this safety valve put too great a load on himself and became an intellectual ascetic.

In his memoirs, Afanasy Afanasyevich Fet gives a singularly perceptive characterization of the three Tolstoy brothers:

"I am convinced that the fundamental type of all the Tolstoy brothers is identical, just as the fundamental type of all maple leaves is identical, the variety of their configuration notwithstanding. And if I were to set myself to develop this idea, I could demonstrate to what degree the passionate enthusiasm that made it possible for one of them, Lev Tolstoy, to become a creative artist, was inherent in all three. The differences in their attitude to life lay in the way each of them relinquished his unfulfilled dreams. Nikolai cooled his ardor with skeptical mockery; Lev abandoned unrealized dreams with silent remorse, and Sergei with morbid misanthropy. The greater the original store of love in such characters, the stronger the resemblance, if only for a time, to *Timon of Athens*."[6]

In the winter of 1901–2, when my father lay ill in the Crimea, hovering for a time between life and death, Uncle Seryozha did not feel strong enough to leave Pirogovo and anxiously followed the course of Father's illness in newspaper reports and our letters. But when Father began to recover and I could leave him and go home, I stopped at Pirogovo on my way and gave him a personal report. I remember with what joy and gratitude he welcomed me.

"Oh, how good that you have come! Now, tell me, tell me everything. Who is with him now? All of them? Who nurses him most of the time? . . . Do they take turns? At night too? . . . He can't get up? Yes, yes, that's the worst of all! It will soon be my turn to die—a year sooner, a year later, what does it matter? But to lie helpless, a burden to everyone, to have others do everything for you, lift you, help you to sit up—that's what's so awful!

"And how does he bear all this? Got used to it, you say? No, I can't imagine having Vera change my linen and wash me. Of course, she would say it was nothing for her, but for me it would be awful.

"And tell me, is he afraid to die? . . . He says he's not? It's possible—after all, he's strong, he might be able to conquer this fear. Yes, yes . . . Perhaps he's not afraid . . . and yet . . .

"You say he struggles with the feeling? Why, naturally, what else can one do? I wanted to go to him, but then I thought, how can I? I'll break down, and then there'll be two invalids instead of one. But you've told me a great deal, and every detail is of interest to me.

"It's not death that's terrible, what's terrible is illness, help-lessness, and, above all, the dread of being a burden to others. That is awful, awful!"

Uncle Seryozha died in 1904 of cancer of the face. My aunt Maria Nikolayevna told me that he was on his feet almost to the end and refused to let anyone nurse him.

Besides his own family—the elderly Maria Mikhailovna and his daughters—his sister Maria Nikolayevna, the nun, was with him at the end, and my father was expected hourly; they had sent a messenger to Yasnaya for him. The difficult question of whether he would wish to receive the last Sacraments arose. Knowing his lack of faith, no one dared to broach the subject, and poor Maria Mikhailovna, in great anguish, hovered about and prayed constantly. They were eager for Father to come, yet secretly feared his influence and hoped that Sergei Nikola-yevich would ask for a priest before his arrival.

"And how amazed and happy we were," Maria Nikolayevna told me later, "when Lyovochka came out of his room and told Maria Mikhailovna that Seryozha wanted them to send for a priest. I don't know what they had said to each other, but when Seryozha told him he wanted to receive the last Sacraments, Lyovochka's response was that he was right, and he came and told us at once." *

Father spent about a week at Pirogovo and returned home

---

*I do not believe that Sergei Nikolayevich's attitude toward the church had changed before death. I think that both he and my father, who did nothing to dissuade him from receiving the Sacraments, made this concession for the peace of mind of those to whom it meant much.—I.T.

just two days before Uncle died. When the telegram came saying that his brother's condition had worsened, he set out once
more for Pirogovo, but arrived too late to see him alive. He
carried the body from the house and bore it to the churchyard.
When he got back to Yasnaya, he spoke with affecting tenderness of parting with that "inscrutable and beloved brother, who
was strangely remote and at the same time infinitely dear to
me."

XVI

Fet. Strakhov. Gay

"WHAT's this saber doing here?" the young guardsman, Lieutenant Afanasy Afanasyevich Fet, asked the footman as he entered Ivan Sergeyevich Turgenev's flat in Petersburg one day in the middle of the fifties.

"It belongs to Count Tolstoy. He's asleep in the drawing room. And Ivan Sergeyevich is in his study having breakfast," replied Zakhar.

"During the hour I spent with Turgenev," Fet writes in his memoirs, "we spoke in an undertone for fear of waking the Count, who was sleeping in the next room. 'It's like this all the time,' Turgenev said to me with a smile. 'He's been carousing ever since he left his battery in Sevastopol and came to stay with me. Gambling, drinking, and gypsies all night long. Then he sleeps like a dead man till two in the afternoon. I did my best to restrain him, but now I've given up.'

131

"It was on this visit to Petersburg that Tolstoy and I became acquainted, but in a purely formal way, as I had neither read a line of his work nor even heard of him as a name in literature, though Turgenev had spoken of his stories of childhood." [1]

Soon after this my father and Fet came to know each other well and developed a firm and lasting friendship and a correspondence that lasted almost to the time of Afanasy Afanasyevich's death. It was only in the last years of Fet's life, when Father was completely absorbed in new ideas that were at variance with Afanasy Afanasyevich's whole philosophy of life, that they became estranged and met only rarely. In the early stages of their friendship, their paths had run parallel. They met when they were both young officers and novices in literature; then both married—Fet considerably earlier than my father—and both settled in the country.

Fet lived at his farm, Stepanovka, in the Mtsensk District, not far from Spasskoye-Lutinovo, Turgenev's estate, and at one time Turgenev, my father, and his elder brother Nikolai used to meet there to go game hunting, often going on to Spasskoye and my Uncle Nikolai's estate at Nikolsko-Vyazemskoye. It was at Fet's that my father's quarrel with Turgenev took place.

Before the railroad was built and travel was still by coach, Fet always stopped to see my father on his way to Moscow, and these visits became an established custom. Later, when he traveled by train, he almost always broke his journey to come and see us, and if for some reason he failed to come, Father wrote and reproached him so vehemently that he apologized as though guilty of some wrong.

In that remote period of which I am speaking, Father and Fet had a common bond, not only in their literary interests, but in farming. Some of my father's letters of the sixties are curious in this respect. In 1860, for instance, he writes a long discourse on Turgenev's *On the Eve,* which had just come out, and adds this postscript, "What is the cost of a set of the best veterinary instruments? Also a pair of lancets and bleeding cups for use on humans?" [2]

In another letter he writes, "By the same post I am writing to Nikolskoye to have him send for the mare. . . . Do write to me about the price." And this is followed by, "*Tender art Thou . . .* and the whole thing is charming. You have never done anything better. All charming." (The quotation is from Fet's poem *The Last of the Lingering Clouds Floats over Us.*[3])

But it was not only community of interests that brought my father and Afanasy Afanasyevich together. The reason they were so congenial was that they "thought alike with the heart's mind," as Father expressed it. "From various almost imperceptible signs," he wrote to Fet in 1876, "it has suddenly become clear to me that we are profoundly similar in our natures —our souls." [4] And in the autumn of that same year, he reiterated, ". . . it's amazing how akin we are in mind and heart." [5]

He used to say of Fet that his chief merit was that he thought independently instead of borrowing images and ideas from others, and considered him one of our finest poets and on a level with Tyuchev. After Fet died, Father often recalled certain of his poems and, singling me out for some reason, would say, "Ilyusha, repeat those lines beginning 'I thought . . .' I can't remember what he thought; or, 'The world's asleep . . .' You must know them." And he listened with delight, sometimes with tears in his eyes, prompting me in his favorite passages.

I remember Fet's visits from the time of my childhood. He almost always brought his wife, Maria Petrovna, with him, and they sometimes stayed for several days. He had a distinctly Jewish type of face, a long black grizzled beard, and small feminine hands with unusually long well-manicured fingernails. He spoke in a deep bass voice and had a fitful protracted cough that rattled like small shot, after which he would pause, lower his head, and with a lengthy "hm . . . hm . . ." stroke his beard and go on talking. He was extremely witty at times and entertained the whole household with jokes that were all the more enjoyable for being completely spontaneous.

My sister Tanya used to give a perfect imitation of Fet reading his own poetry. "This is the portrait, li-i-ke and yet un-li-i-ike . . . hm . . . hm . . . wherein the li-i-keness and unlikeness li-ies in the hm . . . hmm . . . hmmm . . ."

One is not much interested in poetry in early childhood,

which at that time of life seems to have been invented for the
sole purpose of forcing small children to memorize it. I got so
sick of Pushkin's *The Children Ran into the Hut* and Lermon-
tov's *Angel,* both of which I was compelled to learn by heart,
that it was years before I could enjoy poetry, and I sulked over
every poem as if it were a form of punishment. So it is hardly
surprising that I disliked Fet at the time and thought that he
and *papa* were good friends only because he was "funny." It
was only much later that I learned to understand him as a poet
and to love him as he deserved.

I also remember the visits of Nikolai Nikolayevich Strakhov,
a remarkably quiet, modest man. He first appeared at Yasnaya
in the early seventies and spent almost every summer with us
from then on. He had large wide-open gray eyes that gave him
a perpetually astonished look, and a long beard streaked with
gray. When he spoke, every phrase was punctuated by a dep-
recatory little laugh. He slept downstairs in Father's study,
where he used to spend the entire day reading and writing,
never without one of the thick cigars, which he rolled himself,
held in his mouth. An hour before dinner, when the wagonette
drawn by two horses drove up to the door and we all assembled
to drive to the bathhouse, Nikolai Nikolayevich joined us,
wearing a soft gray hat and carrying his towel and walking
stick. Everyone without exception was fond of him, children
and grown-ups alike; indeed, it would be hard to conceive of
anyone not liking him.

He used to recite a humorous poem beginning "Fades the
leaf," by Kozma Prutov [6] so amusingly that we children would
beg him for it and give him no peace till he at last gave in and
recited it from beginning to end. After his emphatic conclusion,
"Junker Schmidt, word of honor, summer will return," he always smiled and broke into his little laugh.

Strakhov's was the first and best critical work on *War and
Peace* and *Anna Karenina.* When the *ABC Book* and the *Readers* were published, he helped Father with the editing,[7] and
before long what had begun as a business correspondence de-

veloped into a friendly and philosophical one. Father had a high regard for his critical acumen and at the time he was writing *Anna Karenina* set great store by his opinion. "It is enough for me that you think so," he writes in a letter to him in 1872 (probably in connection with "A Prisoner in the Caucasus.")[8]

In 1876, referring to *Anna Karenina,* he writes, "In your letter you ask me whether you have understood my novel aright, and what I think of your opinion. Of course you have understood it aright, and of course I am inexpressibly happy over this; but it does not necessarily follow that everyone will understand it as you have." [9]

It was not alone his critical work, however, that drew my father and Strakhov together. *Papa* disliked critics as a rule and used to say that only those with no creative faculties of their own took up this form of work. "The stupid judging the intelligent," he used to say of professional critics. Even when Father happened to put a scientific question to him in conversation (Strakhov was a scientist by education), his answer was so precise and lucid that it was like listening to the exposition of a good teacher.

"Do you know what most impressed me about you?" Father writes in one of his letters to him. "It was the expression on your face as you came through the balcony door from the gardens one day, not knowing that I was in the study. That remote concentrated austere expression was what made me understand you—with the help of all you had written and said, of course. I am convinced that you are destined for a purely philosophical career. . . . You have one quality that I have never found in any other Russian, which is that, along with your clarity and conciseness of expression, you have a gentleness combined with strength; you do not tear at a thing with your teeth, but go at it with gentle powerful paws." [10]

Strakhov was "a real friend," as Father said, and I remember him with deep affection and respect.

And now I come to the man who was closer to my father in spirit than was any other human being: Nikolai Nikolayevich

Gay. "Grandfather Gay," as we used to call him, became acquainted with my father in 1882. Living on his farm in the province of Chernigov, he happened to read Father's pamphlet *On the Census*,[11] and finding in it solutions to the very problems that were troubling him at the time, set out for Moscow without delay. I remember his first visit, which left me with the impression that he and Father understood each other from the first moment and spoke the same language.

Like my father, Gay was going through a grave spiritual crisis at the time and, traveling virtually the same road as Father in his search for truth, had arrived at a study of the Gospel and a new understanding of it. In the article devoted to him in *Friends and Visitors at Yasnaya Polyana*, my sister Tanya writes, "He cherished a passionate, tender love for the personality of Christ, whom he loved with all the strength of his soul."

Often during a heated argument Nikolai Nikolayevich would take from his pocket a copy of the Gospel, which he always carried with him, and read an appropriate passage. "This book contains all a man needs," he used to say on such occasions. As he read, he raised his eyes, fixed them on his listener, and finished the passage without again looking down at the book. His face glowed with such inward joy at these moments that one could see how precious, how near to his heart, were the words he was reading. He knew the Gospel almost by heart and used to say that every time he read it he experienced a new and genuine spiritual joy; that not only was everything in it comprehensible to him, but when reading it he seemed to be reading his own soul and felt himself capable of rising higher and higher toward God and merging with Him.[12]

When he visited us in Moscow, Nikolai Nikolayevich offered to paint a portrait of my sister Tanya, "in return for all the good you have done me," he said. *Papa* asked him to paint my mother instead, and the next day Gay brought paints and canvas and set to work. I do not recall how much time he spent on it, but in the end, despite the thousands of comments the portrait evoked (all of which were listened to and taken into consideration), or perhaps because of them, the portrait was not a success and he destroyed it. As a fine artist, he could not be satisfied with a merely external likeness, and having painted "a lady in a velvet dress with forty thousand rubles in her pocket," he was himself perturbed by it and decided to make a fresh start. It was not until several years later, however, when he knew my mother better and had grown to love her, that he painted the three-quarter-length portrait of her with my two-year-old sister Sasha in her arms.[13]

"Grandfather" was like a member of the family from the first and visited us often both in Moscow and at Yasnaya. When he painted the portrait of my father in his Moscow study, *papa* grew so accustomed to his presence that he paid not the slightest heed to him and continued working as if he were not there.[14] It was in this room that "Grandfather" used to sleep when he stayed with us.

He had an extraordinarily appealing and intelligent face. With his wise candid eyes and the long gray curls that encircled his bald pate, he looked like an Old Testament prophet. When he got excited, as he invariably did whenever the conversation turned on art or the teachings of the Gospel, his burning eyes and forceful sweeping gestures gave him the aspect of a preacher. And though I had absolutely no interest in religious questions at the age of sixteen or seventeen, I was never bored by "Grandfather's sermons" and in fact loved listening to them. This can undoubtedly be attributed to the tremendous love and sincerity that one felt in all he said.

It was my father who influenced Gay to resume his painting, which had long been abandoned. Several of his late works such as *What Is Truth?* and *The Crucifixion* were the fruits of his new understanding and interpretation of Gospel subjects and to some extent were inspired by Father. Before beginning a painting, Gay would nurture it in his soul for a long time, and always shared these projects with my father, who was keenly interested in his ideas and sincerely delighted with his suggestive conceptions and his technique.

Nikolai Nikolayevich's friendship was very dear to my father.

He was the first man who wholly shared Father's convictions, and he loved him without reservation. Having embarked on the search for truth, they both served it with all the strength of their being and found support in each other and their shared experiences. Just as Father closely followed Gay's work, so Gay never let a word that Father wrote escape him; he copied out his manuscripts himself and begged us to send him anything new that came from his pen.

Both men gave up smoking at the same time, and both became vegetarians. They were of one mind even in their love of manual labor and their recognition of it as a vital necessity. Gay happened to be very skillful at building brick ovens, and had built all those at his farm and for the peasants as well. When Father learned of this, he asked him to build one for a widow at Yasenki for whom he himself had just put up a clay cottage. "Grandfather" put on his apron and they set to work at once, he as the master workman and Father as his apprentice.

Nikolai Nikolayevich died in 1894. When the telegram came announcing his death, my sisters Tanya and Masha were so overcome by grief they could not bring themselves to tell Father, and the painful duty of showing him the telegram fell to *maman*.

XVII
Turgenev

I do not intend to recount the misunderstandings between Turgenev and my father which terminated in their complete estrangement in 1861. The factual side of the story is well known, and there is no necessity to repeat it here.[1] According to popular opinion, the quarrel between the two greatest writers of the day sprang from their literary rivalry. I am obliged to refute this generally accepted view and, before discussing Turgenev's visits to Yasnaya Polyana, wish to make as clear as possible the real cause of the constant dissensions between those two splendid men who had a sincere affection for each other—dissensions which finally led to an open quarrel and mutual recriminations.

As far as I know, my father never had a serious falling out with anyone in his life except Turgenev, and in a letter that Turgenev wrote to Father in 1865 he said, "You are the only man with whom I have ever had misunderstandings." [2] When speaking of his quarrel with Ivan Sergeyevich, Father blamed only himself, and immediately after the quarrel Turgenev wrote him a letter of apology and never at any time sought to justify himself.

Why was it then that their "constellations moved through the ether in positive hostility," as Turgenev himself expressed it? In her book, my sister Tatyana said of this, "There could be no question of literary rivalry, it seems to me. Turgenev acknowledged my father's literary talent from the very outset of his career, and never thought of competing with him. From the time he wrote to Kolbasin in 1854, 'If God lets him live, I firmly believe that Tolstoy will amaze us all,' [3] he never ceased to follow my father's career and to express his admiration for him."

In 1856, in a letter to Druzhinin, Turgenev wrote, "When this new wine has fermented, it will be a drink worthy of the gods." [4] And in 1857, writing to Polonsky, "This man will go far, and leave a deep imprint behind him." [5] Yet these two men never got on together. Reading Turgenev's letters to my father, one sees that there were continual misunderstandings from the very beginning of their acquaintance, which, though they always tried to smooth them over and forget them, inevitably cropped up again, sometimes in another form, and gave rise to renewed explanations and reconciliations.

In 1856, Turgenev wrote to my father, "Your letter took a long time to reach me, dear Lev Nikolayevich. Let me begin by saying that I am most grateful to you for having written it, and for sending it to me. I shall never cease to love you and to value your friendship, although—and this is probably my fault—it may be some time before we cease feeling slightly awkward in each other's presence. I think you yourself understand the reason for this awkwardness of which I speak. You are the only man with whom I have ever had misunderstandings, and they have arisen precisely because I was unwilling to confine myself to only friendly relations with you and wanted to go further and deeper; but I set about it unwisely, irritated and upset you, and when I saw my mistake, withdrew too hastily perhaps. And it is this that created the 'gulf' between us.

"But this awkwardness is only a physical sensation, nothing more; and if, when we meet, I still have this 'blind spot,' believe me, it is not because I am a bad person. There is no need to look for any other interpretation, I assure you. I may add that I am much older than you, and have traveled a different road. Apart from our special so-called literary interests—and I am convinced of this—we have few points of contact. Your whole life aspires to the future; mine is built on the past. For me to follow you is impossible; for you to follow me is equally out of the question. You are too far from me, and besides, you stand too firmly on your own feet to become any man's disciple. I can assure you that I have never attributed malice to you, never suspected you of literary envy. I have often been inclined to think (please forgive the expression) that you were wanting in common sense, but never in goodness. You are too perceptive not to realize that if either of us has cause to envy the other, it is certainly not you." [6]

The following year, Turgenev wrote a letter to my father which, it seems to me, provides the key to an understanding of his attitude toward him. "You write that you are very glad you did not follow my advice, did not become only a man of letters. I cannot dispute you—perhaps you are right; still, I must confess that however long I puzzle over it, I cannot imagine what you are if not a man of letters: an officer? a landowner? a philosopher? the founder of a new religious sect? a civil servant? a businessman? Please help me out of my difficulty and tell me which of these suppositions is correct? I am joking, of course, but I should really like so much to see you under full sail at last." [7]

It seems that, as an artist, Turgenev saw in my father only his great literary talent, and was unwilling to recognize his *right* to be anything other than an artist and writer. Any other sort of activity on Father's part was an affront, as it were, to Turgenev and made him angry with Father for not following his advice and devoting himself exclusively to writing. He was much older than Father yet did not hesitate to rank his talent higher than his own, and demanded only one thing of him: that he devote all his energies to his literary work. But Father would have nothing to do with his magnanimity and modesty; he refused to heed his advice and followed the path of his own spiritual needs. Turgenev's tastes and character were diametrically opposed to my father's. While opposition always inspired Father and gave him strength, it had just the opposite effect on Turgenev.[8]

Being wholly in accord with my sister's views, I will add only the comment made by my father's brother, Nikolai Nikolayevich Tolstoy: "Turgenev cannot reconcile himself to the idea that Lyovochka is growing up and withdrawing from his tutelage."

As a matter of fact, when Turgenev was already a famous writer, no one had yet heard of Tolstoy, and in Fet's words, there was merely "some talk of his stories of childhood." I can imagine with what secret veneration a young writer like my father, who was only a novice at the time, must have regarded Turgenev. And all the more because Ivan Sergeyevich was a great friend of his eldest and favorite brother, Nikolai.

This passage from a letter to Fet from V. P. Botkin, a close friend of both my father and Turgenev, written just after their quarrel, confirms my own opinion. "As a matter of fact, I think that Tolstoy has a passionately loving nature, and would have liked to love Turgenev with all his heart, but unfortunately his impetuosity met with only bland good-natured indifference. And this is something absolutely intolerable to him."[9]

Turgenev himself said that in the early period of their friendship Father dogged his footsteps "like a woman in love," and for a time he avoided him out of fear of his contrary attitude.

I hesitate to affirm it, yet it seems to me that just as Turgenev was unwilling to confine himself to "only friendly relations," so my father was far too hotheaded in his relations with Ivan Sergeyevich, and this was the reason they could never meet without a dispute or a quarrel. And while Father was perhaps irritated by the slightly patronizing tone that Turgenev adopted toward him in the early days of their friendship, Turgenev was irritated by my father's "queer ideas," which distracted him from his "profession—literature."

In 1860, before the quarrel, Turgenev wrote to Fet, "Lev Nikolayevich continues to be a crank. It was evidently preordained. When will he turn his final somersault and land on his feet at last?" [10]

He had the same attitude toward Father's *Confession,* which he read not long before his death. Having promised to read it, "to try to understand it and not lose my temper," he "started to write a long letter in answer to the *Confession* . . . but never finished it—for fear of falling into a controversial tone." [11] In a letter to Grigorevich he termed this work, which in his opinion was based on false premises, "a denial of any kind of human life" and "a kind of nihilism." [12]

It is obvious that even then Turgenev did not realize how completely Father was dominated by his new world-view and was inclined to ascribe this fresh outburst of enthusiasm—as he had previously ascribed his interest in pedagogy, farming, publishing a magazine, and so forth—to his characteristic eccentricity, his "somersaults."

Ivan Sergeyevich visited Yasnaya Polyana three times within my memory: in August and September of 1878, and in May of 1880 for the third and last time.[13]

I remember his first visit as being a great event in our lives, with *maman* being more excited than any of us as we awaited his arrival. She told us that our father had quarreled with Turgenev and had once challenged him to a duel, and that now he was coming at *papa's* invitation to effect a reconciliation.

Turgenev spent most of the time alone with *papa,* who had even set aside his work for the time he was there. On one of the days, however, *maman* unexpectedly gathered us all together in the drawing room to hear Ivan Sergeyevich read his story "The Dog."[14] I remember his tall powerful figure, his silky yellowish gray hair, and his supple, rather slipshod, gait. He had a high-pitched voice that was quite incongruous with his majestic exterior, and a rippling childlike laugh that made his voice rise even higher.

In the evening after dinner, we all assembled in the salon. Our other guests at the time were Uncle Seryozha, Prince Leonid Dmitrievich Urusov, the Vice-Governor of Tula, Uncle Sasha Behrs and his beautiful young Georgian wife, Patty, and the whole Kuzminsky family. Aunt Tanya was asked to sing, and we listened with bated breath to hear what Turgenev, who was known to be a connoisseur, would say about her voice. Of course he praised it—sincerely, I believe.

After the singing, a quadrille was got up, and someone asked Turgenev whether the French still danced the old-fashioned quadrille, or if everyone had taken up the cancan.

"The old cancan was not at all like the new improper version of it, which is now being danced in the *cafés chantants;* the old cancan is a graceful decorous dance," he said. And suddenly he stood up, took one of the ladies by the hand, and putting his thumbs in the armholes of his vest began to dance an old-fashioned cancan, dipping and rising with great style. Everyone roared with laughter, and he most of all.[15]

During the talk among the grown-ups after tea, a heated discussion arose and Prince Urusov very vehemently attacked Turgenev on some score. This occurred at the beginning of my father's "spiritual rebirth" (as he himself called it), and Prince Urusov was among the first sincerely to embrace his views. I do not remember what the Prince had been arguing about, but he was sitting at a table opposite Ivan Sergeyevich making broad gestures with his arm, when all at once his chair slipped out from under him and he landed on the floor in exactly the same posture, with one arm outstretched and his forefinger pointing menacingly. And he sat there, not the least disconcerted, and, still gesticulating, finished the sentence.

Looking at him Turgenev burst into laughter. "He kills me, *il m'assomme,* that Trubetskoy!" he piped through his laughter, calling the Prince by the wrong name. Urusov was on the point of taking offense, but when he saw that everyone was laughing, he stood up and joined in the general hilarity.

On one of the evenings that Turgenev was there—a wonderful summer night—we were all sitting around the table in the little drawing room when someone (I think it was *maman*) proposed that everyone present should describe the happiest moment of his life.

"You begin, Ivan Sergeyevich," she said, turning to Turgenev.

"The happiest moment of my life was when I first read in the eyes of the woman I loved that she loved me in return," said Ivan Sergeyevich, and fell into a reverie.

"Now it's your turn, Sergei Nikolayevich," said Aunt Tanya to Uncle Sergei.

"I'll tell you, but I'll have to whisper it in your ear," he said with his knowing, sarcastic smile. "The happiest moment of my life . . ." and the rest was whispered into Tatyana Andreyevna's ear and I did not hear what he said.

"Ai, ai, ai! You're always saying such things, Sergei Nikolayevich. You're an impossible man!" she said, drawing back from him with a laugh.

"What did Sergei Nikolayevich say?" asked *maman,* who never understood a joke.

"I'll tell you later."

And that put an end to the game.

I remember that on Turgenev's third visit we went hunting. It was the second or third of May 1880, and we all went out together to the other side of the Voronka. *Papa* gave Turgenev the best place and went himself to the edge of a glade a hundred and fifty paces away. *Maman* stood near Turgenev, and we children lit a bonfire not far off. *Papa* fired several shots and brought down two birds, but Ivan Sergeyevich had no luck and kept watching Father with envy. Just when it was beginning to grow dark, a woodcock flew over and he shot it.

"Killed it?" Father called from his place.

"Fell like a stone. Send your dog to pick it up," replied Ivan Sergeyevich.

Papa sent us with the dog. Turgenev showed us where to look for the bird, but though we searched and searched, and the dog

too, we could not find it. Then Turgenev came, followed by
papa, but there was no woodcock to be found.

"Perhaps you only winged it, and it got away," said *papa*,
puzzled. "It's impossible that the dog shouldn't have found it,
he couldn't miss a bird that was killed."

"But I tell you, Lev Nikolayevich, I saw it with my own eyes
—it fell like a stone. It wasn't wounded, I killed it outright—I
can tell the difference."

"Then why hasn't the dog found it? It can't be—there's something wrong."

"I don't know. I can only tell you that I'm not lying; it fell like
a stone," insisted Turgenev.

But the woodcock was not found and the incident gave rise
to an unpleasant atmosphere, as if one or the other of them had
been in the wrong; either Turgenev in saying that he had killed
the bird outright, or *papa* in asserting that the dog could not
have failed to find a bird that had been killed. And this occurred just when they were both so anxious to avoid any sort of
misunderstanding that they had abstained from serious conversation and spent all their time in pleasant diversions.

That evening as he was saying good night to us *papa* whispered that we were to get up early and go back and make a
thorough search for the bird. And what was the result? In falling, the woodcock had got caught in a fork at the very top of an
aspen tree, and it was all we could do to dislodge it. When we
brought it home in triumph, it was a great occasion, and *papa*
and Turgenev were even more delighted than we were. They
had both been right, as it turned out, and the incident ended
to their mutual satisfaction.

Ivan Sergeyevich slept downstairs in Father's study. When
we dispersed for the night, I accompanied him to his room and
sat on the bed talking about hunting while he got undressed.
He asked me whether I knew how to shoot. I told him I did, but
that I didn't care to go hunting because I had nothing but a
worthless single-barrel gun.

"I'll give you a gun," he said. "I've got two in Paris and one
is quite enough for me. It's not an expensive gun, but it's a good
one. I'll bring it with me next time I come to Russia."

I was embarrassed but tremendously happy at the thought of having a real "center-fire" gun. Unfortunately, Turgenev never came to Russia again.[16] Later I tried, but without success, to buy from his heirs the gun he had spoken of, not because it was a "center-fire," but because it was Turgenev's gun.

This is all I can recall about that delightful, ingenuously warmhearted man with the childlike eyes and childlike laugh, and in my mind the image of his grandeur merges with the charm of his kindness and simplicity.

In 1883, *papa* received his last letter from Ivan Sergeyevich, written in pencil when he was on his deathbed, and I remember with what emotion he read it. And when the news of his death came, *papa* could talk of nothing else for days, and sought from every possible source the details of his illness and last days.

Apropos of this letter, I should like to say that *papa* was genuinely indignant when he heard applied to himself the epithet "great writer of the land of Russia," which was taken from the letter.[17] He always detested clichés, and considered this one absurd.

"Why 'writer of the land'? I never knew before that a man could be the writer of a land. People take up some nonsensical expression and go on repeating it without any reason."

Earlier I have quoted extracts from Turgenev's letters which show the consistency with which he extolled my father's literary talents. Unfortunately, I cannot say the same of my father's attitude toward him. Here again his passionate nature asserted itself. Personal relations prevented him from being objective.

In 1867 he wrote to Fet, referring to Turgenev's novel *Smoke,* which had just appeared, "There is hardly any love in it, and hardly any poetry. It shows love as nothing but wanton adultery, and consequently the poetry of the story is repugnant. . . . I hesitate to express this opinion because I am unable to form a sober judgment of an author *whose personality I dislike."* [18]

In 1865 he had written to Fet, "I do not like *Enough.* A personal, subjective treatment is good only when it is imbued with life and passion, but in this the subjectivity is pervaded with insipid suffering." [19]

In the autumn of 1883, after Turgenev's death, when our

family had gone to Moscow for the winter and Father remained at Yasnaya Polyana with only Agafya Mikhailovna, he set about earnestly reading all of Turgenev's works.

"I am always thinking about Turgenev," he wrote to my mother at this time. "I am terribly fond of him, feel sorry, and do nothing but read him. I live with him constantly. I shall certainly give a lecture on him, or write one and have it read; tell Yuryev . . ." [20] And in another letter to her, "I have just finished reading Turgenev's *Enough*. Read it, it's charming. . . ." [21]

This lecture was never delivered, unfortunately. The Government, in the person of the Minister Count D. A. Tolstoy, prohibited my father from paying this last tribute to the dead friend he had quarreled with all his life only because he could not be indifferent to him.

XVIII

Garshin

My recollections of Vsevelod Mikhailovich Garshin date from early childhood and are therefore few and fragmentary. He visited Yasnaya Polyana in the early spring of 1880, and I learned subsequently from his biography that when he went from Tula to Kharkov that same spring, he was put in a psychiatric hospital. This explains a certain crudeness in the behavior of that modest and charming man, which struck us at the time as being very strange, and thanks to which I have a vivid recollection of his first appearance at Yasnaya Polyana.

It never occurred to any of us then that we were in the presence of a sick man who was agitated by an impending breakdown, and consequently not entirely normal. We explained his behavior as being mere eccentricity. After all, he was not the first eccentric to visit Yasnaya Polyana!

It was between five and six o'clock in the evening and we were sitting at the big table in the salon just finishing dinner, when the footman Sergei Petrovich told my father that "some man" was downstairs asking to see him.

"What does he want?" my father asked.

"He didn't say; he wants to see you."

"All right, I'll be down in a moment."

Without finishing his dessert, Father got up and went downstairs. We children jumped up and ran after him. In the entrance hall stood a young man, rather poorly dressed, with his overcoat on. My father greeted him and asked what he wanted.

"The first thing I want is a glass of vodka and the tail of a herring," he said, looking into my father's eyes with a bold, bright expression and smiling ingenuously.

My father was not prepared for such an answer and was momentarily taken aback. What was the meaning of such an extraordinary reply from an apparently sober, modest, and intelligent young man? What sort of queer fish was this? My father looked at him again with his deep penetrating gaze, and as their eyes met he broke into a broad grin. Garshin too smiled, like a child who has played a prank and looks into his mother's eyes to see if his little joke has been appreciated. And it was appreciated. Not the prank, of course; it was rather the deep luminous eyes of the child that had found favor. There was such candor, spirituality, and at the same time such pure and childlike goodness in this man's gaze that it would have been impossible not to take an interest in him and treat him kindly. And this is evidently what Lev Nikolayevich felt. He told Sergei to bring vodka and appetizers, opened the door to the study, and invited Garshin to take off his coat and come in.

"You must be frozen," he said kindly, as he scrutinized his visitor.

"I don't know, perhaps I am a little, I've been traveling a long time."

After a glass of vodka and a bite of food, Garshin gave my father his name and told him that he "did a little writing."

"And what have you written?"

"*Four Days.* The story was published in *Notes of the Fatherland.*[1] You probably didn't pay any attention to it."

"Of course, I remember, I remember it well. So it was you who wrote that excellent story! I paid particular attention to it. You must have been in the war."

"Yes, I went through the whole campaign." [2]

"I can imagine what a lot of interesting things you must have seen. Come, tell us about it. This is most interesting."

And Father began to question Garshin in detail and at length about what he had seen and experienced. He sat beside him on the leather-covered sofa and we children gathered around them. I do not remember this conversation very clearly and therefore shall not attempt to repeat it here. I only recall that it was tremendously interesting. The man who had somewhat startled us in the entrance hall no longer existed. Before us sat an intelligent and charming companion who gave a graphic and veracious picture of the horrors of war he had experienced, and his account was so fascinating that we spent the whole evening listening, unable to take our eyes off him.

Recalling that evening now, when I know that poor Vsevelod Mikhailovich was on the verge of a serious psychological breakdown, and searching my impressions for symptoms of his illness, I can only say that if he manifested any signs of abnormality, it was in his excessive and spellbinding talk. He re-created scene after scene for us, his eyes wide and burning, and the more he talked the more fluent his speech became. When he paused, as he did from time to time, the expression of his face changed and he became the same gentle charming child as before.

I do not remember whether he spent the night at Yasnaya or left the same day. A few days later he came again, this time on horseback. We saw him from the window as he rode up the avenue, talking to himself and making strange gestures. When he reached the house he dismounted and, still holding the reins, inquired whether we had a map of Russia. Someone asked him what he wanted it for.

"I want to find out how to get to Kharkov; I'm going to see my mother."

"On horseback?"

"Why, yes. What's so surprising in that?"

We got out an atlas and helped him look for Kharkov. He made a note of the towns he would have to pass on the way, then said good-bye and left.

Later we learned that he had somehow contrived to unharness the horse he was riding from a cab in Tula. The owner of the horse, not suspecting that he had to do with a sick man, spent a long time searching for his horse and recovered it only with great difficulty. After this episode, Garshin disappeared. How he managed to reach Kharkov and came to be put in a hospital, I do not know.

A few years later two thin volumes of his stories appeared.[3] I read them—by then I was a grown youth—and, needless to say, was deeply impressed. Could they have been written by the man with the remarkable eyes who sat in the study that night and told us all those fascinating stories? Yes, yes, of course, it was he, and I recognized him in those two little books. But what had once been no more than the casual interest of a child in a stranger who had crossed his path was transformed into a deep regard for the man and artist, and I cherish even these sad and fragmentary memories of him.

About a year before his death, I had the good fortune to see Garshin once more at our house in Moscow. Father happened to be out at the time and my mother received him. He was silent and morose and did not stay long. I remember *maman* asking him why he wrote so little.

"How can I write when I'm occupied all day long with work that stupefies me and makes my head ache?" he replied bitterly, and fell into a reverie.

Maman then began to inquire about his personal life and treated him with great kindness and sympathy. I was again struck by his large beautiful eyes shadowed by long lashes, and could not help comparing them with the eyes I had noticed the first time he visited us. Then they had glowed with vitality and daring; now they were sad and pensive. Life had robbed them of their brilliance, had drawn a veil of sorrow over them. And this sorrow was reflected in his whole being. It made one feel like speaking very quietly and tenderly to him, like cherishing and caressing him. When I learned of his death I was not surprised. Such men do not live long.

My own answer to the question put to Garshin by my mother —why he wrote so little—would be to repeat what Turgenev had said of my father's brother, Nikolai Nikolayevich Tolstoy: "He wrote little because he had all the good qualities but none of the shortcomings a man needs to become a great writer."

XIX

The First "Dark People." Assassination of
Aleksandr II. The Spy

THE revolutionary movement that led up to the
events of March 1, 1881, hardly touched Yasnaya Polyana, and
we knew of it only from newspaper accounts of attempted
assassinations that occurred almost yearly in Russia during that
period.

My father was visited from time to time by certain "dark people," whom he received in his study and with whom he always
argued heatedly. As a rule these unkempt, unwashed visitors
appeared only once at Yasnaya and, receiving no encouragement from Father, disappeared forever. The only ones who returned were those who became interested in his new ideas of
Christianity and certain "Nihilists" who in later years turned up
frequently at Yasnaya and under his influence gave up terror-
ism altogether. Not accepting violence, Father could not ap-
prove of the terrorist methods of these revolutionists, and with
his firm belief in the principles of nonresistance, he necessarily
felt that violence could lead to no good.

"The revolutionist and the Christian," he said, "stand at the two extreme points of an uncompleted circle, and consequently their proximity is only illusory. Actually, no two points are further from each other, and in order to come together they would have to turn back and traverse the complete circumferance."

We learned of the assassination of Aleksandr II in the following circumstances.[1] On the first of March, *papa* went for his usual walk before dinner. A thaw had set in after a snowy winter, deep holes had formed on the snow-covered roads, and the hollows were filled with water. We had given up sending into Tula because of the condition of the roads, and consequently had seen no newspapers. On the main road, *papa* met an itinerant Italian organ-grinder who was traveling on foot from Tula with his barrel organ and fortune-telling birds, and they got into a conversation.

"Where do you come from? Where are you going?"

"From Tula. Business no good. Me no eat, birds no eat. Tsar got killed."

"What Tsar? Who killed him? When?"

"Russian Tsar, Petersburg. They throw bomb—I saw in newspapers."

When he got home, *papa* immediately told us about the assassination, and the newspapers that came the next day confirmed it. I remember the depressing effect this senseless murder had on my father. Besides his horror at the cruel death of the Tsar, "that kindly old man who has done so much good, who has always wished for the good of the people," [2] he could not help thinking about the murderers, the approaching executions, and "not so much about *them* as about those who plan to take part in *their* murders, and especially about Aleksandr III." [3]

For several days he went about in a state of melancholy contemplation. At last he decided to write a letter to the new Emperor, Aleksandr III. There was a great deal of talk about the form in which the letter was to be written, whether to use the salutation required by etiquette or the one in general use among ordinary mortals; whether he was to write it in his own hand or have it copied by Aleksandr Petrovich Ivanov, who was staying with us at the time. Good paper was sent for from Tula, the letter was rewritten and recopied several times, and finally sent to N. N. Strakhov in Petersburg, with a request that he forward it to the Emperor through K. N. Pobyedonostsev.[4]

How firm was Father's faith in the power of his own convictions! How he hoped that the criminals would be—not pardoned, he had no hope of that—at least saved from execution. And he anxiously followed the newspapers, living in hope and expectation, till he read that all those who had been a party to the crime had been hanged.

He learned only later that Pobyedonostsev had not even given his letter to the Emperor, because, as he wrote to my father, his "religious convictions prevented him from discharging the commission." Eventually the letter came into the Emperor's hands through a friend. On reading it, Aleksandr III is said to have remarked, "If the crime had concerned me personally, I should have had the right to pardon those who were guilty of it, but I could not pardon them in behalf of my father."

I remember that not only my father but we children were horrified by this execution of several people, one of them a woman.

The number of "dark people" who visited Yasnaya Polyana gradually increased. In the end there were hardly any revolutionists among them, the majority being either those who shared my father's views or those who, seeking the truth, came to him for counsel and moral support. What a lot of them there were—of all ages and professions! So many sincere people with deep convictions; so many Pharisees who sought only to derive some personal benefit by associating themselves with the name of Tolstoy; so many eccentrics, one might almost say freaks! There was an old Swede, for instance, who stayed at Yasnaya Polyana for a long time, going about barefooted and half-naked in summer and winter.[5] His principle was "simplification" and getting closer to nature. Father was interested in him for a while, but then the man went too far, became cynical, in fact, indecent, and had to be turned out of the house. Another time, a gentleman turned up who ate only once every two days. The day he arrived at Yasnaya Polyana was not his day to eat. There was food on the table from morning to night: breakfast, lunch, dinner, and evening tea with bread and cakes—but he persisted in sitting apart and refusing to touch food.

"I ate yesterday," he replied modestly, when offered food.

"What do you eat on the days you do eat?" he was asked.

It appeared that he ate exactly one pound of bread, one pound of vegetables, and one pound of fruit.[6]

"And yet you are not so very thin!" my father remarked in astonishment.

One of Father's frequent visitors was a tall fair-haired morphine addict by the name of Ozmirov, who demonstrated the teachings of Christianity by certain mathematical formulae. Then there was the short, dark, ne'er-do-well Popov, and the converted Jew Feinerman, who lived and worked in the village, and finally the spy Simon, sent by the secret police.

We were wandering about the garden one summer day when we came upon a young man sitting in a ditch calmly smoking a cigarette. Our dogs began to bark at him, and after quietly setting them on him we ran off in the opposite direction. A few days later we encountered the same young man on the road not far from the house. He greeted us courteously and started a conversation. It seemed that he had settled in the village, in the cottage of one of our servants, and was spending the summer in the country with his fiancée, Ada, and her mother.

"Come and have tea with me," he said to me. "I'm bored here. We'll have a chat and I'll tell you about myself. And, incidentally, you can do something for me. I'm going to be married in a few days and I haven't got a best man. I hope you won't refuse to grant me this favor."

The proposal was rather alluring and I accepted it. Within a few days Simon had so completely captivated me that we became great friends. I began to visit him daily, sometimes staying for hours.

The day of the wedding I got my parents' permission to be away all day. I put on a clean jacket and felt very proud of being best man at a wedding. When we got back from the church, I dined with the bride and groom and drank their health in a cordial.

Having observed my fascination with my new friend, *maman* took alarm and tried to curb my enthusiasm. One of her objections to Simon was that he could not be a well-bred man or he would not have invited a young boy to visit him without first making the acquaintance of his parents. "I can't let my son associate with a man I don't even know."

When I told this to Simon, he called on my mother the same day and offered his apologies for not having come sooner. He then met my father and soon became a frequent visitor. Everyone got so used to seeing him in the house that he was treated like a friend of the family. He sometimes helped Father with his work in the fields and seemed to be completely in accord with his views.

Before leaving Yasnaya Polyana in the autumn, he came to Father and made a clean breast of everything. He admitted to having been sent by the secret police to keep him and any visitors to Yasnaya Polyana under observation.

Years later, another man, the prison chaplain from Tula, appeared at Yasnaya in the same unsavory role. He used to visit my father periodically and hold long religious discussions with him.[7] Feigning a liberal attitude he drew my father into a frank expression of his views and gave the impression of being greatly interested in his ideas.

"What a strange man!" said my father in amazement. "Yet he seems to be quite sincere. I asked him whether he might not fall foul of the ecclesiastical authorities by coming to see me so often, and he seemed quite unconcerned. I had begun to think that he must have been sent to spy on me, but when I told him of my suspicion, he assured me that he comes of his own accord."

When the church excommunicated my father, it was this very priest who was cited by the Synod as having tried in vain to "bring him to reason" on its orders.

The last time he came to see my father, which was after his excommunication and during one of his illnesses, he was told that Father was ill and could not see him. He sat down on the veranda—it was in the summer—and announced that he would not leave till he had seen Lev Nikolayevich in person. An hour or two passed, yet he continued to sit there, obstinately refusing to go. Finally he had to be spoken to sharply and told to leave. I never saw him again after that.

XX

End of the Seventies. The Crisis. The Highway

I now come to the period of my father's moral crisis, and with it the crisis in our family life. I will begin by giving my own interpretation of this crucial time. My father was almost fifty years old. Fifteen years of cloudless family happiness had passed in a twinkling, and many of his enthusiasms had run their course. He had achieved fame, his material well-being was secure, but he no longer experienced life with the same poignancy and had begun to realize with horror that slowly but surely the end was drawing near.

Two of his brothers, Dmitry and Nikolai, had died young of tuberculosis, he himself had often been ill in the Caucasus, and he was frightened by phantoms of death. He went regularly to Moscow to consult the renowned Professor Zakharin, on whose advice he had gone to Samara to take the kumiss cure. After his first summer alone there he bought land, developed a huge stud farm (another of his enthusiasms), and for three successive

summers took the whole family with him and spent several
months in the Samara steppes.

Meanwhile, his "tedious" *Anna Karenina* was nearing com-
pletion. He wanted to write something new—but what? Despite the rhapsodical reviews by the critics Strakhov,[1] Gromeka,[2] and others, he felt in his heart that *Anna Karenina* was
a weaker novel than *War and Peace*. Several of the types he had
created in *War and Peace* were repeated in *Anna Karenina* and
had lost something of their vividness. Natasha shone through
Kitty; there was no Platon Karatayev, no Princes Bolkonsky;
Anna herself, though giving the book its title was not the im-
mortal creation that Natasha and Princess Marya were; and
there was not that epic, Homeric sweep, that prodigious out-
pouring of the first novel. What should he write next? It was
impossible to repeat those same types in yet another permuta-
tion, again to strain memory and imagination to create new situations, new psychological experiences. He began a desperate
search. At one time he had thought he might be interested in
the period of the Decembrists and had studied the material and
even made a draft of the beginning of the novel.[3] But the
project did not fascinate him sufficiently; other, more profound
questions had arisen and he began to cast about.

In his youth he had been strongly attracted to the ideas of
Rousseau, and to philosophy in general. It can be seen from the
diary he kept during the time he was in the Caucasus that he
often speculated about religion and God. By nature he was a
man with strong religious inclinations, but thus far had only
sought without finding anything definite. His faith in the religion of the church was like that of most people who are not
deeply absorbed in it and who give it little thought. It was what
everyone believed, what their fathers and their grandfathers
had believed—and so be it.

The time had come, however, when new interests no longer
emerged to fill his life, and before him lay emptiness, old age,
suffering, and death. He saw himself hanging over a deep abyss,
where two mice, one black, one white (night and day), gnawed
indefatigably and unerringly at the root he was clinging to; he

saw the yawning gulf beneath him and was horrified. What was
he to do? What would become of him? Was there really no
salvation? Those condemned to die often resort to suicide.
Would it not be better, instead of waiting till the mice had
completed their fatal work, to make an end and avoid the agony
of waiting?

In many ways, what my father was going through resembled
Gogol's experiences in the last years of his life. There was the
same disillusionment, the same relentless self-analysis, and the
same hopeless despair. Gogol burned the second part of *Dead
Souls* because in the light of his new vision he no longer saw
beauty in what had formerly attracted him. Had it been possible for my father to burn *Anna Karenina* at this time, he too
would not have hesitated, and his hand would not have trem-
bled whem committing to the flames the work of years. "There
is nothing either difficult or good in writing about the love
affair of a married woman with an officer," he had said of *Anna
Karenina*. The difference between Father and Gogol was that
poor Nikolai Vasilyevich died in that negative state and before
his time, without ever having arrived at a positive world-view,
while Father, thanks to his tremendous strength of mind and
will, lived through his ten-year moral crisis and out of it created
his "spiritual rebirth." It was not without reason that he read
Gogol's *Correspondence with Friends* at that time and was
deeply moved by it.[4]

My father's spiritual crisis cannot be regarded as something
new or unexpected. The doubts and searchings were virtually
a continuation of a ceaseless search that had begun in his youth
and gone on all his life, only partially and temporarily stifled by
literary work and the joys of family life—a new experience for
him. I must mention in passing that my father had never known
family life as a child; he could not remember his mother and
had lost his father when he was only eight years old.

Accustomed all his life to conquer and dominate, my father
suddenly found himself faced with the unconquerable. Could
it be that death was really death—nothing more? He often
pondered on this question. In "Three Deaths" the artist in him

had implied the answer to the question, but it was an answer that no longer satisfied him. To be sure, the closer to nature, the simpler and more natural death becomes: the death of the conceited lady is dreadful; the death of the peasant bearable; and the death of the birch tree even beautiful—but death all the same.

It is not so much death as the constant fear of death that is terrible. There was no salvation from without, but there must be salvation from within, and he had to find it. Only first he had to find God.

At this point I should like to interpolate a delightful story that I once heard Gorky tell. Nothing better illustrates my father's search at that time.

There once lived a peasant in a remote corner of the province of Kostroma. He was well-off, the possessor of an inn, several draft horses, a beautiful wife, fine children, was an elder of the church for which he had had a thirty-six-thousand-pound bell cast, and was happy and respected by everyone. And then he began to relive the life of Job. First there was a fire, then a cattle plague, his wife and children died in an epidemic, and finally the peasant was all alone and a pauper. So he went to see the priest.

"Father," he said, "I'm displeased with God. I've lived a righteous life, have always attended Mass and given to the church, and now I am punished. For what?"

"Come and see me after vespers and I'll tell you what to do," said the priest.

So he went to the church after vespers and the priest told him to remain there all night and pray to the icons. The peasant stayed alone in the church surrounded by darkness. The only light came from a flickering candle before the icon. He knelt down and began to pray. And he prayed all night. The solitary candle burned out but the peasant did not cease praying and continued till daybreak, till sunrise.

When it began to grow light in the church, the peasant rose to his feet and went up close to the icon. What he saw was a board with a picture painted on it. He touched it—nothing but a board. He scraped off a little paint with his fingernail—nothing but wood underneath the paint. Then he looked at the iconostasis—every-

where the same boards. At that moment the lock clicked and in
came the priest.

"Well, have you prayed, and are you repentant?"

"No, father, I'm not repentant. I have not found God here.
That's not God—those are just painted boards."

"Oh, you blasphemer, you! Get out and don't ever show your
face here again, or I'll send for the police and have you locked
up."

And the peasant walked out of the church and followed his
nose. . . .

My father's interest in the Othodox Church lasted, if I remember correctly, for about a year and a half. I recall that
brief period of his life when he attended Mass on every holiday,
strictly observed all the fasts, and was moved by the words of
certain very beautiful prayers. We heard him talk more and
more often about religion. Regardless of who our guest might
be, whether Ushakov, the Governor of the province of Tula; the
Radstockite, Count Bobrinsky; [5] Strakhov; Fet; Rayevsky;
Pyotr Fyodorovich Samarin; or Prince Urusov, it was all the
same: the conversation never failed to come around to religious
subjects, giving rise to endless arguments in the course of which
my father frequently became very harsh and disagreeable.

As Father grew more religious, so did we. Formerly we had
fasted only during the first and last weeks of Lent, but in 1877
we began to observe every fast without exception and zealously
attended all the church services. In summer, during the Assumption fast, we prepared for communion. I remember the
exalted religious mood we were in as we drove to church in the
droshky, calling to mind all our sins and solemnly preparing for
confession. It was a rainy summer that year with an abundance
of mushrooms along the road to church, and we used to stop on
our way back and fill our hats with them.

In the summer of 1879, the wandering minstrel Shchegolen-
kov, who was called by his patronymic Petrovich, stayed with
us at Yasnaya. He recited epics in a way that resembled the
singing of the blind minstrels, except that his voice was free
from that atrocious twang I always found so objectionable in

them. For some reason I always think of him sitting on the stone steps of the veranda outside Father's study. His endless stories delighted me and I loved to sit and gaze at his long gray beard, which hung in twisted locks. These tales were imbued with remote antiquity, and one felt in them the accumulation of centuries of sound wisdom.

Papa used to listen to him with great interest, every day making him recite something new, and Petrovich never failed to comply. He was inexhaustible. Later Father borrowed several of these subjects for his popular tales (*What Men Live By* and *The Three Old Men*).

It is difficult for me now to analyze my childish emotions of that period. I only remember that in a general way I felt that *papa* had changed and that something was happening to him.

In the spring of 1878, he fasted and observed Lent and that summer paid a visit to Father Ambrose at the Optina Pustyn Monastery. He went there twice during this period. In 1877 and again in 1881.[6]

The second time he made the journey on foot with Sergei Petrovich Arbuzov, our footman, whom he invited to accompany him as a friend; they wore bast sandals and carried knapsacks on their backs, and, the corns he acquired notwithstanding, Father always cherished his memories of this journey.

The monastery itself, however, and the celebrated Father Ambrose were an acute disappointment to him. They lodged in the pilgrims' hospice, which was filthy and infested with lice, ate their meals in the cookhouse, and, like ordinary pilgrims, had to submit implicitly to the barracklike discipline of the monastery. "Come here . . . Sit there . . . Here's your cell, old man," and so on.

Revering "the Count" as only a man born under serfdom can revere his master, Sergei Petrovich could not bear to see his idol treated in this way and, despite my father's having asked him not to talk, babbled to one of the monks.

"Do you know who that old man with me is? He's Lev Niko-layevich Tolstoy."

"Count Tolstoy?"

"Yes."

All at once everything changed. The monks came running to Father. "Your Excellency, please come to the inn, the best room has been set aside for you. What does Your Excellency wish to have prepared for his meals?" and so on. Such obsequiousness, their rudeness on the one hand and servility on the other, produced a very unfavorable impression on Father. And this impression was not eradicated on meeting Father Ambrose, in whom he found nothing particularly good or praiseworthy. His dissatisfaction with Optina Pustyn was apparent on his return, and soon afterward he began to criticize the rites and practices of the church, and finally repudiated them altogether.

His Orthodoxy came to an end unexpectedly. This occurred during Lent, when lenten meals were prepared for Father and those wishing to fast, while meat was served to the younger children and their tutors and governesses. The footman had been passing a platter of cutlets and had set it down on a little side table while he went downstairs to fetch something. All at once Father turned to me (I always sat beside him) and pointing to the platter said,

"Ilyusha, give me those cutlets."

"Lyovochka," *maman* interposed, "you've forgotten that this is a fast day."

"No, I haven't forgotten. I don't intend to fast anymore, and please don't order any more lenten meals for me."

To everyone's horror, he ate the cutlets and pronounced them delicious. This attitude on Father's part made us all lose interest in fasting, and before long our devoutness gave way to a complete indifference to religion.

I am recounting these moral experiences of Father's as a series of episodes because that is how they were seen by a thirteen-year-old boy. It is not my purpose to enter into an analysis of his intensive prodigious mental effort at that time. Those who are interested can read Biryukov's book,[7] or, better still, my father's own works on the subject. There they will learn why he could not reconcile himself to the church and its distortions of Christ's teachings.

Disillusioned with the church, he grew still more restive. Then began the dark period of the burning of the idols. Having idealized family life and lovingly depicted in three novels the background of a nobleman's life that resembled his own, he suddenly began to denouce and decry it; having prepared his sons for a classical and university education according to the methods of the day, he began to condemn current scholarship; having regularly consulted Dr. Zakharin and sent to Moscow for doctors for his wife and children, he began to denounce medicine; having always been a passionate sportsman and avid hunter of wolves, bears, and wild game, he began to call hunting "chasing dogs"; having accumulated money for fifteen years and bought land cheap from the Bashkirs of Samara, he began to call property a crime and money corruption; and lastly, having devoted his entire life to literature, he began to repent of this activity and all but abandoned it forever.

I remember how grievously this period of Father's search affected my own life. I was between thirteen and fourteen years old at the time and undergoing the very difficult transition from childhood to youth, of which I was aware only long after it had been accomplished. I regretted my childhood, even wept over it. My adolescence was as gloomy as my childhood had been bright and sunny. Whether this is the fate of everyone or whether there are those for whom this time passes differently, I do not know. It is the period when a man's character is formed, when a boy is in special need of guidance, and I had lost that guidance. It had split asunder. All the new discoveries made one after another by my father contradicted the old principles by which we had been raised, and I oscillated like a magnetic needle between two poles, swaying helplessly as I was torn this way and that. This instability was characteristic of me for a long time—and perhaps still is.

The world was divided into two camps for me at that time, with *papa* in one and *maman* and everyone else in the other. How to bridge the gap? What happened was inevitable in a boy of my age: I began to take from both my father and my mother only what I liked and what was to my own advantage, and to reject whatever seemed difficult. Hunting fascinated me, so I would hunt; cake was delicious, so I wanted to have it; studying was hard and tedious, so I was unwilling to study, and anyhow *papa* said that scholarship was unnecessary; and since he also said that the peasants were superior to us, the gentry, I would go tobogganing with the village boys.

But what my mother must have gone through at the time! She loved him with all her being. And she was almost his creation. Out of the fine soft clay that was the eighteen-year-old Sonya Behrs, he had modeled the wife he wanted, and she gave herself to him wholly, lived only for him. And now she saw him suffering, and her interests, which had been their common interests, no longer concerned him. He began to deprecate them and to chafe at their life together. Eventually he even frightened her with threats of a separation, a complete break, and she had a huge complex family on her hands—from Tatyana and Seryozha, who were seventeen and eighteen, to an infant in arms. What was she to do? Could she have followed him then, disposing of all the property as he wished and condemning her children to hunger and want?

Father was fifty years old at the time, and she was thirty-five. He was a repentant sinner, and she had nothing to repent of; he was a man of tremendous intellect and moral strength, and she was an ordinary woman; he was a genius striving to embrace the whole range of world thought in his outlook, and she was an average woman with the conservative instincts of her sex and the nest she had built to protect. What woman would have acted differently? I know of none, whether in life, literature, or history. One may pity my mother in this instance, but not judge her. She had been happy during the early years of her married life, but after the 1880's, that happiness faded and never revived.

It was my father, of course, who suffered most. He became taciturn, morose, and irritable, and our former jovial buoyant companion and leader was transformed before our eyes into a stern and censorious preacher. His harsh denunciations of the empty life of the gentry, their gluttony and idleness, and their

despoiling of the working people, grew more and more frequent. "Here we sit in our well-heated rooms, and today a man
was found frozen to death on the road. He froze to death because no one would give him a night's lodging." . . . "We stuff
ourselves with cutlets and all kinds of pastry, and in Samara
people are dying by the thousands, their bellies distended from
starvation." . . . "We ride saddle horses to the bathhouse, and
Prokofy's last gelding has died and he's left without a horse for
plowing."

I cannot say that we children did not understand these simple statements. Naturally we understood what he was saying,
but it spoiled our selfish childish happiness and severely disturbed every aspect of our daily lives. We would be getting up
amateur theatricals at Yasnaya with the two Baroness Meng-
dens, the Kislenskys, and Nunya Novosiltsev, or playing croquet, or talking about falling in love, when suddenly papa
would appear in the midst of our merriment and games, and
with a single word, or, worse, a mere look, would ruin everything. It became very dull, and we were even rather ashamed
at times. "It would have been better if he hadn't come." The
worst of it was that he felt this himself. It was not that he
wanted to spoil our fun—after all he loved us very much—but
it happened nonetheless. Even if he said nothing, he was thinking—and we all knew what he was thinking. That was what
made us so uncomfortable.

Meanwhile the life of the family flowed along its accustomed
channel and continued its course of development. We still had
the same Nikolai the cook, the same "Anke cake" passed on to
us from the Behrs family to become a tradition at Yasnaya
Polyana, the same tutors and governesses, the same lessons, and
maman as usual with a nursing infant, and all these stable foun-
dations on which our anthill rested were as firm as ever and as
necessary for our selfish enjoyment.

It is true that we felt a severe split in our lives, felt that something important was missing as *papa* grew more and more remote from us. This was often exceedingly painful, and yet we
could not change our lives as he wanted us to; it seemed absolutely unthinkable to us.

In the conflict between ideas and tradition, between "life according to God" and "Anke cake," what happened was exactly
what always happens in such cases: tradition won out, and the
ideas did nothing more than spoil the sweetness of our cake with
their bitter flavor. How would it have been possible to reconcile "life according to God," the life of pilgrims and peasants
with which *papa* was so enraptured, with those infallible principles that had been instilled in us from the cradle: the absolute
necessity of always having soup and cutlets for dinner, of talking English and French, of preparing for the *gymnasium* and
university? And we children often felt that it was not we who
had failed to understand our father, but rather he who had
ceased to understand us because of his preoccupation with "his
own affairs."

These "affairs" were his new philosophy and the piles of
books that had appeared in his study. He brought in great
mountains of them from somewhere, all sorts of treatises and
teachings of the church fathers, and spent whole days shut up
in his study reading and meditating. Sometimes at dinner or at
evening tea he would discuss his thoughts with us or share his
new ideas with any visitors who happened to be present, but
even now it is painful to recall his pitiful attempts to interest
others in what at that time was for him more important than
life itself.

We might be absorbed in the preparations for putting on a
play; or one of us might have fallen in love; or Seryozha might
be diligently preparing for an examination; or *maman* worrying
about Andryusha's stomachache or new tooth; or I might have
been given a new hunting dog and game bag—who could be
interested in the Sermon on the Mount or in a new interpretation of Christ's teachings?

Looking back on that period now, I am filled with horror at
the thought of my father's mental state. Having repudiated all
that he formerly venerated—the nobleman's patriarchal way
of life, which he had re-created for himself and lovingly described in his novels, and all of his former interests beginning
with war and ending with literary fame, family life, and religion—how awful must have been his solitude! And the more

so because it was the solitude of a man living in the midst of people who were estranged from him.

He had begun with this negation but had not yet found those positive principles of love that he later derived from his study of the Gospel and made the foundation of his whole world-view, and he cast about like a man condemned to die, for two years struggling with the temptation of suicide. Later he wrote of this time, "I, a man favored by fortune, used to hide a rope least I should hang myself on the crossbeam of the bookshelves in the room where I undressed alone every night, and I gave up hunting with a gun lest I should be tempted by so easy a way of delivering myself from life." [8]

And when he could no longer endure the onslaught of agonizing thoughts, he poured them out to us, but we withdrew, fearing to have our childish happiness destroyed. It is true that he sometimes entered into our life, expressed an interest in our lessons, tried to adapt himself to our thinking, but we felt that this interest was not that of a father but of a teacher. And he himself was conscious of this.

In a letter to V. I. Alekseyev in 1882, describing the life of the family, he writes, "Seryozha is hard at work and believes in the university. Tanya, half-serious, half-good, half-clever, becomes no worse, perhaps improves a little. Ilyusha grows and does no work; his spirit is not yet crushed by organic processes. Lyolya and Masha seem to me better; unlike the older children, they have not picked up my coarseness and seem to be developing in more favorable conditions. . . ." [9]

I quote this letter with its touching self-condemnation to show how discerning and conscientious Father was about our education, and how tormented he must have been in those periods of estrangement when his inner struggle so diverted him from his family that he was powerless to treat them as he would have liked to.

And we did not understand him. Great is the solitude of the writer when he withdraws from life and mentally ranges a world of images and impressions, but how much more rigorous the solitude of the thinker! His world cannot be embodied in images, for spirit and flesh are often in opposition. There is no way back for the thinker, since the deeper his thought the further he withdraws from life, and woe to the thinker who is fettered by temporal, earthly bonds!

There was a time when as an artist my father had intuitively created Platon Karatayev. Now he went back to that same Karatayev, not as an artist, but as a thinker. Why is it that we, the so-called intellectuals, are afraid of death, and a Karatayev relates to it so simply? In what does the solution lie? Can it be that Karatayev possesses a faith that we lack? Can it be that he knows the very God I seek? And thus began the period of my father's love for the simple people.

Not far from the gates of Yasnaya Polyana was the old Ekaterinskaya highway, known as the Moscow–Kiev "way." In the old days, this was one of Russia's main arteries. It was a post road traveled by swift carriages-and-three and dashing government couriers, as well as endless crawling strings of carts. The Tsar himself used to pass on this road. I can remember the old Yasenki postboy Pavel Shentyakov, who was still alive in my time, telling me how he had driven the Emperor Nikolai I on this road. Later it was replaced by a stone roadway, which in some places ran parallel to the old highway and in others deviated from it. When the railway was built, it lost its importance as a vehicular thoroughfare. Passing Yasnaya at a distance of no more than a verst, it was clearly visible on the horizon from the big windows of our salon. From time immemorial, pilgrims, wayfarers, and roving cripples had traversed it. Whoever had made a vow to visit Jerusalem or Troitsa; whoever wished to acquire merit before death by going to the holy places; men and women, the old and the young, the sound and the infirm, passed by, sometimes singly, more often in groups, in summer and in winter, going north and south, with staffs in their hands, knapsacks on their backs, and living on alms in Christ's name.

At that time, forty years ago, such pilgrims were very numerous and groups of them passed daily going in both directions. After his work, that is, about four o'clock in the afternoon, my father liked to go for a walk or a horseback ride. Instead of riding to the bathhouse or going hunting as he had done in the past, he began to walk on the highway. There he fell into conversation with pilgrims, sometimes meeting extremely intelligent and interesting people. Once more the age-old wisdom of the people was revealed to him in the vivid simple expressions found in Russian proverbs and sayings, and the more absorbed he became in this wisdom the more it seemed to him that perhaps it contained the solution to his tormenting doubts.

Referring to this in his *Confession,* he says, "Thanks to a certain strange *physical love for the real working people,* which forced me to perceive and understand that they are not so stupid as we think, or thanks to my sincere conviction that I cannot know anything—so that the very best thing I could do would be to hang myself—I had a presentiment that if I wished to live and understand the meaning of life, I had to look for this meaning not among those who had lost it and wanted to destroy themselves, but among those milliards, both dead and living, who create life and bear us on the current of their lives." [10]

These walks became not only a pleasure but a necessity for him. "I'm off to the Nevsky Prospekt," he would say jokingly as he set out, and sometimes he did not return till late at night. "I met an extraordinarily interesting old man and walked with him as far as Tula," he might say, coming in at ten o'clock without having had any dinner. His diary for that period is peppered with proverbs and expressions of God's will coined from the wisdom he had picked up from these pilgrims. Many of his late popular tales were inspired by his "Nevsky" friends.

"Yes, those people know God. Despite all their superstitions, their faith in St. Nicholas-of-the-Spring and St. Nicholas-of-the-Winter, in the Iberian and Kazan Madonnas, and in the Icon of the Three Hands, they are closer to God than we are. They lead moral, working lives, and their simple wisdom is in many ways superior to all the artifices of our culture and philosophy." And there were times when he, the great writer Lev Tolstoy, famous, cultivated, and rich, genuinely envied those ragged,

destitute, and often hungry men who were nonetheless happy
and inwardly at peace.

At the same time he was doing an enormous amount of reading. "Never in my life had I labored as zealously as during those
ten years," he wrote in one of his later works. He studied philosophy, theology, the lives of the saints, the history of the
church, and everything he could find relating to the life of
Christ and his teachings. He made a translation of the Gospel
from Greek, compared it with every available text, and even
studied ancient languages for the purpose.

I remember how persistently he strove, and how little by
little his new world-view developed and took shape. It was
comparable to the way we children used to build with blocks.
At first all was chaos and seemed hopeless. Then one block was
put in place, then another, and something began to take shape:
this one here, that one there, one is difficult to fit in so you set it
aside and take another, till a pattern begins to evolve, the
empty space is filled, everything becomes clearer and more
comprehensible, and at last the picture is complete; only one
spot remains to be filled, you take the block that was set aside
because it seemed too difficult to place, and it clearly and simply fits into the pattern.

I have chosen this comparison with childhood because it is
the best example I can find of the way in which Father gradually attained to an understanding of the teachings of Christ.
His first building block, that is, the foundation of his new con-
ception, was the Sermon on the Mount and the doctrine of nonresistance to evil. How strange it seems now that it took him so
many years to understand the simple words, "Resist not evil."
This shows the degree to which the Orthodox Church, with its
services and symbols of faith, its catechism and theology, ob-
scures Christ's teachings.

Having perceived this fundamental thesis in its direct meaning, my father began to examine the teachings of the Gospel
anew and to apply them to the solution of all the problems of
life. Wherever there seemed to be contradictions, he examined
the sources, and in most cases they turned out to be either in-

accuracies or errors in translation. And the deeper he probed the clearer everything became to him, and the more feverishly and joyfully he put his last blocks in place, till at last the whole picture unfolded before him, definite and unmistakable.

This work of my father's is the only attempt of its kind to apply a deep philosophical foundation to the teachings of Christ and to adapt them to all spheres of human life, from the personal to the social, economic, and even political realms.

I have already mentioned that I was always irresolute. I never pretended to be a follower of my father, though I always believed in him. But the older I grew, the clearer his world-view became to me and the closer I drew to it.

Meanwhile, the gulf between him and the rest of the family deepened and the situation began to be complicated. The children were developing and growing up, and my mother had eight of us on her hands by then. Father had removed himself from the problems of raising us and she had begun to realize that she lacked the strength to bear alone the burden he had shifted onto her shoulders. The question of moving the family to Moscow arose, partly because it was time for Seryozha to go to the university, for Tanya to "come out," and because Ilyusha was idling at home and had to be put into a *gymnasium*. And then there were Lev, Masha, Andryusha, and the baby Alyosha to think about.

"It's all very well to talk about ideas, but children can't be left ignorant and half-educated; they have to be fed, clothed, and their health looked after. The children of Konstantin Romashkin, for instance, run about the village without ever being washed, start herding sheep at the age of ten, and by the time they are thirteen are set to the plow—surely that's not what you want?"

"Konstantin's children are taught to work at an early age and to help their parents, but we batten on the peasants and are raising just such parasites as ourselves. Early this morning I saw our tailor in the avenue coming toward the house. 'Where have you been?' I asked him. 'There weren't enough hooks for the fur coat, so I ran into Tula.' He had already been to Tula

and back, fifteen versts each way, and now will be busy working till night, and our children can't go as far as the Voronka
(the river where we bathed) without demanding that the
horses be harnessed for them. So Filip harnesses the horses
for them and then sits on the box all day while the young ladies
and gentlemen refresh themselves."

Such discussions arose continually between my mother and
father, their acerbity increasing on each occasion. Yet the croquet, horseback riding, ice skating, and singing in the evening
went on as before, only *papa* was no longer with us. Although
he refrained from saying anything or criticizing us openly, his
disapproval made itself felt, and it was awkward for us and for
him.

I must say that in spite of his masterful nature, Father never
coerced any of us. He never scolded or punished his children,
and as a consequence we feared and respected him more than
Mother, who sometimes shouted at us, spanked us, or made us
stand in a corner.

Our situation was also difficult during this period because we
had no way of pleasing Father. All right, I'll give up riding to
the bathhouse and walk instead—but the cart will go all the
same; I won't overeat at the table—but the pancakes and jam
will be served all the same. And even if I give up "chasing
dogs," what then? I still cannot change our whole way of life
and suddenly become a Romashkin. It was not I who was to
blame, but the whole tenor of our life, which of myself I was
helpless to change. And not only I, but Father himself was incapable of doing so.

Striving to justify somehow his "idle" aristocratic life, he began to apply himself zealously to manual labor. He broke up
his day into "stretches" of time and endeavored to substitute
physical for mental work.[11] He plowed and scythed, built a
barn and an oven for the peasants, and had Pavel the village
shoemaker (brother of the footman Sergei Arbuzov) come and
work with him in his study during the winter, teaching him
how to stitch boot tops and make shoes.

Maman regarded this "eccentricity" of Father's as something transitory and watched over his health, tried to prepare more nutritious food for him, and hoped it would soon pass.

But for Father the situation became desperate. There are those, my elder brother Sergei among them, who believe that he made a mistake not to leave the family then, that is, at the very beginning of the eighties. I know that the question of leaving was uppermost in his mind during the last thirty-five years of his life, and that he deeply and conscientiously weighed all aspects of the question. And I therefore consider that he made the right and only possible decision.

How can one conceivably judge the actions of a man unless one has experienced all of his doubts and penetrated the depths of his thinking? Others may judge him, but for myself, I would not presume to blame either Father or Mother, because I know that they both wanted to act, and in fact did act, in the way that seemed best and most honest to them at the time.

One of the fundamental characteristics of my father's nature was an uncompromising honesty with himself and an abhorrence of hypocrisy. And he suddenly found himself in the tragic position of a man who was living in a way that was patently counter to all of his convictions, the position of a repentant sinner who continues to abide in his sin, the position of a teacher whose own life is a denial of his precepts.

He talked about the criminality of wealth and the evil of money, yet he himself possessed half a million; he talked about the simple workman's life, yet he himself lived in a fine manor house, slept on an expensive mattress, and ate tasty, satisfying food; he condemned private property and talked of six feet of land, yet he himself possessed over twenty thousand acres; his family spent more in a week than any peasant family could spend in a year, living as they did in a house with footmen, housemaids, a cook, coachman, gardeners, and laundresses. Did he have the right to preach his ideas when he himself did not practice them? What a wealth of material he offered his enemies to accuse him of hypocrisy! Would it not be the ruination of the idea itself were he to continue to live in these conditions of comfort and luxury with his family? What to do? Go away?

This might appear to have been the simplest and perhaps even the sole solution to the problem, but it raised another whole series of questions that were even more complex and subtle. Did he have the right to give away all his property and leave his wife and children indigent, perhaps even hungry? The way he had raised them they were not accustomed to privation. Give his property to his wife? But if this property was a burden to him, and if he considered it a sin, did he have the right to shift this burden and sin onto her shoulders? Did he have the right to leave his thirty-five-year-old wife alone with a big family, to deprive her of his moral support and love? He was everything to her, her whole life, the focal point of her concentration. Without him there was no life for her, and he knew this. Moreover, he loved her with his whole being. If he were to go away and sacrifice the lives of his wife and children to escape the accusation of hypocrisy, would this not be vanity on his part?

When Sakyamuni realized that there was suffering in the world and felt that he had been called to go forth to teach and bring comfort to the people, he left his beautiful young wife at night, without even waking her to say good-bye, left his palace and all his wealth and became the Buddha. If my father had left his family at that time, his fame and popularity would have grown into something legendary, and he realized this, of course. He was probably tempted more than once by these vainglorious dreams, but he overcame the temptation, and in this I see his great virtue. What he did was not what he wanted to do, not what would have been simplest for him to do, but what he considered best.

He often expressed the thought that it should be possible to live the true Christian life in all circumstances, and he began to adapt his own life to this belief insofar as it was possible. He humbly doomed himself to criticism, to countless compromises and moral torments, but he took up his cross and bore it with fortitude. And how sorry I am for him now when I think that he did not succeed in bearing it to the end.

There is a moving story by Tagore about a Hindu who dedicated himself to seeking the truth and ended by becoming a teacher.[12] As he stood on the bank of the sacred river, his beautiful wife approached him, and kissing the hem of his robe said, "Master, I know that you have renounced the life of the flesh and have attained a higher stage of wisdom: what do you command me to do?" "Disappear from my path forever," answered the wise man. Without a word, his wife descended the stone steps to the river and slowly sank into the waters of the Ganges. The sage impassively watched as the water lilies and lotuses covered the spot where his wife's head had sunk from sight, then calmly went up the mountain to continue the great work of the salvation of his eternal soul.

I am enchanted by the beauty of this story, but glad that my father did not do what the legendary sage had done, but instead sacrificed everything for the peace and happiness of his wife.

XXI

The Move to Moscow. Syutayev. The Census.
Buying a House. Fyodorov. Solovyov

In the autumn of 1881, the whole family moved
to Moscow. This move, the logical outcome of all that had pre-
ceded, seemed to be necessary for three reasons. My eldest
brother Sergei was at the university and could not be left alone
in Moscow without supervision. My sister Tanya had to "come
out" and could no longer remain sequestered in the country
without a proper social life, and it would be far easier to edu-
cate the rest of the children in Moscow without my father's
help than it would be at Yasnaya. *Maman* went to Moscow in
the summer and rented an apartment in Denezhny Lane, and
in the autumn we moved.

I had gone to Tula in the spring and passed the examination
for promotion to the fifth class and was to go to a state *gymnasium. Papa* went to the director of one of the Moscow State
gymnasia to enroll me, but an unexpected difficulty arose:
among the papers required for my entry he was asked to sign

one guaranteeing my loyalty to the Tsar. He refused to sign it, and I had to go to Polivanov's private *gymnasium* instead, where I was accepted on the strength of the examination and without any superfluous formalities.

"How can I guarantee the conduct of another human being, even my own son's?" said my father indignantly. "I explained to the director that it was absurd to require a parent to sign such a paper, and he agreed that it was an unnecessary formality, but nevertheless it seems that they cannot take a boy without it."

When we moved to Moscow, we all fell under the influence of our new impressions of city life. Each of us was affected in his own way. *Maman* threw herself into arranging the apartment, buying furniture under Uncle Kostya's guidance, paying the required social calls, and making preparations for Tanya to go into society. Seryozha was all wrapped up in university life, while I, in the intervals between going to school and preparing my lessons, played knucklebones with the children in the street and by spring had fallen in love with a girl at school who was not known to my parents.

That winter Father met the sectarian Syutayev, who interested him very much and unquestionably influenced his views. The man was a simple peasant from the province of Tver, a stonemason by trade. Father had heard about him in Samara from Prugavin and went to his village to see him. Later in the winter Syutayev came to Moscow and stayed with us for some time. At first glance he appeared to be the most ordinary sort of poor peasant, with his sparse mud-colored beard, his small colorless eyes, and his greasy black sheepskin coat, which he wore indoors and out. Like every good serious-minded peasant, he knew how to behave with simple dignity, was perfectly composed in any company, and spoke in a way that made one feel that what he said had been carefully considered and that his convictions were unshakable.

Syutayev and my father were in agreement in many respects. "It's amazing," Father said, "that Syutayev and I, two such completely different men, dissimilar in cast of mind and degree of development, should have arrived at the same point entirely independently of each other and by entirely different roads."

Like Father, Syutayev had renounced the church and its rites and, also like him, preached brotherhood, love, and "life according to God."

"Everything is within you," he used to say; "where love is, there is God." Being a simple man and not understanding compromise, Syutayev repudiated all violence and would not accept it even as a means of resisting evil. He refused to pay taxes on principle because the money was used to support an army. And when the police distrained his property and sold his cattle, he offered no resistance and submitted to his own ruin without demurring. "It's their sin, let them do it. I won't open the gates, but if they must, let them go in. I have no locks," he said when telling about it. His family shared his convictions and they lived in community, not recognizing private property. When his son was conscripted, he refused to take the army oath because the Gospel says "Swear not" and refused to take up a gun because it "smelled of blood." As a result he was sent to the Schlüsselburg Disciplinary Battalion and suffered great privations.

Syutayev saw the realization of his ideal of "life according to God" in the early Christian community. "Fields ought not to be divided; forests ought not to be divided; houses ought not to be divided. Then we should need no locks, no watchmen, and no trade, ships, or war. Everyone would be of one heart and one mind—everything would belong to the village or town," he said, and his profound belief in the attainability of these ideals, which he had derived from the Gospel, could be felt in his words.

Father was so captivated by what he preached that he often invited friends to meet him and had him expound his views to them. It is hardly surprising that the presence of such a man in Moscow, and still more, in the home of Tolstoy, should have attracted the attention of the authorities. Prince Dolgorukov, the Governor-General, sent an elegant Captain of Gendarmes to my father with orders to find out what Syutayev was doing in his house, what sort of convictions he held, and how long he intended to remain in Moscow.

I shall never forget the reception my father gave to this gendarme in his study, because I had never imagined that he was capable of such anger. He neither offered him his hand nor asked him to sit down, but spoke to him standing. After hearing his request, he dryly informed him that he did not consider himself obliged to reply to his questions. When the captain started to object, my father turned white as a sheet and pointed to the door. "Go, for God's sake, leave this house at once!" he said in a constrained voice. "I beg you to go!" he shouted, no longer able to control himself, and hardly giving the bewildered gendarme time to get out of the room, he slammed the door after him with all his might.

Afterward he repented of his outburst and was sorry he had lost control of himself and was rude to the man; nevertheless, when the Governor-General persisted and sent his secretary Istomin a few days later for the same purpose, he refused to give him any explanation, saying curtly that if Vladimir Andreyevich wished to see him there was no one who could prevent him from coming himself. I do not know how this harassing on the part of the administration would have ended if Syutayev had not gone away soon after this.

In January 1882, my father participated in taking the three-day census in Moscow. He selected the very poorest quarter of the city near the Smolensk Market, which included Protochny Lane and the then famous flophouses, the "Rzhanov Fortress" among others.

I remember students coming to see him with whom he shut himself up in his room for a long time, and remember him taking me with him to inspect one of the flophouses. We spent the evening going into wretched little rooms where the filth and stench were appalling, and Father questioned each of the lodgers as to what he lived on, what had brought him there, how much he paid, and what he ate. In the general room, where they were allowed to sleep at no cost, it was still worse. There it was not even necessary to make inquiries; it was obvious that they were all utterly degraded, and that mass of destitute degenerated humanity aroused only horror and disgust.

I looked at *papa* and saw reflected in his face all that I myself was feeling, but there was also an expression of suffering, of a suppressed inner struggle, which made such a deep impression on me that I have never forgotten it. I felt that he wanted to escape from there as quickly as possible, just as I did, but at the same time felt that he could not, because there was no place for him to escape to: wherever he might go, the impression of what he had seen would remain with him and continue to torment him as much as if not more than at that moment. And, indeed, this was exactly what happend.

In his article "What Then Must We Do?" (1886) he describes what he experienced in these words: "City life, which had always seemed strange and unnatural to me, was now so repulsive that all the luxuries of life which had once been a pleasure now became a torment. And try as I might to find in my heart any sort of justification for our way of life, I could not look at our own or anyone else's drawing room, or at a clean and tastefully set table, a carriage with a well-fed coachman and horses, shops, theaters, or social gatherings, without a feeling of anger. Side by side with all this I could not help seeing the cold, hungry, degraded inhabitants of Lyapin House. And I could not rid myself of the thought that these two things were related, that one was the result of the other. I remember that this feeling of my own guilt remained with me exactly as I had felt it the first time." [1]

In 1881, my father had made the acquaintance of two interesting men in Moscow, Vladimir Fyodorovich Orlov and Nikolai Fyodorovich Fyodorov, and became very intimate with both of them.

I remember less about Orlov, but Fyodorov, the former librarian of the Rumyantsev Museum, I can see as if he were standing before me at this moment. He was a thin little old man of medium height, always badly dressed, and extremely

quiet and retiring. Instead of a collar, he wore a gray checked
scarf around his neck and the same overcoat summer and winter. His face had an unforgettable expression. He had large intelligent penetrating eyes and radiated an inner goodness that
was almost a childlike naiveté. If there are saints, they must be
like him. Not only was Nikolai Fyodorovich incapable of harm-
ing anyone, but I believe that he himself was impervious to evil
of any kind, because he simply did not understand it. It was
said that he lived in a little room somewhere, sleeping on bare
boards and eating little like a true ascetic, and giving all he
had to the poor. As far as I remember, he never argued with
my father and, what was more remarkable, Father, who invariably became vehement and impetuous in conversation,
used to listen to Nikolai Fyodorovich with marked attention
and never once lost his temper with him.

But it was very different with Vladimir Solovyov.[2] He was
a frequent visitor of my father's at one period, and I cannot recall a single occasion which did not end in a violent dispute.
Every time they met they vowed not to lose their tempers, but
it always ended the same way. There would be several guests
for tea in the evening, the conversation would be animated,
with Solovyov making jokes and everyone very gay, when suddenly and quite unexpectedly some abstract question would
arise; my father would begin talking, always addressing himself to Solovyov for some reason, who then challenged something he had said, and one word led to another till they were
both on their feet and the bitterest of arguments ensued. The
tall gaunt figure of Solovyov, with his beautiful wavy hair,
swung to and fro across the room like a pendulum, Father got
excited, their voices rose, and it was impossible to separate
them the rest of the evening.

When the guests departed and Father went out to the hall
to see everyone off, he held Solovyov's hand in his as he said
good-bye, and looking into his eyes with a guilty smile asked
him to forgive him for his vehemence. And so it was on every
occasion.

Solovyov never meant very much to my father as a thinker, and he soon lost all interest in him. Father considered him a "brainy" man and called him "the dean's son."

"There are many such men," he used to say. "A dean's son is a man who lives exclusively on what he derives from books. He does a lot of reading and all his conclusions are drawn from what he has read. But the most important thing is wanting—what he brings to it himself. There are clever men among these 'dean's sons'—Strakhov, for instance; he was really clever, and if he had thought *for himself* he would have been great, but it was his misfortune that he too was a 'dean's son.' "

I heard my father apply this definition to both of these men on several occasions after their deaths.

XXII

Manual Labor. Shoemaking. Haymaking

Iɴ June 1884, Father wrote to our former tutor, V. I. Alekseyev: "I am now convinced that only life can show the way—the example of a life. The influence of this example is neither very rapid nor very definite (in the sense that I do not believe you can know whom it affects) and is very difficult, but it alone gives the necessary impulse. Example, proof of the possibility of a Christian life, that is, of a rational and happy life in all possible circumstances, is what influences people, and it alone is necessary for you and me, so let us help one another to achieve it." [1]

The example of life, and *a rational and happy life in all circumstances.* Herein lay the sole solution to the complicated problems that confronted my father at the time, and it was along this path that he directed his own life and maintained that course till the fatal autumn of 1910.

In spite of the immense labor that consumed his strength, he ranked himself among the parasites who live on the backs of the

189

working people, and in order to justify even to some extent in his own eyes what he called his uselessness, he set about doing manual labor, and from that time forth never gave it up till he became too weak to go on with it.

In a letter to N. N. Gay, July 21, 1891, he writes, "... And you cannot imagine how disgusted, ashamed, and depressed I feel now at harvest time living in such base, loathsome conditions. Especially when I think of former years." [2]

Father always enjoyed physical work as a useful and healthy form of exercise and as a means of communion with nature. I remember the great moral and educational importance he ascribed to it, his actual love for it. He was enthusiastic about the very process of work, which he explored in the most minute detail, often finding in it a safety valve which I believe helped him to endure the most difficult moments of his life.

His attitude to work, as to religious responsibility, was clearly manifested only at the beginning of the 1880's. I remember how, during our first winter in Moscow, he used to go out to the Sparrow Hills beyond the Moscow River and saw wood with the peasants. He would come home tired, bathed in sweat, but full of his new impressions of the healthy life of labor. At dinner he told us about how the men worked, for how long at a time and what they earned, inevitably contrasting their poverty and hard work with our luxury and genteel idleness.

In order to be able to work at home and turn the long winter evenings to account, Father began to learn shoemaking. He found a shoemaker—a modest, black-bearded man, a typical workman—bought implements and materials, and set up a workbench in the little room next to his study. In the window beside the bench he installed a curious little iron stove heated by a kerosene lamp for the double purpose of warming and ventilating the room. I recall that in spite of this arrangement, of which he was extremely proud as an innovation, it was always very stuffy in his little low-ceilinged workshop and smelled of leather and tobacco.

The shoemaker would come at fixed hours, and master and pupil sat down on low stools and set to work stitching, splicing bristles, knocking quarters into shape, nailing soles, attaching heels, and so on. Impatient by nature but exceedingly persevering, Father stubbornly labored to achieve perfection in some of the technical difficulties of the craft. I remember how delighted and proud he was when he had at last learned how to splice a bristle, prepare a "tip," and hammer the wooden tacks into a sole. He always worked with great zeal, insisted on doing everything himself, and never left off till he had succeeded in making his work the equal of his teacher's. Hunched over the workbench, he carefully prepared to splice a bristle, and when he broke it started afresh, groaning with the effort. Like any pupil, he was triumphant over each success.

"Allow me, Lev Nikolayevich, I'll do it," the shoemaker would say, seeing Father's unavailing efforts.

"No, no, I'll do it myself. You do your work and I'll do mine, otherwise I won't learn."

People often came to see Father during these lessons, and sometimes there was such a crowd of interested spectators in the little workroom that there was no room to turn around. I too liked going in to see him and often spent the whole evening there.

I remember Prince Obolensky, the husband of my cousin Elizaveta Valerianovna, coming in one day. Father had just learned how to drive the tacks into the sole. He was sitting with the boot held upside down between his knees, carefully driving the wooden tacks into the new red sole. A few went wrong, but he succeeded in driving most of them in.

"See how well it's turned out?" boasted Father, showing his work to the visitor.

"What's so difficult about that?" said Obolensky, half in jest.

"You try it."

"I'd be glad to."

"Good, but on one condition: for every tack you drive in I'll pay you a ruble, and for every one you break you'll pay me ten kopecks. Agreed?"

Obolensky took the boot, awl, and hammer and broke eight tacks one after another. Then in his good-natured way, he joined in the general laughter and paid the eighty kopecks, which went to the shoemaker.

Having begun with simple boots, Father soon began to improvise: he made ladies' shoes and finally a pair of canvas summer shoes with leather tips, which he wore all summer. (Photographs taken of him at that time show him sitting on the terrace wearing these shoes.)

I recall another incident, which relates to my only memory of the poet Yakov Petrovich Polonsky. We were sitting at the bench working one evening (I say "we" because I too learned this craft and at one time was rather good at it), when the footman, Sergei Petrovich, came in and said that a gentleman by the name of Potogonsky wished to see the Count.

"What Potogonsky? I don't know anyone by that name. Ask him to come up," said Father.

At least five minutes passed and we had forgotten all about "Potogonsky" when all at once we heard a peculiar sound in the corridor like uneven wooden footsteps. The door opened and a tall gray-haired man on crutches appeared. Looking up at the visitor and instantly recognizing him, Father sprang to his feet and kissed him.

"Good Heavens! So it's you, Yakov Petrovich! Do forgive me for having made you come up all these stairs. If I had known, I would have come down, but Sergei said 'Potogonsky.' I had no idea it was you. What can I offer you?"

"Well, in the circumstances, I'll take a *potogonnoye*," * he punned. "I should enjoy a little tea," he added, panting from his exertions and seating himself on the sofa.

In order to reach Father's room, the poor old lame man had had to climb two flights of stairs, go through the drawing room, then down several steep steps and along a dimly lit passage with various doorsills. Neither before nor after that occasion did I ever see Polonsky, and I recall very little of that visit because I soon left the room for some reason and was not present during his conversation with Father.

Potogonnoye means "sudorific" in Russian.—*Tr.*

My father's other instructor in shoemaking had been Pavel Arbuzov, son of our nurse Marya Afanasyevna and brother of our footman, who had worked with him at Yasnaya Polyana. Father's enthusiasm soon came to an end, however. I believe that this was partly because of the absurd interpretation placed on it in certain circles, which could not have failed to irritate and grieve him.

In the summer he worked in the fields. If he heard of a widow or a sick old man in distressing circumstances, he would plow, mow, and harvest grain for him. When he first began doing this work, he was quite alone; no one was in sympathy with him, and most of the family looked on his work as a whim and felt rather sad that he should waste his valuable energies on such strenuous and unproductive work.

Although Father had become much gentler by that time, was less critical, less apt to lose his temper in an argument, and at times was even gay and companionable as he had been in the past, we still felt the acute discordance of our life—with its croquet and visitors and endless round of amusements—with Father's exertions, which were divided between his study and the fields, between work at his desk and behind the plow.

The first member of the family to ally herself with Father was my late sister Masha. In 1885, she was fifteen years old. A rather tall, slender, lissome girl with fair hair, she resembled my mother in figure but had Father's strongly defined cheekbones and sky-blue deep-set eyes. She was quiet and retiring by nature and always had an air of being somewhat put upon. Father's solitude touched her heart, and she was the first among us to forsake the company of those her own age and unobtrusively but very firmly and definitely side with him.

Always a champion of the oppressed and unfortunate, Masha wholeheartedly espoused the cause of the poor in the village and devoted her limited physical strength and, what was more important, her generous responsive heart to helping them.

At that time we did not have a doctor living in the house, and all the sick of Yasnaya Polyana, and often those of neighboring villages, came to Masha for help. She used to go from house to house visiting her patients, and to this day there are peasants living in the village who remember her with gratitude and old women who are firmly convinced that Marya Lvovna always "knew" and could tell without fail whether or not a patient would recover.

That summer a young Jew named Feinerman appeared at Yasnaya Polyana. He was a sincere disciple of my father at the time, a disinterested and confirmed idealist. He lived in the village, worked for the peasants without asking any recompense other than the simplest and most Spartan fare, and dreamed of founding a Christian community. In order to avoid being oppressed by the authorities, he had himself christened in our church.

At one time Feinerman was so genuinely dedicated to Christian ideals that everyone was impressed by his thoroughgoingness, and he exerted a certain influence on the villagers, especially on the young. He had a beautiful wife named Esther and a baby, and they lived in a hut in the village, literally starving. Feinerman used to bring them crusts of bread he received for his labors, but often, when working for very poor peasants, he was given nothing at all and went hungry himself. Esther went about the village and sometimes came to our estate begging food for herself and the child. At last she insisted that her husband ask for at least a pot of milk for the baby in return for a day's work. But even this he considered wrong, and finally his wife could no longer endure such an existence and left him.

Once when Feinerman came to see my father in the evening and asked him to read something aloud to him, he suddenly turned pale and fell to the floor unconscious while Father was reading. It appeared that he had been working all day without food and had fainted from hunger.

This episode had a very disturbing effect on my father, and he could never forget it. "We well-fed people stuff ourselves and do nothing," he said, "while this man works all day and then faints from hunger." What a vivid, appalling contrast!

Another time, in the autumn, a passing gypsy persuaded Feinerman to give him his only coat. Winter was approaching and he was left with absolutely nothing to wear but a hempen shirt. The incident caused a great deal of talk, of course, which ended in someone taking pity on him, and by winter he was better clothed than he had been before.

I arrived at Yasnaya Polyana early in June that year, after my examinations and when all the family was assembled there and our summer life was following its customary routine. I was nineteen years old, considered myself engaged, and dreamed of getting married and beginning a new life with my wife in accordance with my father's views. Not knowing what to do with my excess energy, I told my father that I wanted to work and asked him what I should do.

"Splendid! Go to Zharova's; her husband left her last winter to go and make some money, and hasn't been seen since. She's having a hard time alone with those children on her hands and no one to plow her strips. Take a plow, harness Mordvin, and go and do the plowing for her; it's just the moment for turning over the fallow."

I did as he told me and soon had several strips near the lake behind the village plowed up. I can remember the pleasant, soothing sensation—new to me—of doing useful work. Feeling like a horse harnessed to the plow you are following, turning up furrow after furrow, you think your leisurely thoughts while keeping your eyes on the glistening ribbon of earth, the endless band falling off the moldboard, the fat white cockchafer grubs wriggling helplessly in the fresh furrow, the rooks following the plow tracks and picking up what they can without paying you the slightest heed, and you never notice your fatigue till dinnertime or dusk drives you home. Then you turn the plow upside down, tie it to the carriers, get up sideways on your horse and ride home with your legs dangling against the shafts, pleasantly contemplating food and rest.

Often when I had taken my horse back to the stable, without waiting for the family meal I would run straight to the room where the servants were eating at a bare table, and, seating myself in a corner between the coachman and a laundress, gulp cold kvas, and with a round wooden spoon eat ground onions and potatoes or watery, heavily salted crumb broth with a dash of green oil.

By St. Peter's Day we had begun to mow. As a rule the Yasenki peasants got in our hay for a share of the crop. Before the haymaking began, they formed gangs composed of several families, each gang clearing its own strip for payment of a third part, or two fifths, depending on the quality of the grass.

Our gang consisted of two peasants—the tall Vasily Mikheyev and the squat, long-nosed Osip Makarov—my father, Feinerman, and myself. We set about mowing the new meadow beyond the avenues and the "water meadow" by the Voronka. I mowed for the benefit of Zharova again, and Father and Feinerman for someone else.

It was a very hot summer, and we had to get the hay in quickly because the rye would soon be ready and the peasants had no time to lose. The grass in the fields had been burned by the sun and was dry and stiff as wire. It was only very early in the morning when the dew was on it that it yielded easily to the scythe, and we had to get up at dawn in order to complete the task we had set ourselves the night before.

Our best mower, Vasily, went in front, then Osip, my father, Feinerman, and myself. Father mowed well and never fell behind, but he sweated heavily and apparently got tired. He said I looked like a carpenter when I mowed; something about the sweep of the scythe and the bend of my waist for some reason suggested this to him.

When the sun was high, we tedded the hay and gathered it into haycocks, and when the evening dew fell, we again set out with our scythes and mowed till nightfall.

Following our example, another gang was formed, working side by side with ours, a large and merry one joined by my brothers Sergei and Lev, and our governess's son Alcide, a very nice boy whom the peasants called Aldakim Aldakimovich. My sister Masha was in our gang, while Tanya and our cousins, the two Kuzminsky sisters, were in theirs. Ours was very strict and serious—we were called "the saints"—while theirs was frivolous and gay. On Sundays and holidays, sometimes on ordinary working days too, they sold their haycocks for drinks, and were constantly laughing and singing, but we "saints" were very sedate, and, I must confess, had a very dull time. I must also confess that whenever they sold a haycock, my brother Lev, who did not drink vodka, kept his share for me, and I enjoyed betraying my comrades now and then by taking his drink. This in no way prevented my looking down on his gang, and all the more as their merriment ended in disaster. The drunken peasants got into a fight and Semyon Rezunov, the head of their gang, broke his father's arm.

The summer of which I am speaking was remarkable for the fact that everyone who was staying at our Yasnaya Polyana house was infected with a passion for work. Even *maman* used to come out to the fields in a *sarafan* and take up a rake, and my Uncle Aleksandr Mikhailovich Kuzminsky, a middle-aged man who at that time occupied a prominent official position, mowed so vigorously that his hands were covered with huge blisters.

Naturally, not everyone who came out to work shared my father's convictions or had ideals about physical labor, but it happened that all of us were caught up in it that summer. Why should the sixteen-year-old French boy Alcide, and the others who ascribed no moral value to work, go into the fields and scythe instead of going horseback riding or playing the usual games? The only psychological explanation I can find for this enigma is that the infectious sincerity that was basic to my father's character could not fail to have an influence in one form or another on those close to him.

One of my father's younger disciples, a certain _____,[3] visited us periodically at that time. Once he arrived just when work was at its height. After breakfast we all assembled and went to the stables where our tools were kept. I was helping Father build a shed for one of the villagers at the time; Feinerman was thatching someone's cottage, and my sisters were binding rye sheaves. Each of us took the tools he needed: Father and I took axes and saws, Feinerman took a pitchfork, my sisters took rakes, and we set out. The visitor came with us, and my sister Tanya, who was fun-loving and always fond of

jesting, seeing that he was going empty-handed turned to him
and said,

"And where are you going?"

"To the vill-a-age."

"What for?"

"To he-e-elp."

"How are you going to help? You haven't got any tools. Here,
take a rake at least, it will be useful for handing up straw."

"I shall he-e-elp with advi-i-ce," he replied, drawling like an
Englishman, quite unaware both of Tanya's irony and of how
utterly ridiculous he would be with his "advi-i-ce" in the "vill-
a-age," where everyone was working, and where a man decked
out in English knickerbockers and a Norfolk jacket would
hinder or spoil the business in hand.

I mention this incident regretfully as a typical example of the
"Tolstoyans" we hear so much about. How many such "advisers" have I seen in my time! How many of them turned up
at Yasnaya Polyana, and how few were really convinced, sincere believers! Many fell by the wayside in my father's lifetime, while others still strut vaingloriously in his shadow and
only damage his memory. Not without reason did my father
often say that "Tolstoyans" were to him the most incomprehensible of sects and the furthest removed from his way of
thinking.

"I shall soon die," he sadly predicted, "and people will say
that Tolstoy taught men to plow, reap, and make boots—but
the chief thing, what I have been endeavoring to say all my
life, what I believe in and is the most important thing of all,
they will forget."

XXIII

My Father as Mentor

I will now turn back and try to trace my father's influence on my upbringing and recall to the best of my ability the imprint it left on my childhood and on the difficult period of my adolescence, which happened to coincide with the radical change in his entire world-view.

I have already spoken of the "Anke cake" that my mother introduced at Yasnaya Polyana. In making her bear the whole responsibility for that "cake" I have done her an injustice, for my father too had his "Anke cake" at the time of his marriage, though he was perhaps so accustomed to it by then that he was no longer aware of it. His "cake" was that archaic mode of life which he had been born into and later dreamed of restoring at Yasnaya Polyana.

In 1852, having grown tired of life in the Caucasus and thinking back on his birthplace, he wrote a letter to his aunt Tatyana Aleksandrovna describing "the happiness that awaits me."

"This is how I picture it to myself. After some years, when I am neither very young nor very old, I shall find myself back at Yasnaya Polyana, my affairs all in order, with no troubles or anxieties. You will be living at Yasnaya too, a little older but still healthy and vigorous. We shall lead the same life we led in the old days: I shall work in the mornings, but we'll see each other almost all day.

"We'll dine together. In the evening I'll read you something that interests you. And then we'll talk; I'll tell you about life in the Caucasus, you'll recount your memories of my father and mother and tell me some of those 'terrifying stories' we used to listen to, wide-eyed and open-mouthed with fear. We shall talk about the people we loved who are no more. You will weep, I'll weep a little too, but our tears will be soothing. We shall talk about my brothers, who will visit us from time to time, and about dear Masha,* who will bring all her children and spend several months of the year at her beloved Yasnaya. We shall have no acquaintances; no one will come to bore us with gossip. It's a wonderful dream. But this is not all I allow myself to dream of.

"I shall be married. My wife will be gentle, loving, and kind, and will love you as I do. We'll have children who will call you 'Grandmother,' and you will live in the big house, in the room upstairs where my grandmother used to live.† The whole house will be run along the same lines as in my father's day; we'll begin the same life all over again, but with a change of roles. You will take Grandmother's place, but will be even better than she was, and I'll take my father's place, though I can never be worthy of the honor. My wife will take my mother's place, and the children will take ours. Masha will fill the role of both of my aunts,‡ except for their sorrow, and there will even be

---

*My father's sister.—I.T.
†Pelageya Nikolayevna, Nikolai Ilyich's mother.—I.T.
‡Pelageya Ilyinichna Yushkova and Aleksandra Ilyinichna Osten-Saken.—I.T.

Gasha|| to take the place of Praskovya Isayevna. The only one lacking will be someone to take the part you played in our family. We shall never find such a beautiful loving soul as yours. There is no one to succeed you.

"Three fresh faces will appear among us from time to time, my brothers, and especially one, who will come often—Nikolenka, who will be retired, a bald old bachelor, but still the same kindly noble fellow. I can see him telling the children stories of his own composition as of old, see them kissing his grubby hands (which deserve to be kissed nonetheless), see him playing with them, while my wife busily supervises the preparation of his favorite dish. He and I will reminisce about the past, and you will sit in your customary place, listening to us with pleasure. You will still call us by our old names, 'Lyovochka' and 'Nikolenka,' despite our age, and will scold me for eating with my fingers and him for not washing his hands.

"If I were made Emperor of Russia, if I were given Peru, in short, if a fairy came with her magic wand and asked me what I wanted, I should lay my hand on my heart and reply that I wanted these dreams to become reality.

"I know you don't like looking into the future, but what is wrong with it? And it's so pleasant. But I fear this is much too selfish, that I have given you too small a share in this happiness. I am also afraid that past misfortunes have left too painful an imprint on your heart, and this will prevent you from committing yourself to a future that would constitute my happiness. Tell me, dear Auntie, would it not make you happy too? All this can happen, and hopes are so comforting.

"I am crying again. Why should I cry thinking of you? They are tears of joy; I am happy in the consciousness of my love for you, whatever misfortunes may occur, I can never consider myself entirely unfortunate as long as you are alive. Do you remember our parting at the Iverskaya Chapel when we were leaving for Kazan? At the very moment of parting, I realized

---

||Agafya Mikhailovna.—*I.T.*

as if by inspiration what you meant to me, and, though still a
child, my tears and a few desultory words made you understand what I was feeling. I have never ceased to love you, but
the feeling I experienced at the Iverskaya and what I feel now
are entirely different; the present feeling is stronger, more exalted than at any other time.

"I will confess one thing to you of which I am ashamed, but
I must tell you in order to relieve my conscience. In the past,
when reading the letters in which you spoke of your feeling for
me, it seemed to me that you were exaggerating. Only now in
rereading them do I understand you, your boundless love for
us, and your exalted soul. I am convinced that anyone else reading this letter and the preceding one would reproach me. But
I do not expect this from you; you know me too well, and know
that perhaps my only good quality is my sensibility. To this
quality I owe the happiest moments of my life. In any case, this
is the last letter in which I will allow myself to express such
high-flown sentiments. High-flown to the indifferent, but not
to you who know how to evaluate them.

"Good-bye, dear Auntie, I hope to see Nikolenka in a few
days, and will write you afterward." [1]

Exactly ten years after he wrote this letter, Father married,
and almost all of his dreams were realized and in the way he
had wished. Only the big house with grandmother's room was
lacking, and his brother Nikolai with the grubby hands, for he
had died two years earlier, in 1860.

Father saw in his married life a repetition of his parents'
life, and in us children he looked for a repetition of himself and
his brothers. This was the atmosphere in which we were
brought up and which lasted till the middle of the seventies.

We were reared as "gentlefolk," proud of our position and
holding aloof from the outside world. Everything that was not
us was beneath us and unworthy of imitation. I became interested in the village boys only when I began to acquire certain
information from them about things I had not known before,
knowledge that was forbidden to me. I was about ten years old

at the time. We used to go tobogganing in the village, but when we began to develop friendships with peasant boys, *papa* was quick to notice our new enthusiasm and put a stop to it. So we grew up completely surrounded by the stone walls of English governesses, tutors, and various teachers, and in such surroundings our parents had no difficulty keeping an eye on every step we took and directing our lives in the way they wished, especially since they were still of one mind about our upbringing, their views not having diverged at that time.

Besides those subjects that *papa* undertook to teach us himself, he paid particular attention to our physical development, to gymnastics and all sorts of exercises for developing courage and self-reliance. At one period he used to take us every day to a place in one of the avenues where an outdoor gymnasium had been installed, and we were required to go through a number of exercises on the parallel bars, trapeze, and rings. The most difficult of these, which we called the "Mikhail Ivanovich," was turning a backward somersault on the trapeze. *Papa* and Monsieur Rey were able to do it, but it was so difficult for us boys that it was a long time before we succeeded in doing it; Seryozha was the first, and later I just barely managed to execute it.

Whenever we were preparing to go horseback riding or for a walk, *papa* never waited for anyone who was late, and if I lagged behind and cried, he mimicked me, saying, "Nobody waits for me," and I howled still louder and became furious, but caught up with them all the same.

The word "milksop" was a term of abuse among us, and there was nothing more humiliating than for one of us to be called a milksop by *papa*. I remember once when my grandmother Pelageya Ilyinichna was trimming a lamp, she took the chimney in her hands and burned herself so badly that her fingers were blistered, yet she carefully set it down on the table without dropping it. Whenever *papa* had occasion to reproach one of us for cowardice, he would recall this incident and hold it up to us as an example. "Now, that is remarkable self-control. She had every right to drop the chimney, it only cost five kopecks

and she can earn five times more than that in a day by her knitting alone—but she didn't drop it. You would have dropped it.
And I probably would have dropped it," he said, delighted by
her fortitude.

Papa almost never forced us to do anything, yet we always
seemed to do exactly what he wanted us to do of our own accord and on our own initiative. *Maman* often scolded and punished us, but when he wanted to make us do something he only
looked into our eyes very intently and we knew what that look
meant; it was far more effective than any command.

As an example of the difference between Father's method
and Mother's, if you needed a twenty-kopeck piece for something and went to *maman* for it she would first question you in
detail about what you wanted it for, then scold you at length,
and sometimes refuse. If you went to *papa*, he never asked any
questions, but simply looked into your eyes and said, "Take it,
it's there on the table." And yet, however much I wanted the
money, I never went to Father for it, but always preferred to
try to get it from Mother.

My father's great strength as a parent was that one could no
more conceal anything from him than one could from one's own
conscience. He knew everything, and to deceive him was like
deceiving oneself; it was not only impossible but to no avail.

My father's influence on me was most clearly manifested in
the question of my marriage and in my relations with women
before marriage. There are times when some trivial incident or
chance word said at the right moment leaves a deep impression
and influences one's whole life. So it was with me.

One morning I was running down the long staircase at home,
taking two steps at a time as usual, and I vaulted over the last
few steps in a nimble, daring leap. I was sixteen at the time and
strong, and it was a truly magnificent leap. My father happened
to be coming toward me and when he saw me flying through
the air, stopped at the foot of the stairs and spread out his arms
to catch me in case I lost my footing and fell. I landed on my
feet with agility, straightened up and said good morning.

"What a lusty fellow you are!" he said with a smile, apparently admiring my youthful vigor. "In the village a young fellow like you would have been married by now, but here you are not knowing what to do with your energy."

I said nothing, but those words made a tremendous impression on me. I was not so much struck by the implied reproach for my idleness as by the new idea that I was so grown up that it was "time for me to be married." I knew that Father felt very strongly about chastity in young people, knew what value he placed on purity, and consequently an early marriage seemed to me the best solution to this difficult problem which must plague every thoughtful youth after he has reached puberty.

I do not suppose that when he uttered these words my father foresaw the effect they would have on me, but coming from his heart, as they undoubtedly did, they made a very deep impression. I understood not only their explicit meaning, but all that was left unsaid and yet was so meaningful.

Two or three years later, when I was eighteen and we were living in Moscow, I fell in love with a young lady I had met, Sofya Nikolayevna Filosofova, and went to see her almost every Saturday at her parents' home. My father knew about this but said nothing.

One day when he was going out for a walk, I asked if I might go with him. As I very seldom accompanied him on his walks in Moscow, he realized that I wanted to talk about something serious. After walking for a while in silence, he evidently felt that I was too shy to initiate the conversation and very casually remarked,

"How is it that you've been going to the Filosofovs' so often?"

I said that I was very fond of the eldest daughter.

"Well, do you want to marry her?"

"Yes."

"Is she a good girl? . . . Now, see that you don't make a mistake—and don't deceive her," he said thoughtfully and with a singular gentleness.

I left him at once and ran happily home along the Arbat. I
was glad that I had told him the truth; his warm and discreet
attitude had strengthened my feeling not only for him, to whom
I was boundlessly grateful for his tenderness, but for her whom
I loved still more from that moment, and I was more firmly
resolved than ever not to deceive her.

My father's delicacy in his relations with us amounted almost
to shyness. There were certain matters he could never touch on
for fear of causing us pain. I shall never forget how in Moscow
one day I happened to run in to change my clothes and found
him sitting at the table in my room writing. My bed stood behind a screen, and I could not see him from there. Hearing my
footsteps he spoke without looking around.

"Is that you, Ilya?"

"Yes."

"Are you alone? Shut the door. . . . Now no one can hear us,
and we can't see each other, so we won't feel ashamed. Tell me,
did you ever have anything to do with women?"

When I said, "No," I suddenly heard him start to weep, sobbing like a child. I too cried, and for some time, with the screen
between us, we continued to shed tears of joy; and we were not
ashamed, but were both so glad that I consider that moment
one of the happiest of my entire life. No discussions, no reasoning, could ever have done for me what that did. The tears of a
father of sixty can never be forgotten, even in moments of the
greatest temptation.

In the period of my youth between the ages of sixteen and
twenty my father followed my development very attentively;
he perceived all of my uncertainties, encouraged all of my good
impulses, and frequently reproached me for my inconsistency.

I still have some of the letters he wrote to me at that time.
The first is one that he wrote from Yasnaya at the beginning of
October 1884, when I was living in Moscow with my brothers
Seryozha and Lev.

"Ilya Lvovich, greetings. The dog is terribly contrary, but
since she's the joy of your life, they'll let her stay. Her charac-

teristics are the following: the scent of a woodcock means nothing to her, but she understands the firing of a gun and runs home for all she's worth the instant she hears it. Davydov, who has been going out with her, gave me this information. *Maman* says that you should have your shoes mended and you'll get new ones in the spring. How are you getting on? Apart from school, I have no notion of how you spend your time. Of course, those unexpected out-of-towners turn up, the Tolstoys for the theater and the Golovins for music. Yesterday riding to the post office I saw some girls running up the hill by the village. 'Where are you going?' 'To the fire.' I rode up—Bibikin's place was in flames. Going farther I saw that the threshing barn, granary, grain, and one hundred and fifty crates of apples were all burning. They had set fire to it. It was a spectacle more comical than sad, strange to say. The peasants all running about demolishing everything, obviously delighted. The authorities, among them Fyodor the village policeman, the chief with the paunch, giving orders. Certain landowners not of this region, including Khomyakov, commiserating. Two priests commiserating. Alyoshka Dyachok and his brother with the extraordinary curls, just back from the Slavyansky choir, commiserating. And the apples baking and the peasants obviously approving. Write to me so I'll have some idea of your emotional state. (I am sure you would become friends with Alyoshka's brother from the Slavyansky. A fine lot of hair—like a haycock. The effect of curl papers.)" [2]

The second, a postcard, was written from Yasnaya in 1886, when Father had a bad leg and we elder sons were living in Moscow with Nikolai Nikolayevich Gay (the son).

"You get letters from here every day so you know all about me. I myself write 'for constancy's sake.' General condition good. If anything to complain of, it's sleep; as a consequence, head's not clear and can't work. I lie here listening to the women talk and am so lapped in femininity that I've begun to speak of myself in the feminine gender. But my mind's at peace; sometimes a little anxious about some of you, about your spiritual state, yet don't allow myself to worry, but wait and rejoice in the progress of life. As long as you don't undertake too much and live without doing evil, all will be well. I kiss you and Kolechka." [3]

The following letter belongs to the same period.

"I have just written you a letter, my dear friend Ilya, which was true to my own feelings, but I fear unjust, and am not sending it. I said some unpleasant things to you, but I have no right to. I don't know you as I should like to, and as I ought to know you. That is my fault. And I should like to remedy it. There are many things about you that I do not like, but I don't know everything. As for your proposed journey, I think that in your position as a student—and not only as a student in a *gymnasium* but throughout your student years—it is better to do less gadding about; moreover, every unnecessary expenditure, which you can easily refrain from, is immoral in my opinion, and in yours too if you only think about it. If you decide to come, I'll be glad for my own sake, as long as you are not inseparable from Golovin.

"So do as you think best. But you must work both with your mind, thinking and reading, and with your heart, that is, you must learn to know what is really good and what is bad though seeming to be good.

"I kiss you. L.T." [4]

The next three letters were written in 1887.

"Dear friend Ilya,

"There is always someone or something that prevents me from answering your letters, which to me are important and precious, especially the last one.

"First it was Buturlin, then poor health, then sleeplessness, and now Dzhunkovsky, the friend of Khilkov that I wrote you about, has arrived. He is sitting at tea talking to the ladies (none of them understanding one another). I left and want to write at least part of all I have been thinking about you.

"Assuming that Sofya Alekseyevna is asking too much of you,* there is no harm in waiting, especially from the point of

---

*I had written to my father that my fiancée's mother would not permit us to marry for two years.—*I.T.*

view of fortifying your faith and your views. Everything depends on this. It can be dreadful to set out from one shore and not reach the other.

"The one shore is a good and honest life that will lead to your own happiness and benefit others. But there is a bad life, a life so sugar-coated and so prevalent that if you follow it you don't even notice that it's not a good life, and only your conscience suffers—if you have one; but if you leave it and do not reach the real shore, you will be tormented by solitude and the reproach of having deserted people, and you will feel ashamed. In short, I am trying to say that it is impossible to want to be *somewhat* good, impossible to jump into the water unless you know how to swim. One must be upright and want to be utterly good. Do you feel this within yourself? All I am saying, therefore, is that we know what Princess Marya Alekseyevna's† opinion of your marriage would be: that if young people marry without sufficient money, it means children, poverty, getting tired of each other in a year or two, and in ten years the quarreling begins, the defects—hell. And in all this Princess Marya Alekseyevna is absolutely right, and her predictions are accurate, unless the young people getting married have another, one and only purpose, unknown to her—and that purpose is not of the mind, not recognized by reason, but one that constitutes the light of life and the attainment of which is more exciting than anything else. If you have this—good, marry at once, and prove Marya Alekseyevna wrong. If not, ninety-nine chances out of a hundred nothing but misfortune will come of your marriage. I am speaking to you with my whole heart. And you too accept with your heart what I am saying and weigh it well. Besides loving you as a son, I love you as a man standing at the crossroads. I kiss you, Lyolya, Kolechka, and Seryozha, if he has returned. We are all safe and sound." [5]

The following letter belongs to the same period.

"Your letter to Tanya has arrived, my dear friend Ilya, and I see that you are still advancing toward that purpose which

†My father took Griboyedov's Princess Marya Alekseyevna as a symbol.—I.T.

you had set for yourself, and I want to write you both (because you probably tell her everything) what I think about it. And I think about it a great deal, with both joy and fear. This is what I think: to marry in order to have more enjoyment of life never turns out well. To make marriage, union with one you love, the principal aim of life, displacing everything else, is a great mistake. And an obvious one, if you think about it. Object—marriage. Well, you marry, and what then? If you had no other purpose in life before marriage, it will be doubly hard, terribly hard, almost impossible to find one afterward. In fact, you may be sure that if you had no common purpose before your marriage, nothing will bring you together afterward and you will continually grow further apart. Marriage can only bring happiness when those who marry have a single aim. Two people meet on a road and say, 'Let's walk together,' 'Let's,' and they go on hand in hand; but not if they hold out their hands to each other and then turn off the road.

"In the first case it will be like this:

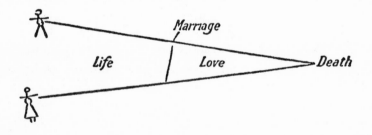

"In the second case like this:

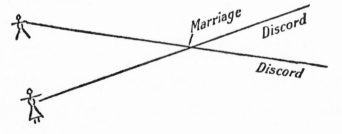

"The reason for this is that the idea shared by many that life is a vale of tears is just as false as the idea shared by the great majority—an idea to which youth, health, and riches incline one—that life is a place of entertainment. Life is a place for service, and in that service one sometimes has to endure much pain, but often experiences much joy. And that can be genuine only when people regard life as service, and have a purpose in life outside themselves and their personal happiness.

"As a rule those who are getting married completely forget this. So many joyful events are in store for them in marrying and having children that these events seem to constitute life itself. But this is a dangerous delusion. If the parents spend their lives begetting children without having any purpose in life, they are only putting off this question of the purpose of life, but not escaping it, because they will have to bring up their children, guide them, without having anything to guide them by. And then the parents lose their human qualities and the happiness they afford one, and become breeding stock.

"So this is what I say: for those who prepare to marry because life *seems* to them to be full, it is still more essential to think and make clear to themselves what it is that each of them lives for. And in order to make this clear, you must think, consider your present circumstances and your past life, evaluate what you regard as important and unimportant, find out what you believe in, that is, what you consider to be the eternal, irrefutable truth by which you will guide your life. And not so much recognize and understand it as practice it in your daily life, because until you do this you cannot know whether you believe it or not. I know your belief, and that belief, or those aspects of it that can be expressed in deeds, you must now, more than ever, make clear to yourself by putting it into practice.

"Your belief is that your well-being consists in loving people and being loved by them. For the attainment of this end I know of three courses of action, which I try constantly to follow, which it is impossible to practice enough, and which are especially necessary for you now.

"First, in order to be able to love people and be loved by

them, one must accustom oneself to expect as little as possible from them—and this is very hard work—for if I expect much and am disappointed, I am inclined to reproach rather than to love them.

"Second, in order to love people not in word but in deed, one must train oneself to do what benefits them. This is still harder work, particularly for you at your age, when it is natural to be studying.

"Third, in order to love people and be loved by them, one must learn humility, gentleness, and the art of bearing with disagreeable people and situations, the art of always behaving in a way that will not hurt anyone, and in those cases where it is impossible not to offend someone, to choose the least offense. And this is the hardest work of all, work that never ceases, from the moment you wake up in the morning till you go to sleep at night. But it is the most joyful work, because day by day you can rejoice in your growing success and receive the added reward, unnoticed at first but very gratifying, of being loved.

"So I advise you, advise you both, to think and live as sincerely as you can, because that is the only way you can learn whether you are really walking on the same road, whether it is wise to join hands, and at the same time, if you are sincere, you will be preparing your future.

"*Les extrêmes le touchent.* The most selfish and abhorrent life is the life of two people who have united only to enjoy life, and the highest vocation is that of people who live to serve God, furthering good and peace, and who have united for that purpose. So don't become confused—don't take one thing for the other. Why should a man not choose the highest? But when you have chosen the highest, you must set your whole heart on it, and not just a little part of it. A little leads to nothing. There now, I am tired of writing, and there is still more I wanted to say.

"I kiss you." [6]

In his next letter of that period, Father was writing about my fiancée.

"Two things unite you to her: the convictions—faith and love. In my opinion, even one is enough. The real, sincere bond is love, human and Christian; if she has this too, the being in love will grow, beautifully and firmly. If it should be love alone —being in love—this is not exactly bad, but neither is it good, though possible. And for honest natures, it is possible to live even with that—with great struggles. But if there is neither one nor the other, and only the *prétexte* of one or the other, then it is undoubtedly bad. I advise you to be as severe as possible with yourself, and to know the reasons for your actions." [7]

Tolstoy and his wife, two years before his death.

(Above) Tolstoy and Maksim Gorky at Yasnaya Polyana, 1901.

(Right, above) Reproduction of a
painting by Repin of Tolstoy
in his study.
(Right, below) The Tolstoy home
in Moscow, now the L. N. Tolstoy
Museum. Tolstoy and his family
lived in this house from 1882–1901.

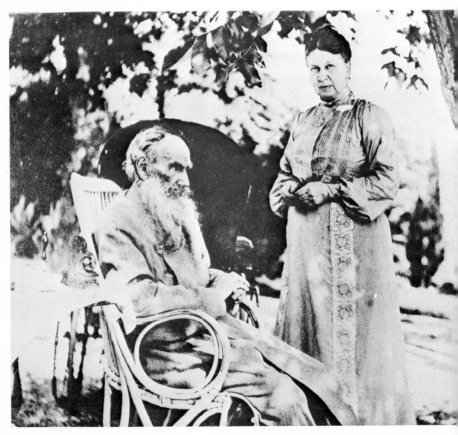

(*Left, above*) **Vanechka Tolstoy.**
(*Left*) **Tolstoy and his wife at Gaspra in the Crimea, 1902.**
(*Above*) **Tolstoy's secretary, N. N. Gusev, copying a speech by Tolstoy from the phonograph presented to Tolstoy by Thomas Edison in 1908.**

Tolstoy setting out for a ride with his doctor, Dushan Makovitsky, 1907.

Ilya Tolstoy with his father at Yasnaya Polyana, 1903.

Tolstoy and his wife in their garden at Yasnaya Polyana, 1910.

Ilya Tolstoy in Hollywood, 1920.

XXIV

My Marriage. Father's Letters. Vanechka. His Death

IN February 1888, I married and took my young bride to Yasnaya Polyana, where for two months we lived in three rooms on the ground floor. In spring I was to move to the Aleksandrov farm, which was part of our Nikolskoye property in the Chern District, where I intended to build a house and settle.

Shortly after my marriage, I received the following letter from my father:

"And how are you, my dear children? Well? In lively spirits? This is an important time for you now. Everything is important now, every step is important, remember that; your life, your mutual relations, are being formed—the new *homme-femme* organism, a single being, as well as the relations of this complex being to the rest of the world, to Marya Afanasyevna, to Kostyushka, etc., to the inanimate world, to your food, clothing, etc., is all new. If you want anything, want it now.

"And what will also be of great importance now will be your moods of *mauvaise humeur* when everything, and you yourselves, will appear in an unnatural light to each other, but don't believe in it, don't believe in the evil, but wait for the good to return again.

"I do not know about Sonya, but Ilya is prone to this and must be careful. And you, Sonya, will suddenly find yourself bored—bored, bored, bored. But don't believe in this and don't give in to it, only know that it is not boredom, but simply the soul's demand for work, for any kind of work, mental or physical, it's all the same.

"The important thing, more important than anything else, is to be kind to people, not kind from a distance, but to be accessible and near. If this is so, life will be full and happy. Well, stick to it! I kiss you and love you both dearly. I have just heard that Khilkov is marrying the sister of Dzhunkovsky's wife. I don't know her." [1]

At the end of March *papa* had come to Yasnaya to stay with us until we left for Nikolskoye. We had nobody in the house with us but old Marya Afanasyevna, who by then was very feeble and had been pensioned off, so that we had to do without servants and cook our own meals, fetch water, and clean the rooms.

Papa did what he could to help us, but I confess that I became convinced at that time that he was utterly unqualified for the Robinson Crusoe life. It is true that he was not at all demanding and found everything perfectly splendid, but having been accustomed to a certain regimen, a certain diet, for so many years, every departure from it, even when he was only sixty, had a disastrous effect on his organism. How many times he went away from home in good health and came back ill as a result of living in different conditions—even when he had been staying with people who knew all his habits and looked after him like a baby.

At the end of April my wife and I left for our farm, and from that time forth I returned to Yasnaya only for brief visits, either on business or simply to see my parents. I never lived there again.

After we had gone, we received the following letter from *papa:*

"Did you have a good journey, dear friends? We miss you and are sorry you are no longer with us. The enclosed telegram came for you and nothing has been done about it. I think there is no harm in that. Write and tell us what you have done about settling and what your plans are. My health is quite good now. Our temperance society is having a great success; many have signed, one of whom, Danilo, has managed to get drunk again even after signing. I am not at all discouraged by this and am looking forward, eagerly looking forward, and shall be very glad for you when you have given up those two bad habits, alcohol and tobacco, which have no place in the true life. Life is no joking matter, especially for you now; every step you take is important. There is much good in you—above all purity and love; preserve them with all your strength. But there are many, many dangers threatening you—you do not see them, but I do, and I am afraid. Well, *au revoir,* I kiss you, everyone sends regards. Write. According to the last letters from Moscow, they are all cheerfully making haste to come home. L.T." [2]

On the occasion of the birth of my first daughter, Anna, Father wrote the following letter:

"I congratulate you, dear and beloved young parents. I congratulate you not just in words; I myself was so unexpectedly overjoyed at hearing of my granddaughter that I want to share my joy and thank you; I understand your happiness. I now look on all girls and women with pity and contempt. What is that creature? You should see Anna—she'll be the real thing! But joking apart—and yet what I said was not a joke—what I want to say in all seriousness is this: see that you bring up this granddaughter, your daughter, well; don't make the mistakes that were made with you, the mistakes of the period. I believe that Anna will be brought up better, will be less coddled and spoiled by genteelness than you were. How is Sonya? It is awful to write when one thinks that something may have gone wrong. However, all will be well so long as all is well in one's heart, and that above all I wish for you. How glad I am that Sofya Alekseyevna is with you; kiss her and congratulate her for me. I kiss you.

L.T." [3]

It was after my marriage, in the spring, that *maman* gave birth to her youngest son, Vanechka. This little boy, who lived only to the age of seven and died of scarlet fever in 1895, was the darling of the whole family. Father loved him as his youngest child, with all the strength of a father's and an old man's affection.

I must say that he had taken little part in the upbringing of my two younger brothers, Andrei and Mikhail. By the time they were of an age to go to school, he was in complete disagreement with the methods by which the rest of us had been educated, and feeling that he was unable to direct them as he would have liked to, according to his own convictions, he forsook them altogether, washed his hands of them, and did not concern himself with their education or their lives. *Maman* enrolled them first in Polivanov's *gymnasium,* where my brother Lev and I had gone, and they were later transferred to the Katkov Lycée.

I believe that Father looked on Vanechka as his spiritual heir and dreamed of bringing him up according to his own views, in the principles of Christian love and virtue.

I did not know Vanechka as well as my other brothers and sisters because I was no longer living at home when he was born, but I remember how remarkably affectionate and responsive this delicate frail child was.

Vanechka was only a year and a half old when *papa* decided to give up all his landed property and divide his estate among the members of the family. Vanechka, as the youngest, was given part of Yasnaya Polyana with the house and demesne. A more distant part of the estate was allotted to my mother. After Vanechka's death *maman* told me that when walking in the garden with him one day she had explained to him that all of that land was his. "No, *maman*," he said, stamping his little foot, "don't say that Yasnaya Polyana is mine, everything is everyones'."

When I received the telegram announcing his death, I went to Moscow at once. *Maman* told me that after he died my father said, "This is the first irreparable sorrow of my life."

Vanechka was buried not far from Moscow in the village churchyard at Nikolskoye, beyond All Saints, where my other little brother, Alyosha, was buried.[4] When the coffin was lowered into the grave, my father sobbed and said very very softly, so that I could barely hear him, "Dust thou art, and unto dust shalt thou return." He had written the same words to his brother Sergei Nikolayevich on the occasion of their brother Nikolai's death. Vanechka's death was the greatest loss he had suffered since then.

I have often thought that if Vanechka had lived, a great many things in my father's life might have been quite different. Who knows, perhaps that sensitive responsive child might have attached him to his family, and he would not have been obsessed with the idea of leaving Yasnaya Polyana. This supposition is suggested to me by a letter he wrote to my mother a year and a half after Vanechka's death. Here is the letter, which I quote in its entirety:

[Yasnaya Polyana, June 1, 1897]

"Dear Sonya,

"I have long been tormented by the incongruity between my life and my beliefs. To make you change your life, your habits, which I myself instilled in you, was something I could not do, nor could I leave you up to now, thinking that I would deprive the children of the influence, however slight, that I might have on them while they were still young, and that I would cause you pain. But to continue living as I have been living these sixteen years, at times struggling and upsetting you, at times falling under the influence of those temptations to which I was accustomed and by which I was surrounded, has also become impossible, and I have now decided to do what I have long

wished to do—to go away; first, because with my advancing
years this life grows more and more burdensome to me and I
long more and more for solitude; second, because the children
have grown up, my influence in the house is no longer needed,
and you all have more lively interests which will make my absence less noticed.

"But the chief reason is that as the Hindus retire into the
forests when they approach their sixties, and as every religious
old man wants to dedicate the last years of his life to God rather
than to jokes, puns, gossip, and tennis, so I, who am now entering on my seventieth year, long with all the strength of my soul
for this serenity and solitude and, if not perfect harmony, at
least not this crying discord between my life and my beliefs
and conscience.

"If I were to do this outright, there would be entreaties, reproaches, arguments, accusation, and perhaps I should weaken
and fail to carry out my resolution, and it must be carried out.
Please forgive me, therefore, if this step that I am taking causes
you pain, and above all, in your heart, Sonya, let me go of your
own accord and do not try to find me, do not lament over me,
and do not condemn me.

"My leaving does not mean that I have been dissatisfied with
you. I know that you could not, literally *could not,* and cannot
now see and feel as I do, and therefore could not and cannot
alter your life and make sacrifices for what you do not fully
accept. And I do not condemn you for this, on the contrary, I
recall with love and gratitude the long thirty-five years of our
life together, especially the first half when, with the maternal
selflessness that is characteristic of you, you so staunchly and
energetically bore with what you considered your calling in life.
You gave to me and to the world what you were able to give,
and gave much maternal love and self-sacrifice, and I cannot esteem you enough for that. But during the latter period of
our life, the last fifteen years, we have drifted apart. I cannot
think that I am to blame, because I know that I have changed
not for myself, not for other people, but because I could not do
otherwise. And I cannot blame you for not having followed me,

but thank you and lovingly remember, and shall continue to remember, what you have given me.

"Good-bye, dear Sonya. Your loving Lev Tolstoy."

On the envelope was written: "Should there be no special decision made by me concerning this letter, it is to be given to S.A. after my death." [5]

The letter came into my mother's hands only after Father's death. Later, perhaps, I shall return to this extremely important document, which explains many questions that are incomprehensible to most people. I have quoted it here in connection with Vanechka's death because it seems to me that there is unquestionably an intrinsic relation between the two events.

The idea of leaving home cannot have occurred to my father immediately after the death of his son, for at that time he fully shared with my mother the "dreadfully overwrought state of mind" she was in, and wrote concerning it:

"Now when she is suffering so, I feel more than ever and with all my being the truth of the words that man and wife are not separate individuals, but one. . . . I long intensely to convey to her even a part of that religious consciousness which I have —though only to a slight degree, still enough to make it possible for me to rise at times above the sorrows of life—because I know that only this, the consciousness of God and of being His son, can give life; and I hope that it will come to her, not from me, of course, but from God, although this consciousness does not come easily to women." [6]

A year and a half later, when the acuteness of my mother's grief had begun to pass, my father felt morally freer and wrote the above farewell letter.

XXV

Help for the Famine-Stricken

AFTER the Moscow census, after my father had become convinced that helping people by giving them money was not only ineffectual but immoral, his participation in the distribution of food during the famines of 1891 and 1898 may seem to have shown a certain inconsistency, if not contradiction.

"If a horseman sees that his horse is exhausted, he should not remain seated on its back, but should simply get off," he used to say, condemning the charity of the affluent who, sitting on the backs of the people, enjoy all the benefits of their privileged position while giving only of their superfluity. He did not believe any good came from that sort of charity and considered it a form of self-delusion, all the more harmful because those who practice it seem to derive a moral right to pursue their idle, aristocratic life while increasing the poverty of the people.

In the autumn of 1890, my father conceived the idea of writing an article on the famine, which at that time had spread throughout most of Russia. Although he already knew the extent of the disaster from newspapers and from the accounts of those who came to see him from the famine-stricken areas, nevertheless, when his old friend Ivan Ivanovich Rayevsky called on him at Yasnaya Polyana and proposed that he drive through the Dankovsky District to see for himself what was happening in the villages, he readily consented and went with him to Begichevka.

He had intended to stay only a day or two, but when he saw how urgent the need was, he set to work immediately with Rayevsky, who had already organized several soup kitchens in the villages, to bring help to the peasants, at first on a small scale and then, when donations poured in from all over, on a broader scale. The result was that he devoted two whole years of his life to this work.[1]

One cannot think of my father as being inconsistent in this matter. He did not for a moment delude himself and at no time considered that he was engaged in some great and virtuous undertaking, but when he saw the misfortunes of the people, he simply could not bear to go on living in comfort at Yasnaya or in Moscow; to have done so at such a time instead of going out and helping would have been too painful for him.

"There is much about it that is not what it ought to be; there is Sofya Andreyevna's money, the relations of those who feed to those who are fed, *there is sin without end,* but I cannot sit at home writing. I feel a need to take part in it, to do something," [2] he wrote to Nikolai Nikolayevich Gay from the province of Ryazan.

At the very outset of his work at Begichevka, he suffered a great sorrow. In November, Ivan Ivanovich Rayevsky, who was traveling constantly on business connected with the famine, sometimes to Zemstvo meetings, sometimes to the villages and hamlets, caught a cold, fell ill with a severe influenza, and died. It seems to me that this loss imposed a moral obligation on my father to continue to carry through to the end the work begun by his friend.

Rayevsky was one of my father's oldest friends.[3] He was known to have been an athlete at one time, and I believe that he and my father became acquainted in Moscow when both were interested in physical culture and were going to Poiret's Gymnastic School. I remember him from the days of my early childhood, when he occasionally visited Yasnaya Polyana and he and my father shared a passion for wolfhounds and race-horses. Later, when Father had renounced all such interests, his friendship with Ivan Ivanovich continued, but I believe they had never been as close as they were during that brief period when they were brought together by the people's distress and their joint efforts to combat it. Rayevsky put his whole heart into the work, and with his great practicality and selflessness he was an invaluable collaborator and companion for my father.

That same winter, because of poor health, I believe, Father had to leave Begichevka for two months and asked me to take his place during that time. I immediately prepared to go, turned over to my wife the work of feeding the starving in the Chern District, and went to Begichevka.

My father had been directing a really stupendous operation there. I found only one assistant when I arrived, a splendid energetic young woman named Persidskaya, with whom I worked for some time.

Before long I received the following letter from my father, which was brought to me by a young lady he had sent to help us.

"Dear friend Ilya,

"This letter will be brought to you by Velichkina, a girl who knows how to work. Let her act as your assistant for the time being, and when we arrive after the 20th, we'll make some other arrangement for her. I am very sorry I did not write you to come here first so as to talk everything over with you. I am very much afraid that out of ignorance of the conditions there you may make a lot of mistakes. There is so much that I ought to write that I won't even begin, especially as I don't know what you are doing.

"One thing I beg of you: be as careful as you can, and carry out the work without making any changes. And, above all, take care of what comes in, of the grain supply and its proper distribution, and see that you do not let those into the kitchens who can feed themselves with what they get from the Zemstvo, but on the other hand, do not turn away any who are in need.

"It is now time to help the very poorest with firewood. This is very important and difficult, and in this case, however undesirable, it is better that those who do not need it should get it than that those who do should not.

"What about the hay from Usov? I am afraid of Yermolayev making a mess of it. They write about broken bales. It must be picked up as soon as possible and taken to Lebedev at Kolodez. Look out for potatoes in private stores, see if they won't sell, and buy them. There is much more to say, but not knowing how things are going I can't deal with them by correspondence. I rely on you. Please do all you can. I kiss you. Give our regards to Elena Mikhailovna and Natasha[4] and everyone there. L.T."[5]

The "assistant" who brought me this letter drove in from the station just as Persidskaya and I were sitting down to supper. The old carpenter who acted as our manservant announced, "The Lord has sent another young lady," and in walked a girl student with a big jar of Montpensier under her arm and handed me Father's letter.

I asked her to sit down and have some supper. There was sauerkraut with kvas and black bread on the table. The unhappy Muskovite looked at it, swallowed a couple of spoonfuls, and fell into a despondent silence. She gazed fondly at her jar of sweets, as if to say, "I've landed in a famine district where there's nothing to eat but sauerkraut; what would I have done had I not thought to bring my caramels with me?" When the cutlets were brought in she brightened up.

Next morning at the break of day she asked to be given "work." I ordered a horse to be harnessed and asked her to drive to the village of Gai with a coachman and make a list of all who were being fed there.

Half an hour later, Dmitry Ivanovich Rayevsky (Ivan Ivanovich's brother) rushed in, covered with snow. "What have I seen?" he exclaimed aghast. "There's a snowstorm out there, and I saw a child standing in a sledge, tearing cross-country all alone. It's one of the horses from here. Who is it?"

I simply gasped. The girl had gone off without the coachman, Heaven knows where! I had to send a man to look for her and bring her back.

Another time, as I was leaving the house I told her to distribute the firewood for the kitchens. All of our own wood was damp, being freshly cut, and we had dry birchwood sent by rail from the province of Kaluga to use for kindling. This wood was expensive and we used it very sparingly. We allowed only one third as much dry wood as damp. I had explained all this to the young student before going out, but when I got back I found to my horror that she had given out all the dry wood.

"But they asked for the dry," she said, justifying herself.

"And what are we to do now with our damp wood? It won't burn, you know, without kindling."

We were obliged to make hasty efforts to find more dry wood, which cost us three times more than we had paid before.

After my father returned to Begichevka, I remained with him for a time and then returned home.

The next time I worked with my father in this same capacity was in the Chern and Mtsensk Districts in 1898. Following the crop failures of the two preceding years, it became clear by the beginning of winter that another famine was impending in our district, and that the peasants would require charitable assistance. I turned to my father for help. By spring he had succeeded in collecting some money; and early in April he came to see me himself.

I might mention that my father, who was economical by nature, was exceedingly prudent, if not parsimonious, in the administration of charitable funds. This is readily understood, of course, if one considers the unlimited confidence he enjoyed among the donors and the great moral responsibility he neces-

sarily felt toward them; so before undertaking anything, he had
to be fully convinced of the need for help.

The day after his arrival, we saddled a couple of horses and
set out. We rode across the fields as we had ridden together
twenty years before, when coursing cross-country with wolfhounds. It was all the same to me where we went, as I believed
that all the neighboring villages were equally distressed, but
Father, in memory of old times, wanted to have a look at Spasskoye-Lutinovo, which was only nine versts from my property. He had not been there since Turgenev's death. I remember his telling me on the way about Ivan Sergeyevich's mother,
who was famous throughout the region for her lively wit, energy, and extravagant behavior. I do not know whether he had
ever seen her himself or was only repeating the tales he had
heard about her. As we rode through Turgenev's park, he recalled in passing how he and Ivan Sergeyevich had disputed
which park was the finer, Spasskoye or Yasnaya Polyana. "And
now which do you think is?" I asked him. "Yasnaya Polyana is
really better, although this is fine too, very fine indeed."

In the village we visited the elder's cottage and two or three
others, but there was no evidence of famine. Besides their earn-
ings, the peasants had been granted a full allotment of good
land and there was hardly any want. It is true that some of the
yards were not well stocked, but there was not that acute need
which amounts to famine and instantly strikes the eye. I even
remember my father reproaching me slightly for having
sounded the alarm without sufficient cause. Momentarily I felt
rather awkward and ashamed.

When talking to the peasants, he naturally asked each of
them whether he remembered Ivan Sergeyevich and eagerly
picked up anything they recalled about him. Some of the old
men remembered him well and spoke of him with great affection.

We rode on, and about two versts from Spasskoye came upon
a deserted little hamlet, Pogibelka, lying off in the fields. In the
village we found that the peasants were living on a "beggarly"
allotment, the land being badly situated and somewhat out of

the way. By spring matters had reached a point where there was only one cow and two horses for eight households. The rest of the cattle had been sold. Children and adults alike went about furtively "picking up" whatever they could.

In the next village, Bolshaya Gubarevka, it was just as bad. Farther on it was still worse. We decided to open soup kitchens without delay. Soon the work was in full swing. The most difficult part was ascertaining the number of mouths to be fed in each family, and this Father did almost entirely by himself, spending whole days, often till late at night, going from village to village. The preparation and distribution of provisions was undertaken by my wife; helpers appeared, and in a week we had about a dozen kitchens operating in the Mtsensk District and as many in Chern.

As it was beyond our means to feed all the peasants without making distinctions, we admitted mostly children and the old and sick to the soup kitchens, and I remember how Father delighted in arriving in a village at dinnertime, and how touched he was by the reverential, almost prayerful attitude toward food which he observed in those who were fed.

Unfortunately, we were unable to avoid difficulties with the authorities.[6] It began with two young ladies, who had come from Moscow and were managing one of our biggest soup kitchens, being simply turned out under threat of closing it down. Then a district police officer came to me and demanded to see a permit to open soup kitchens from the head of the provincial police. I tried to convince him that there could be no law prohibiting charity. This, of course, was of no avail.

At that moment my father came in and he and the police officer had a friendly discussion, the one arguing that people cannot be prohibited from eating, and the other asking him to put himself in the position of a man who is under orders from his superiors. "What would you have me do, Your Excellency?" "It's very simple: don't work where you can be made to act against your conscience."

After that I had to go to see the governors of the Orel and Tula provinces, which resulted in my sending a telegram to the

Minister of the Interior asking him to "remove the obstacles set up by local authorities to private charity not prohibited by law." In this way we managed to save the existing soup kitchens, but we were not allowed to open any new ones.

After leaving my house to go to the eastern part of the province of Chern, where he wanted to see the condition of the grain crops, my father fell ill and had to spend several days in bed at the house of my friends the Levitskys. The following letter was written to my wife and me after his departure:

"Dear friends Sonya and Ilya,

"Please continue the work as begun, and even expand it if there is a real need. I can send you another three hundred rubles. I am keeping fifteen hundred in reserve, as I have written to those who contributed, and two thousand I have yet to receive. I sent off my article and an accounting of some three thousand rubles. Total expenditures shown to date, about twenty-five hundred. Please, Ilya, send me a very careful accounting of the rest of the money so that I may send it to the newspapers.

"My stay with you has left a wonderful impression with me. I have come to know you both more intimately, and understand and love you.

"My health is better, but I can't say that it's good. Am still very weak.

L.T.

"Many kisses to my dear grandchildren and to Annochka. Which of them are at their grandmother's?" [7]

XXVI

Father's Illness in the Crimea. Attitude Toward
Death. Desire for Suffering. Mother's Illness

In the autumn of 1901, my father was taken ill
with a persistent fever, and the doctors advised him to go to
the Crimea. Countess Panina kindly offered him her villa
"Gaspra" near Koreiz, and he spent the winter there.[1]

Shortly after his arrival, he caught cold and suffered two
successive illnesses, inflammation of the lungs and enteric fever.
His condition was so bad at one point that the doctors were almost certain he would never get up again. Although his temperature was quite high at times, he was always conscious, dictated
his thoughts almost every day,[2] and consciously prepared for
death. The whole family was with him and we took turns nursing him.

I look back with pleasure on the few nights when it fell my
turn to sit up with him; I sat on the balcony near the open
doors, listening to his breathing and to every sound in the room.
As the strongest member of the family, my chief duty was to lift

him and hold him when the sheets were changed; I held him in my arms like a child while they made the bed. I remember that once my muscles quivered with exertion, and he looked up at me with astonishment and said, "Surely you don't find me heavy? What nonsense!" It reminded me of the day when as a child he had worn me out riding through the Zaseka forest, and then said, "Not tired, are you?"

Another time, during this same illness, he wanted me to carry him in my arms down a winding stone staircase. "Pick me up as they do a baby and carry me." He hadn't an iota of fear; it never occurred to him that if I lost my footing it might result in his death. It was all I could do to insist that he be carried down in an armchair by three of us.

Did my father fear death? It is impossible to answer this question in a word. With his resolute nature and physical strength he instinctively fought not only death but old age as well. Up to the very last year of his life, he refused to give in and continued to do everything for himself, and even to go horseback riding. Consequently, to suppose that he was entirely devoid of the instinctive fear of death would be absurd. He not only had such a fear but had it to a high degree, and fought against it constantly. As to whether he overcame it, I can say definitely—yes.

During his illness he talked a great deal about death and deliberately and earnestly prepared himself for it. When he felt himself growing weaker, he wanted to say good-bye to everyone, and summoned each of us individually to his bedside to say his parting words. He was so weak that he spoke almost in a whisper, and having spoken to one, he had to rest and muster his strength before speaking to another. When it came my turn, as nearly as I can remember he said,

"You are still young, vigorous, and ruled by passions. Consequently, you have not yet had time to ponder on the principal questions of life. But the time will come, of this I am sure. Then know that you will find the truth in the Gospel. I am dying at peace only because I have come to know that truth and believe it. God grant that you may understand it soon. Good-bye."

I kissed his hand and quietly left the room. When I reached the front door I rushed headlong to a stone tower and there in the darkness sobbed like a child. Looking up I saw that someone else was sitting on the steps not far from me also weeping.

And thus I said farewell to my father nine years before his death, and this memory is dear to me, for I know that had I been at his bedside when he lay dying at Astapovo, he could not have said anything different to me.

Returning to the question of death, I will say that my father did not fear it—in the latter part of his life he even desired it, was actually interested in it. This "greatest of mysteries" fascinated him to such an extent that his interest came near to love. How attentively he listened to accounts of the death of his friends Turgenev, Gay, Leskov, Zhemchuzhnikov, and others. He inquired about every particular, and no detail, however insignificant it might seem, was without interest and importance for him. Several days of his *A Circle of Reading,* including the seventh of November, are devoted exclusively to thoughts on death. "Life is a dream, death the awakening," he wrote in anticipation of that awakening and under the date that fatefully coincided with that of his own death.[3]

Apropos of his *A Circle of Reading,* I cannot refrain from relating a characteristic incident which was told to me by one of my sisters. When my father first conceived the idea of compiling this collection of the thoughts of the wise, he told one of his friends about it. A few days later the "friend" [4] came to see him again, and his very first words to my father were that he and his wife had been thinking it over and had decided that the new book should be called *For Every Day* instead of *A Circle of Reading.* To this Father replied that he preferred the title *A Circle of Reading* because the word "circle" suggested the idea of continuous reading, which was what he meant it to express. Half an hour later, the "friend" again came across the room to Father and repeated exactly the same remark. This time my father made no reply. In the evening when the "friend" was preparing to leave, as he held Father's hand in his, he began once more, "Nevertheless, I must tell you, Lev Nikolayevich, that my wife and I have thought it over . . ." and so on, exactly as before.

"No, no, I want to die, the sooner the better!" my father groaned when he had seen the man off. "Isn't it all the same whether it's *A Circle of Reading* or *For Every Day?* No, it's time to die, I cannot live like this any longer."

And what happened? In the end one of the editions of the thoughts of the wise was called *For Every Day*, instead of *A Circle of Reading*.

"Ah, my dear, since that gentleman turned up, I really don't know which of Lev Nikolayevich's writings are by Lev Niko-layevich, and which are by _____," our gentle, pure-hearted old friend, Maria Aleksandrovna Schmidt, remarked sadly.

This sort of intrusion into my father's literary work was modestly termed "hypothetical corrections" [5] by the "friend," and there is no doubt that Maria Aleksandrovna was right, for no one will ever know where what my father wrote ends and where his concessions to that gentleman's unremitting "hypothetical corrections" begin, particularly since this foresighted adviser had arranged for my father to return his letters to him along with the replies to them. In this way he concealed forever the fruits of his intrigues.

Along with the desire for death that my father manifested in the last years of his life, he cherished another dream—one to which he openly aspired—and that was the desire to suffer for his convictions. This idea was first suggested to him by the per-secutions that many of his friends and followers were subjected to by the authorities during his lifetime. Whenever he heard of anyone being put in prison or exiled for disseminating his writ-ings, he became so agitated that it was pitiful.

I remember the time when I arrived at Yasnaya a few days after the arrest of N. N. Gusev.[6] During the two days I spent with my father, I heard of nothing but Gusev. It was as if no one else existed. I confess that sorry as I was for Gusev, who was then in the Krapivna jail, I felt the stirrings of an ignoble resentment against my father for paying so little attention to me

and the others, and devoting all his thoughts to Nikolai Nikolayevich. I readily admit that my spontaneous reaction was unjust, and had I entered into my father's sentiments, I should
have realized it at the time.

As early as 1896, in connection with the arrest of a doctor in
Tula, a woman by the name of Kholevinskaya, my father
wrote a long letter to Muravyev, the Minister of Justice, in
which he spoke of the unreasonableness, ineffectiveness, and
cruelty of the measures taken by the government against those
disseminating his proscribed works, and begged that every
means of punishment, intimidation, or suppression of the evil
be directed against whoever had perpetrated it,[7] "all the more,
as I declare beforehand that till the day I die I shall ceaselessly
continue to do what the govenment considers evil, and what I
consider my sacred duty before God." [8]

Neither this nor subsequent challenges had any effect, of
course, and the arrests and deportations of those associated
with him went on as before. My father felt morally responsible
for all of these people, and his conscience was increasingly
burdened with every passing year.

In 1908, before his Jubilee, he wrote to A. M. Bodyansky,
"Indeed, nothing would so completely satisfy me as to be put
in prison, a good, genuine jail—stinking, cold, and without
food. . . ." This "would bring me real happiness in my old age
and before I die, and at the same time would save me from all
the difficulties I foresee with my coming Jubilee." [9]

And this was written by the man who had been so indignant
over the search carried out at Yasnaya Polyana in 1862, and
over the judgment of the examining magistrate which confined
him to his estate on his own recognizance (when in 1872 our
herdsman was gored), that on both occasions he wanted to become an expatriate.

My father suffered moments of great anguish during *maman*'s serious illness in the autumn of 1906. When we heard
that she was sick, we sons and daughters all assembled at
Yasnaya Polyana. *Maman* had taken to her bed several days

before and was suffering from unbearable abdominal pains. We sent for Professor Snegirov and he diagnosed a necrosis of a visceral tumor and suggested an operation. In order to be certain of the diagnosis, he asked us to send for Professor N. N. Fenomenov for consultation, but *maman*'s illness progressed so rapidly that early in the morning of the third day after his arrival, he woke us all up and said that he had decided not to wait for Fenomenov but to operate at once or my mother would die. And with these words he went to my father.

Papa had absolutely no confidence in the efficacy of an operation: he thought that *maman* was dying and was praying and preparing for her death. He believed that the "great and solemn moment of death was approaching, that we should submit to God's will, and that any interference on the part of doctors would only violate the grandeur and solemnity of the great act of death." When the doctor explicitly asked him whether he would give his consent to an operation, he replied that *maman* and the children must decide for themselves, that he would stand aside and refrain from declaring himself either *for* or *against* it. During the operation he went into the Chepyzh grove, where he walked alone and prayed.

"If the operation is successful, ring the big bell twice, and if not . . . No, don't ring, I'll come myself," he had said, and walked slowly toward the wood.

Half an hour later when the operation was over, my sister Masha and I ran to look for him. He came toward us, pale and frightened.

"Successful! Successful!" we shouted from a distance, having caught sight of him at the edge of the wood.

"Good, go back, I'll come in a moment," he said, his voice choked with emotion, and he turned and went back into the wood.

A little later, when my mother had recovered from the effects of the anaesthetic, he went up to her room. He came out in a state of repressed indignation.

"Good Heavens, what a horrible thing! They won't even let a person die in peace! A woman lies there, her stomach cut open, tied to the bed and without pillows . . . and groaning louder than before the operation. It's some kind of torture!"

It was not until several days later, when my mother was restored to health, that he calmed down and ceased condemning the doctors for their meddling.

XXVII

Masha's Death. The Diaries. Fainting Spells.
Debility

As I enter upon the description of the last period of my
father's life, I must again make clear that what I write is based
only on the impressions I received during my occasional visits
to Yasnaya Polyana. Unfortunately, I lack the wealth of steno-
graphic material that Gusev, Bulgakov, and especially Dushan
Petrovich Makovitsky [1] had at their disposal.

IN November 1906, my sister Masha died of
inflammation of the lungs. In a strange way her departure from
life was as inconspicuous as her sojourn in it. This is probably
the destiny of all who are pure in heart. No one was particularly
shocked by her death. I remember that when I received the
telegram I felt no surprise. It seemed to have been ordained.

Masha had married a kinsman of ours, Prince Obolensky, and
lived on his estate at Pirogovo, thirty-five versts from us, but

239

she and her husband spent half the year at Yasnaya. She had a delicate constitution and was always ailing.

When I arrived at Yasnaya the day after her death, I became aware of an atmosphere of exalted, prayerful emotion enveloping the whole family, and it was then for the first time that I was conscious of the beauty and majesty of death.

I clearly felt that, far from having left us, Masha's death had brought her closer to us, that she was united with us all in a way she could never have been in life. I observed this same state of mind in my father. He went about silent, pitiful, summoning all his strength to combat his sorrow, but I heard not a word of lament, only expressions of the tenderest feelings.

When the coffin was carried to the church, he dressed to go out and accompany it. He stopped us at the stone pillars, said farewell to the departed, and went back home. I watched him walking along the avenue on the wet melting snow with his quick, elderly gait, his toes turned out as always, and not once did he look back.[2]

My sister Masha was of immense importance in my father's life, and in the life of the whole family.[3] How many times in recent years have we had occasion to think of her and sadly say, "If only Masha were alive. . . . If only Masha had not died. . . ."

In order to explain her relation to Father, I must go back to an earlier period. One of the distinctive and seemingly peculiar traits of my father's character—perhaps inborn, or perhaps because of growing up without a mother—was that any display of tenderness was entirely alien to him. I use the word "tenderness" in contradistinction to "feeling." Feeling he had to a very high degree. In this connection, his description of my Uncle Nikolai Nikolayevich's death is typical. Writing about the last day of his life to their brother Sergei Nikolayevich, he tells of helping him to undress.

". . . And he resigned himself and became a different man, meek, kind, and uncomplaining. He had a word of praise for everyone he mentioned, and to me he said, 'Thanks, my friend.'

You know what that means between us. I told him that I had heard him coughing in the morning, but had not come in out of *fausse honte*. 'You should have come,' he said, 'it would have comforted me.' " [4]

Evidently in the language of the Tolstoy brothers the words "my friend" conveyed a tenderness beyond which imagination could not go, and the words had astonished my father even on the lips of his dying brother.

I never witnessed a single expression of tenderness on the part of my father during his lifetime. Kissing children was something he did not like and did only as a duty when greeting us. It is therefore understandable that he did not attract tenderness from others, and that the feeling of closeness to him was never accompanied by any outward manifestation. It would never have occurred to me, for instance, to go up to my father and kiss him or stroke his hand. This was partly because of my awe of him and partly because of his spiritual power and greatness, which prevented me from seeing him simply as a man who at times was pitiful and weary, a weak old man so much in need of warmth and rest.

The only person who could give him that warmth was Masha. She would go to him and stroke his hand, caress him, say an affectionate word, and one could see that it pleased him, made him happy, and he even returned her caresses. It was as if he became a different person with her. Why was it that Masha was able to do this when nobody else even dared to try? For one of us to have done it would have seemed unnatural, while with her it was simple and sincere. I do not mean to say that the rest of us loved him less—not at all—only that the expression of love was not as warm and natural as it was with her. And so her death deprived my father of the one source of warmth which, with advancing years, had become more and more necessary to him.

Another and still greater power she possessed was her extraordinarily sensitive and impressionable conscience. This trait was even more precious to my father than her affection. She knew so well how to smooth over any misunderstanding and always came to the defense of those on whom any sort of censure fell—whether justly or unjustly, it was all one to her. Masha knew how to bring everything and everyone into a state of harmony.

When I learned that my father had left home on October twenty-eighth, my first thought was, "If only Masha had been there . . ."

My father's health deteriorated perceptibly during his last years. He experienced a number of sudden fainting spells, from which he always recovered the next day, but with a temporary loss of memory.

Seeing my brother Andrei's children in the salon one day—they were staying at Yasnaya Polyana at the time—he asked in surprise, "Whose children are these?" Once on encountering my wife he said, "Don't be offended, I know that I am very fond of you, but I've forgotten who you are." And after one of these fainting spells, he went into the salon and looking about the room in surprise asked, "And where is my brother Mitenka?" (He had died fifty years earlier.)* The following day, all traces of the attack would have disappeared.

During one of these fainting spells, my brother Sergei found a little notebook when he was undressing him. He put it in his pocket and next day gave it to Father saying that he had not read it. "Well, you could have read it," my father replied, taking it from him. This little diary, in which he wrote his most secret thoughts and prayers, was kept "for myself alone," and never shown to anyone.[5] I saw it after his death. It was impossible to read it without tears.

Although these notes written just before his death are of immense interest, I will not quote them here. It would be distasteful to me to publish what Father wrote only for himself.

---

*I cannot help recalling in this connection that Father and Dmitry Nikolayevich had agreed that whichever of them should die first would appear to the other.—I.T.

The very fact that such a diary was kept speaks for itself. It is "the real diary"; real because all the other diaries in which he wrote his abstract (not personal) thoughts and experiences were never put away but lay open on his table. They were read by anyone who cared to read them, and not only read, but taken home and copied by certain of his "friends." It was this that had caused the smoldering, agonizing struggle between my mother and those "friends," and which ended in my father's keeping the new diary "for myself." He needed his own "Holy of Holies," where no one could intrude, and kept this diary hidden in his boot top.

The last time I was at Yasnaya Polyana was in the early autumn. Father greeted me cordially and affectionately as usual. He was always delighted when one of his sons arrived and gave him a warm welcome. He might say that he had lately dreamed about me, or that I was just the person he was hoping to see, the others having been there recently—in fact, it always seemed that one had come at exactly the right moment.

Although I had grown accustomed to my father's indispositions, I was particularly struck by his feebleness at this time. And not so much by his physical weakness as by a certain abstraction and remoteness from the external world.

I retain a very sad memory of that visit. It seemed to me that Father was trying to avoid all conversation with me, almost as though I had offended him in some way; moreover, I was shocked by his lapses of memory. He knew quite well, for instance, that I had been working at the Peasants' Bank for five years—in fact, had used one of the stories I told him about it in an article [6] he was writing at the time—yet he completely forgot it and asked me where I was working and what I was doing. He was altogether absentminded and withdrawn.

This acute impairment of his memory, strange to say, was manifested only where facts and persons were concerned. His literary work was not affected by it, and everything he wrote, to the very last days of his life, was distinguished by his characteristic logic and forcefulness. Perhaps the details of everyday life escaped his memory because he was so deeply absorbed in his abstract work.

In October my wife was at Yasnaya Polyana, and on her return she told me that something was wrong there. "Your mother is nervous, and your father is in an uncommunicative, depressed mood." I was very busy with my work at the time, but I made up my mind to go and see my parents on my first free day. When I got to Yasnaya Polyana, my father was no longer there.

On the twenty-eighth of October 1910, I was in Moscow, and my brother Sergei telephoned me in the evening to tell me that he had received a very alarming telegram summoning him to Yasnaya at once.

My wife and I left Moscow at midnight and arrived at the Kozlovka-Zaseka station in the morning. We learned from the coachman, Adrian Pavlovich, that Father had left by train the preceding morning and that nobody knew where he was. It was not even known in which direction he had gone, since two trains left the Yasenki station at six o'clock in the morning, the hour of his departure, one northbound and one southbound.

This news was totally unexpected, and I remember feeling apprehensive about a singular coincidence which, while apparently insignificant, struck me as portentous in the circumstances. Father had left Yasnaya on the twenty-eighth. Again that fateful number which coincided with all the important events of his life! This meant that something significant, something of importance, had happened. It meant that he would not come back! Father was not in any way superstitious, never hesitated to sit down at a table of thirteen, often made fun of signs and omens, but he loved the number twenty-eight and regarded it as his own special number.

He was born in the twenty-eighth year, on the twenty-eighth day of August. His first book, *Childhood and Boyhood,* was published on the twenty-eighth; his first son was born on the twenty-eighth; the first wedding of one of his sons took place on the twenty-eighth; and, finally, he had left home on the twenty-eighth, never to return.[7]

We found my sister Aleksandra and my brothers Andrei and Mikhail at Yasnaya Polyana when we arrived. *Maman* met us in the hall, sobbing, distracted, and pitiful. We spent the whole day huddled in groups in the deserted rooms, hearing over and over again accounts of what had happened, making conjectures about where *papa* might be at that moment, whether he might return, and what we ought to do.

Our immediate responsibility was to take care of *maman,* whose condition seriously alarmed us. The psychiatrist we summoned from Tula advised us not to leave her alone and to engage a nurse to look after her. It was decided that in the beginning two of us should remain at Yasnaya.

On the twenty-ninth of October, my sister Sasha prepared to go to *papa,* but she stubbornly refused to tell us when and where she was going.

Exhausted, physically and morally ill, Father had left with no clear purpose and no destination in mind, but simply to hide somewhere and find respite from the moral torments which he could no longer bear.

"Had father considered that *maman* may not survive a separation from him?" I asked my sister Sasha.

"Yes, he considered it, but decided to go anyhow, because he thinks there can't be a worse situation than the one that exists here now," she replied.

That evening we wrote a letter to Father and gave it to her to take to him. We also asked her to tell him not to worry about *maman,* that we would take care of her, and told her to protect and look after him.

I returned to Kaluga that same night. Although no one had told me where Father had gone, I was so sure that he was with Aunt Masha at Shamardino that next day I went to the Governor of the Kaluga province, Prince Gorchakov, and asked him to take steps to insure that the Kozelsk police made no difficulties for Father on account of having no documents.

Shamardino is about fifty versts from Kaluga. I happened to have a carriage and three at Kaluga, and though my wife kept urging me to go at once to my aunt Masha, I did not go because of my fear that it would force Father to take flight. He might have been very annoyed at my finding out where he was. It turned out later that I had gone from Zaseka to Kaluga by the same train on which my sister Sasha was traveling, and had I followed my wife's advice, I might have reached Shamardino at the same time, if not sooner, as she had gone by a round-about way, via the Tikhonova hermitage and Sukhinichy, whereas I would have gone directly without making any stops. I regret now that I did not do this.

Two days later I received a telegram informing me that Father lay ill at Astapovo. I left at once and found almost the entire family there when I arrived. They had come from Yas-naya Polyana by special train and were lodged in a first-class railway coach on a siding.

Father was in a little red-painted annex of the stationmaster's cottage. There were doctors in constant attendance on him, as well as my sisters Tatyana and Aleksandra, my brother Sergei, and several other people who were helping them.

It is sad to think that I had to deprive myself of seeing Father during his last illness. When I arrived, he was already so weak that he spoke with difficulty and was semiconscious most of the time. I did not go to him at Astapovo for more or less the same reason that I had not gone to Shamardino. It seemed to me that if Father were to see me he would think that everyone knew where he was, and it would have been very painful for me to have destroyed his illusion of having at last realized his dream of hiding somewhere.

The most difficult problem we faced during the entire time of Father's illness was a question of singular importance, which for me, frankly speaking, remains unresolved to this day: the question whether my mother should go to him.

There was not a day from first to last that this question was not discussed by every one of us in all its aspects, and it always ended in her going into Father's room only after he had fallen into the somnolent state of a man at death's door and was hardly able to see her. It is generally believed that she was prevented from going to him by those who were taking care of him at the time. This is not true.

When Father talked to my brother Sergei, he dictated a telegram to be sent to my mother, in which he asked her not to come because he felt so weak that seeing her might prove "fatal." My brother brought the telegram to the railway coach and gave it to her. How could she have gone to him after that?

My sister Tatyana was the next person to broach the subject of *maman* to him. Talking about her, he became terribly agitated, and when Tanya tried to calm him, he told her that it was "important," that it was "the most important thing now." Then Tanya asked him whether he wanted to see *maman*. He did not answer.

There were six doctors in attendance at the time, five of whom were old family friends. Their unanimous opinion, both as physicians and as friends, was that any excitement would be so dangerous for Lev Nikolayevich that it might kill him. As long as there was hope for his recovery, he had to be protected from any kind of agitation. Sofya Andreyevna was to go to him only if he himself expressed a desire to see her. No matter how cruel such a decision might have seemed to us, it was impossible not to submit to it. This was clear to all of us. My mother suffered terribly from it, but there was nothing to be done.

Every hour of the day and night, and sometimes oftener, one of us would run out to the little red house, tap on the window vent of the room where the person on duty sat, and bring back a report of the progress of the illness. How many times, taking my mother by the arm, I went up to that little window and stood there for a long time, experiencing with her the most painful moments, the bitterest sorrow!

Thinking back on it, it sometimes seems to me that we made one mistake: we should perhaps have told Father then, during the first days of his illness, that *maman* was there at Astapovo. In his state of reduced consciousness, this might have distressed him, for it would have deprived him of the illusion of having hidden, but it might have been better. Better because it was the truth, which, as it seems to me now, we had no right to keep from a dying man. And what if his reason for not sending for her was pity, fear of upsetting her? He might even have thought that she was ill and in no condition to come.

It is hard to say now what one ought to have done in the circumstances. Obviously what was done was only done because it seemed best for Father. And that my mother submitted to the opinion of the doctors without complaint was on her part a painful expiation, the significance of which it is not for us to judge.

XXVIII

Aunt Masha Tolstaya

A<small>UNT</small> Masha, my father's only sister, was a year and a half younger than he. It was said that my grandmother, Maria Nikolayevna, had died at her birth.[1] I remember as a child hearing that Aunt Masha had been the cause of her mother's death, and I could not understand what her guilt consisted of. I never explicitly asked anyone about this, but deep in my heart, in spite of her being my godmother, I harbored a certain hostility toward her because of this.

I remember my aunt Maria Nikolayevna only after she was widowed. She used to visit Yasnaya Polyana almost every year, with her children before her daughters married, and later alone. She had been married to a distant relation of the same name, Valerian Petrovich Tolstoy. His estate, Pokrovskoye, which later belonged to one of her daughters, Princess E. V. Obolenskaya, was situated in the Chern District only a few versts from Spasskoye-Lutinovo, Turgenev's estate. There Maria Nikolay-

evna met Ivan Sergeyevich and, with her brothers Nikolai
and Lev, became part of the interesting and lively company of
writers and hunters that Afanasy Afanasyevich Fet has so vividly described in his memoirs.[2]

It was said that at one time Turgenev had been in love with
Maria Nikolayevna, and that he had portrayed her in his *Faust*.
It was a chivalrous tribute conferred on her in all purity and
innocence. Aunt Masha cherished the most poetic memories of
Turgenev, and they remained bright and untarnished to the
end of her life.[3]

Her marriage was evidently not a happy one. Shortly before
her husband's death, they separated and she settled on her own
estate at Pirogovo, three versts from Uncle Sergei's estate,
where she had a house and small farm. She lived there till 1889,
when she made the acquaintance of Ambrosius, the Elder of the
Optina Monastery, and entered the Shamardino Convent,
which he had founded. She died there in 1912, a year and a half
after my father's death.

It is curious that the religious crisis in my father's life and in
hers occurred at about the same time. They both evinced the
same pronounced severity in their attitude toward themselves,
the same steadfast, passionate search for truth, and the same
integrity that admitted of no compromises or half-measures.

At one time, after Father had renounced the Orthodox faith
and before Aunt Masha had taken vows but was contemplating
entering a convent, they used to have bitter arguments over
questions of principle. These arguments often resulted in a falling out, which never lasted very long, however.

I remember one occasion after Aunt Masha had become a
novice, when she happened to say to my father that she intended asking permission of Ambrosius to buy a lottery ticket.
Father told her that this was not a monastic matter, that such
questions should not even be put to a monk, and she took
offense and left the room. Later their quarrels became less frequent, and in their last years I never once heard them mentioned. The older they grew the more understanding they were

of each other's feelings and the more tolerant of each other's convictions.

It seems strange that he, with his complete rejection of all religious rites, and she, the punctilious nun, were united by the same passionate search for God, whom they loved equally, but to whom each prayed in his own way and to the limit of his own capacity. Yet they listened to each other with sympathy.

I recall one touching incident that occurred when Aunt Masha was staying at Yasnaya Polyana, which I should like to recount, not as an anecdote, but as a graphic illustration of the characters of both Aunt Masha and my father. On this particular occasion, she had been given the room that later became Father's bedroom, but which at the time was unoccupied. It was autumn, and swarms of big autumn flies had taken refuge in the corners under the ceiling. Aunt Masha knew from times past that there had been an icon shelf in the right-hand corner, but, being nearsighted, she had mistaken the swarm of flies for an icon and prayed to it every evening. Suddenly one night she realized that where she had thought there was an icon there was nothing. She summoned the maid, Avdotya Vasilyevna, and asked her why the icon had been removed.

"There was no icon there, Maria Nikolayevna, the icons were all moved to the Countess's room some time ago—there were only flies in that corner, and today I swept them out."

Aunt Masha told *papa* about this in my presence, and he sincerely bemoaned what had happened and tried to console her: the fact that she had been praying to flies for three days could not be counted a sin, since she had been quite unaware of it.

Another episode that characterizes their relations was that of a little cushion she made for him, and which he always kept near him. To this day it lies on the bed where he left it on October 28, 1910. The first time he visited Aunt Masha in her Shamardino cell, she told him how strictly the nuns observed the rules of the monastery; not a single step, even of the most trifling nature, was even taken without the counsel and blessing of the Elder. Father expressed his indignation that the nuns

were not guided by their own judgment and half-jokingly remarked, "It just goes to show that there are six hundred fools
here, all living according to someone else's judgment. The only
intelligent person among you is your Superior." (At that time
the Mother Superior of the convent was a blind old woman,
Mother Euphrosyne, whom my father liked for her sincerity
and common sense.) Aunt Masha did not forget his words, and
on her next visit to Yasnaya presented him with a little embroidered cushion "from one of the six hundred Shamardino
fools." Father had by then forgotten his jesting remark and said,
"That was badly put—it's I who am the fool, and you are all
very clever."

My father was always very fond of Aunt Masha and had a
subtle understanding of her heart. As he approached old age,
his feeling of friendship for her grew into one of deep affection,
which permeates all of his last letters to her. One of them, written in 1909, ends ". . . Your brother Lev, who loves you more
the older he grows." [4] And in another, referring to a letter of
hers to D. P. Makovitsky, ". . . Your letter is so filled with love
and sincere religious conviction that it moved me almost to
tears." [5]

It is quite natural that when Father decided to leave Yasnaya
Polyana for good, forsaking "the life of the world in order to
live the last days of my life in peace and solitude," he should
have instinctively gone to Aunt Masha, who was the only one
capable of understanding what he was going through at the
time, and who could weep with him and give him a certain
peace of mind.

In a letter written to my mother on April 22, 1911, this is how
she describes her last meeting with her brother:

"Christ is risen!

"Dear Sonya, I was very happy to receive your letter; I
thought that after undergoing such sorrow and despair you
would not feel like writing to me, and this made me very sad.
I think that, apart from the terrible anguish of losing such a
beloved person, there are other reasons for your suffering. You

ask me what conclusions I have drawn from all that has happened. How can I tell, from all I have heard from various people close to the family, what is true and what is false? But I believe, as the saying goes, that where there is smoke there is fire —something must have gone wrong.

"When Lyovochka came to see me he was terribly despondent at first, and when he told me about how you had thrown yourself into the pond, he broke into sobs; seeing him, my own eyes filled with tears. But he did not talk about you and only told me that he had come for a long time and meant to rent a peasant's cottage and live here. It seems to me that what he wanted was solitude; he felt oppressed by the life of Yasnaya Polyana (he had told me this the last time I visited you), everything about it was contrary to his convictions; he simply wanted to live in a way that was satisfying to him, to live in solitude where nobody would disturb him—this is what I gathered from what he said.

"He had no intention of going away from here till Sasha appeared, but was planning to visit Optina and *very definitely* wished to talk with the Elder. But Sasha upset everything by coming the next day. When he left me to go to the inn to sleep that night, he had no thought of going away, but said to me, 'Good night, we'll see each other tomorrow.' What was my astonishment and despair when I was awakened at five o'clock in the morning—it was still dark—and was told that he was leaving. I got up at once, ordered a carriage, and went to the inn, but he had already gone and I saw him no more!

"I do not know what had happened between you; Chertkov was undoubtedly much to blame, but there must have been something unusual, otherwise Lev, at his age, could never have made up his mind to leave Yasnaya Polyana all of a sudden, at night, and in such weather.

"I can well believe that it is very painful for you, dear Sonya, but you must not reproach yourself; all this has certainly come about by God's will. His days were numbered, and it pleased God to send him this last trial by one who was nearest and dearest to him.

"That, dear Sonya, is the only conclusion I have been able to draw from this whole shocking, dreadful event! He was an extraordinary man and his end has been extraordinary. I hope that in return for the love he bore Christ, and for the work he did on himself to live according to the Gospel, that He, the All-merciful, will not reject him.

"Dear Sonya, do not be angry with me; I have written you frankly all that I have thought and felt. I cannot be evasive with you—you are too close to me, too dear, and I shall always love you, no matter what happened. After all, my beloved Lyovochka loved you!

"I do not know whether I shall be in condition to visit Lyovochka's grave in the summer; I have grown very feeble since his death, do not walk at all, and only drive to church—my one consolation. Come to us and prepare yourself for the Sacrament, open your heart to the Elder; he will understand everything and restore your peace of mind. God forgives all and envelops all in His love. Fall down before Him with tears, and you will see how peace will be enthroned in your heart. You have been under a dark cloud! All this is the work of the enemy! Good-bye, be well and at peace.

"Your loving sister,

"Mashenka.

"*P.S.* I live with another nun, whom I hardly ever see; she is always busy with her convent duties. Where are you living, Sonya, and what are your plans for the future? Where do you plan to settle, where shall I address letters to you? All of your sons, except Lev and Misha, have been to see me in turn, and I was very glad to see them. It is sad that I don't see them anymore. Ilyusha's wife Sonya came; she was very sweet."

This letter is imbued with such sincerity, such genuine religious feeling, that I should have been glad to close these reminiscences with it. There could not be a better attitude toward the final events of my father's life.

I went to see Aunt Masha a month after Father was buried. As soon as she was told that I was at the monastery inn, she sent for me. We were very eager to see each other, she to learn the details of Father's last illness and death, and I to hear about his last visit to her at Shamardino. I spent several hours with her in her cozy little cell, and it was the most interesting and pleasant visit I had had for a long time. It would be impossible to write all that she told me. There was such sincerity and genuine simplicity, and at the same time such intense grief over the death of her beloved brother, that at times her tears, or just a look, spoke more than words.

"He sat in that very armchair where you are sitting now, and told me everything. And how he wept—especially when Sasha brought him all your letters from Yasnaya Polyana! When she arrived with her friend,[6] they set to work studying the map of Russia and planning an itinerary to the Caucasus. Lyovochka sat there, melancholy and thoughtful. 'Never mind, *papa,* it'll be all right,' Sasha said, trying to cheer him up. 'Oh, you women, you women!' he replied bitterly. 'What's right about it?'

"I had hoped he could stay here; it would have been good for him here. He had even taken a cottage for three weeks. I never dreamed when I said good night to him that evening that I wouldn't see him again. He had even said, 'How nice, now we can see each other often.' And then he made a little joke as he left.

"I must explain that not long before this, something happened here which I had told him about. One night the front door was opened and someone walked along the corridor tapping on the wall with a stick. My cellmate and I were of course frightened and locked the door to our inner rooms. This knocking went on all night. In the morning, when my cellmate went out, everything seemed to be intact, and the outside door was locked. So we decided that it had been "the enemy" knocking. Then when Lyovochka left me the night he was here, he became confused on his way out and couldn't find the front door. My cellmate lit the way for him and he came back and said, 'Here I am, just like the enemy—all mixed up by your doors.' Those were his last words. And during the night he left."

In her sitting room, Aunt Masha had many photographs

of those near to her, and among them several of monks and elders.

"That photograph is of the Elder Joseph. Lyovochka noticed it too. He said, 'What a good, kind face!' It's a pity they didn't meet. Joseph could have talked to him. He would have won him by his goodness. He was not like Varsonofy. You know, Lyovochka had met Father Joseph once, but it was a long time ago, about twelve years,[7] when I arranged the meeting. They had a long talk, and Father Joseph told him that he had too much pride of intellect, and until he ceased trusting his mind he would not return to the Church. And, you know, Lyovochka became much more mellow after that. God grant that everyone might believe as strongly as he did!"

It was a grievous trial for Aunt Masha when the Elder Joseph, who was her spiritual director, forbade her to pray for her dead brother because he had been excommunicated. She had too independent a spirit to be able to reconcile herself to the harsh intolerance of the church and was genuinely indignant for a time. Another priest to whom she applied also refused to give her permission. Maria Nikolayevna did not dare to disobey her spiritual fathers, but at the same time she felt that she was not really obeying their injunction because she prayed for him all the same, in thought if not in words.

There is no knowing how her spiritual conflict would have ended had not her confessor, evidently understanding her moral torment, given her permission to pray for her brother, but in her cell only and in solitude, so as not to lead others astray.

XXIX

My Father's Will

I remember that after Nikolai Semyonovich Leskov's death, Father read aloud to us his posthumous instructions for a funeral of the starkest simplicity, according to which there were to be no speeches at the grave, and so on, and it was then, for the first time, that he himself thought of making a will.

The first will was written in his diary on March 27, 1895.[1] Since it is printed in full in the Tolstoy Annual for 1912, I will cite only extracts from it here. The first two paragraphs deal with his funeral and the announcement of his death; the third with the sorting and publishing of his posthumous papers; and the fourth, to which I wish to call particular attention, contains a request to his heirs to transfer the rights to his works to the public domain, that is, to renounce the copyright. "But I only ask this, and do not direct it. It is a good thing to do, but if you do not do it, that is your affair. It will only mean that you are not able to do it. The fact that my writings have been sold during these last ten years has caused me more pain than anything in my life."

Three copies of this will were made and placed in the keeping of my sister Masha, since deceased, my brother Sergei, and Chertkov. I knew of its existence but had never seen it up to the time of my father's death and had never asked anyone about it.

I knew my father's views on literary property, and his will could not have added anything to my knowledge. I also knew that this will had not been drawn up legally, and for this I was glad, since it was proof of his confidence in his family. Needless to say, I never doubted that his wishes would be carried out. My sister Masha, with whom I spoke about this, was of the same opinion.

But my father's spiritual sons, those so-called friends, thought otherwise and persuaded him to register his wishes in a legally executed will. Chertkov besieged him with long letters, insistently demonstrating to him the necessity of this step.

Their correspondence was conducted in secret, and Chertkov took special precautions to see that it did not come to the knowledge of Sofya Andreyevna. Under his influence, Lev Nikolayevich gradually lost confidence in his own sons and before long was confronted with an insoluble dilemma. Not to make a legal will meant to leave his spiritual legacy in the hands of his children and to offend his "friends." And if his children did not voluntarily comply with his wishes and renounce the copyright to his works, his friends would be powerless to oppose them. Moreover, it was my father's wish that Chertkov should go through all his diaries and letters and edit and publish them himself. This too could be prevented by his children. There were seven of them, their mother made eight, the majority of whom did not share his convictions. What should he do? Call his children together, explain his wishes to them, and rely on their promise to carry them out? Yes, that was the only right way, the only satisfactory way for him: he believed in the integrity of his children. But this did not satisfy his "friends."

There was the other alternative: to resort to the protection of the law and have his will executed legally. It was a difficult decision. He felt that such a step went counter to his beliefs, that having repudiated the authority of the government he could hardly place himself under its protection, and he also knew that this would hurt his wife. It was repugnant to him to make a secret of it, painful to be in a defensive position in relation to his whole family, and he hesitated for a long time, repeatedly changing his mind. In the end he yielded.

I am convinced that my father would never have made this irreparable mistake had he not been goaded into it by Chertkov's inexorable urging; and I am also persuaded that had his strength of mind not been impaired by his physical weakness and fainting spells, he would never have made that will.

In 1909 my father visited Chertkov at his house in Krekshino, and there, for the first time, drew up a formal will, signed by witnesses.* I know nothing about the will and do not intend to discuss it here. Later it turned out that this will too was invalid, and in October 1909 a new will had to be made.

We are fully informed about the drafting of the third will by F. A. Strakhov, who published an article on it in the *Petersburg Gazette*, November 6, 1911. Strakhov had left Moscow one night, on the supposition that Sofya Andreyevna, "whose presence at Yasnaya Polyana was most undesirable" for the business on which he was bound, was still in Moscow at the time. In a preliminary meeting between V. G. Chertkov and the attorney N. K. Muravyev, it had been made clear that in view of Lev Nikolayevich's extreme old age, it was a matter of urgent necessity to insure that his wishes would be carried out by drawing up a document that would be legally unassailable. Strakhov brought with him to Yasnaya Polyana the draft of the will and presented it to Lev Nikolayevich.

"Having read through the document he instantly signed it and under the text wrote that he was in agreement with its contents, and then, after thinking for a moment said, 'All this business is very painful for me. And it is unnecessary—to insure the

---

*In this will he assigned the rights to his works *to everyone;* nothing was said about transferring the rights to his daughter Aleksandra.—*I.T.*

dissemination of my ideas by means of all sorts of measures. . . . Why, no word can vanish without a trace if it expresses a truth and if the man who has spoken it believes deeply in its truth. But all these external measures for insuring it arise from our lack of belief in what we have said.' And Lev Nikolayevich left the study."

At that point Strakhov began to consider what he ought to do next—whether to go back empty-handed or to stay and argue it out. He decided to stay and undertook to explain to my father how distressing it would be for his friends to hear people criticizing him after his death for having done nothing, his views in the matter notwithstanding, to implement his wishes, thus making it possible for his copyrights to be transferred to his family.

Lev Nikolayevich promised to think about it and again left the room.

At dinner Sofya Andreyevna "was apparently far from suspecting anything." In Lev Nikolayevich's absence, however, she asked Strakhov why he had come. Since he had other business "beside the above-mentioned," he spoke of one thing and another, "with a clear conscience," saying nothing, of course, about the object of his visit.

Strakhov goes on to describe his second visit to Yasnaya, with the new, corrected draft of the will. When he arrived, "the Countess had not yet come down. . . . I breathed more freely." His business finished, "as I was saying good-bye to Sofya Andreyevna, I scrutinized her face carefully; her complete tranquillity and cordiality to her departing guests was so apparent that I had not the slightest doubt about her ignorance of what was going on. . . . I left with an agreeable feeling of work well done, work that was destined to have indubitable historic consequences. I felt only a slight twinge of conscience, the pangs of remorse induced by a certain uneasiness over the conspiratorial nature of our transaction."

But even this text of the will did not satisfy my father's "friends and advisers," and again, in June 1910, it was finally written for the last time. This draft was written by my father in the Limonovsky forest, about three versts from Chertkov's estate.

Such is the lamentable history of this document that was destined to have "historic consequences."

"All this business is very painful for me. And it is unnecessary," my father had said when he signed the document that was thrust upon him. That was his real attitude toward his will, and it remained unchanged to the end of his life. Is proof of this needed? It seems to me that even a slight knowledge of his beliefs would leave one in no doubt. Would Lev Nikolayevich Tolstoy have had recourse to the protection of the law? Would he have concealed such an act from his wife and children?

If an outsider like Strakhov felt some "twinge of conscience and pangs of remorse over the conspiratorial nature of the transaction," what must Lev Nikolayevich himself have felt? He had found himself in a hopeless position. To tell everything to his wife was out of the question: it would have wounded his friends. To have destroyed the will would have been still worse. After all, his friends had suffered for his beliefs—morally, and some of them materially, having been exiled from Russia. And he felt a responsibility toward them.

On top of all this were his fainting spells, the progressive loss of his memory, the vivid awareness of his nearness to the grave, and the increasing nervousness of his wife, who intuitively felt the unnatural aloofness of her husband without understanding it. And were she to ask him what he was concealing from her, he would have had to say nothing, or to tell her the truth. And that was impossible.

What was he to do?

It was then that his long-cherished dream of leaving Yasnaya Polyana presented itself as the only way out.

XXX

Flight. My Mother

The foregoing chapters were written shortly after my father's death. My mother was still living at the time, and there was much about which I was necessarily obliged to be silent. I did not wish to instigate a polemic, which would have distressed her greatly. Now the situation has changed. My mother has been dead for some time, and that venom from which I tried to protect her during her lifetime has been gratuitously splattered over her memory by my father's so-called friends and supporters. I can imagine how it would have grieved him had he foreseen that his "disciples" would exalt his memory at the expense of vilifying that of his wife.

Is it not possible that the grandeur of Socrates was, at least to some degree, enhanced by the character of Xanthippe?[1] And was not a Xanthippe concocted by the above-mentioned people, for whom a negative background was necessary in order to perceive the positive?

I shall try to explain as impartially and truthfully as I can my father's flight. I approach the question with fear and trembling, for I am aware both of the complexity of the

issue and of my own responsibility. The life and actions of a
human being are, after all, formed of such an infinite number
of causes that to compute the consequences of these forces is
utterly impossible. Especially when it is a question of analyzing
the actions of a man of such enormous powers and of such a
purely Christian conscience as my father. And that is why it is
both absurd and cruel to heap all the blame on Sofya Andreyevna, a pitiful half-mad woman of seventy.

That she was no longer responsible for her actions during
the last year of my father's life is unfortunately true. Ultimately
she herself did not deny it, and it goes without saying that Lev
Nikolayevich was aware of it too. But the question is: what had
brought her to this state? Why did my father, after living with
her for forty-eight years, suddenly, at the age of eighty-two,
find it unbearable and have to run away? In order to answer
this question I shall try to throw some light on the mental states
of these two elderly people.

My father was eighty-two years old. He had had a long life
filled with every conceivable sort of experience, and with temptations and struggles with himself; he had achieved the greatest
fame a mortal can win for himself—and now was on the brink of
the grave. His one remaining wish was to die well. He prepared
himself for death with reverence and, I will even say, love. He
did not invite death; he still had "many things to say to people,"
but he had conquered his fear of it and awaited it with
humility.

The question of going away had undoubtedly been in his
mind for the last thirty years of his life. This is evident from
some of the passages earlier quoted from his letters, from numerous entries in his diaries, and from his correspondence with
friends.

For thirty years this cherished dream had continually loomed
large before him, and for thirty years he had dismissed it, considering that he had not the right to translate it into reality.
"Spiritual growth requires suffering," he told himself, and in
this suffering he sought consolation. To leave Yasnaya Polyana

and shake its dust from his feet would have been much easier and more to his liking than to stay—which is why he did not go. And the more difficult it became for him to live at home, the stronger became the opposing temptation, until he was virtually giving his soul for those nearest to him.

Whenever those who were ill-disposed toward him reproached him for advocating "the simple life" while living himself in "mansions," he called this "a bath for the soul" and meekly bore the rebuke, knowing in his heart that "what torments you is the very material on which you are called upon to work, and the harder it is, the more valuable." And he knew that the chief thing, what he needed most, was not to act but to abide in love.

There is no question that for him life at Yasnaya Polyana was very trying. He suffered at heart not only for himself but for others; he suffered for the peasants living a life of toil and deprivation, for his wife who prosecuted those peasants for continually stealing firewood, and even for those who hated and reviled him. And he compelled himself to love them all.

"Yes, love those who do evil unto you, you say. Well, put it to the test. I try, but with little success," he wrote in his diary on June 22, 1909.[2]

"If you love those who love you, that is not love, but to love your enemies, love those who hate you," he recalled the words of the Gospel.[3]

"The wicked are the wise man's riches, for without them to whom would he manifest his love?" he cited one of the sayings of his favorite Chinese thinker, Lao-Tse.

I remember him once trying to persuade me that he loved a certain man who was very sharp and rude to him. "I love him more than anyone else," he assured me. At first I was amazed, for I knew how difficult this man was for him, and it was only later that I understood the true sublimity of the feeling.

Several days before leaving Yasnaya Polyana, my father visited Maria Aleksandrovna Schmidt at Ovsyannikovo and confessed to her that he wanted to go away. The old woman

threw up her hands in horror. "Good heavens, Lev Nikolayevich," she said, "that's only an attack of weakness. It will pass."
"Yes," my father replied, "weakness. Perhaps it will pass."

In his last letter but one to Seryozha and Tanya, dated "Shamardino, 4 o'clock in the morning, October 31, 1910," he writes,
"I thank you very much, dear friends, my true friends, Seryozha and Tanya, for your sympathy in my sorrow, and for your
letters. Yours, Seryozha, give me special joy: brief, clear, con-
cise, and, above all, kind. I cannot help being fearful, and cannot free myself from responsibility, but I *lacked the strength* to
act otherwise." [4]

This is why it is impossible to place the entire blame for his
leaving on Sofya Andreyevna. Admittedly she was difficult for
him and was the cross he bore—but he loved his cross and was
able to find consolation in his very suffering; he would never
have abandoned his cross had the cause of his torment not been
within himself. And that cause was the secret that stood between him and his wife—the first in their forty-eight years
together. How often thinking about my father's flight I am reminded of his favorite proverb: "When the bird is limed—farewell feathers."

"Chertkov drew me into the struggle, and this struggle is very
painful and repugnant to me," he wrote in the diary he had begun *For Myself Alone*. "I understand my mistake very, very
well. I ought to have gathered my heirs together and explained
my intentions to them, instead of acting in secret." [5]

I shall now try to examine the question from the point of
view of my mother and to elucidate the reasons for the confused state she was in at that time.

In describing my mother in her admirable reminiscences, my
aunt Tatyana Andreyevna Kuzminskaya[6] says that Sonya was
always dreamy and always saw the dramatic side of everything.
She was even jealous of her younger sister, who knew how to
enjoy herself and "rejoice with all her being." Sonya lacked this
capacity. We children were not able to analyze so deeply, but
we knew that *"maman* can't understand a joke," and if something struck us as funny, we never shared it with her. This is not

at all to say that she was of a melancholy nature. On the contrary, she was generally affable, knew how to talk to people, and made a very good impression on everyone who knew her. If I had to describe my mother in a few words, I would say that she was a wonderful woman, an ideal mother, and that she would have been an ideal wife for an ordinary man, but not for a giant like my father.

Afanasy Afanasyevich Fet, who knew and loved our family, said that Sofya Andreyevna had walked a razor's edge all her life. It must not be forgotten who she was. The daughter of a Court physician, she was reared in the aristocratic traditions, with all the vagaries of the ancient nobility, which prevailed during the reign of Emperor Nikolai I. At the age of eighteen, pure, innocent, and still a complete child, she married and settled down to spend the rest of her life at Yasnaya Polyana, where the old traditions were embodied in the person of Auntie Tatyana Aleksandrovna and numerous servants. From the very first, Lev Nikolayevich was delighted with the way his young wife diligently, and not without success, undertook the role of mistress of the house. He was "suffocated" with happiness. The young housewife developed into the young mother, the family grew, and Sofya Andreyevna managed to cope not only with the duties of housewife and mother but with those of copyist as well, and there was no one who knew our family during those years who did not admire the beautiful young woman who, with selfless devotion, gave herself wholly to the needs of her husband and family.

If she had happened to die at the beginning of the eighties, she would have been remembered as the ideal Russian woman. It would have been said that without her Tolstoy would never have created *War and Peace* and *Anna Karenina,* which would have been absolutely true, for only in the atmosphere of family happiness that surrounded my father the first fifteen years of his married life would such intense creative work have been possible.

Of the thirteen children she bore him, eleven were nursed at her own breast. During the first thirteen years of her married life, she was pregnant for one hundred and seventeen months, in other words, for ten years. And during the more than thirteen years that she was nursing her children, she was also managing the complicated domestic affairs of a large family and copying *War and Peace, Anna Karenina,* and other works, as many as eight, ten, and even twenty times.[7] It reached a point where Father had to take her to Dr. Zakharin, who found her in such a state of nervous exhaustion that he rebuked my father in a friendly way for not taking better care of his wife.

When my father went through his spiritual-religious crisis, it was not she who withdrew from him, but he from her. She continued to be the same loving wife and model mother she had always been. Had she not had children she might have followed him, but by the beginning of the eighties she had seven, later nine, children and could not bring herself to disrupt the life of the whole family and condemn her children and herself to a life of poverty.

Throughout the entire animal kingdom, the female is the guardian of the nest, by her very nature personifying the conservative element, the preserver of the family principle. This female element was very pronounced in my mother's character.

The virginal radiance of the budding flower had attracted the thirty-five-year-old Lev Nikolayevich and he had been carried away with all the passion of his stormy temperament. The bud had blossomed before his eyes, and for fifteen years its luxuriant color and pure fragrance filled his life with joy. Was Sofya Andreyevna to blame that at the end of these fifteen years the man who was her husband became a great sage and ascetic? Would any woman in the world, after having spent her entire mature life lovingly building her nest, doom it to destruction to embark on such an exploit? As with every ordinary woman, spiritual interests took second place, and religious problems were resolved by means of those convenient compromises obligingly concocted by the church and public opinion.

Can Sofya Andreyevna be blamed for not sharing the religious and philosophical views of her husband when even such men as Fet and Turgenev regarded them as an eccentricity that deprived the world of a great writer? This spiritual divergence was very painful for my mother.

I shall never forget the night when, only a few hours before the birth of my youngest sister Aleksandra, Father quarreled with my mother and walked out of the house. Although her labor pains had already begun, she ran out to the garden in pursuit of him in a state of despair. I ranged for a long time along the dark linden avenues before I found her sitting on a wooden bench at the far end of the garden. It was not easy to persuade her to return to the house, and she consented only after I told her I would take her by force.

During the first years of his moral crisis Father was often very morose, at times even severe. As a straightforward man, he in no way mitigated his disapproval of his family's way of life, and Mother was constantly made to feel his condemnation. And this, of course, could not but affect her psychologically.

It must be remembered that all her life, regardless of the circumstances, she had loved him, and all her life had shown a positively maternal, at times an inordinate, solicitude for him. He would never have lived to such an advanced age had it not been for her unremitting care. She had special dishes prepared for him daily and conscientiously looked after his slightest indisposition. Because "Lyovochka likes to eat a piece of fruit before going to bed," every evening there was an apple, a pear, or a peach on his night table. For "Lyovochka" there always had to be a special oatmeal porridge, special mushrooms, cauliflower, and artichokes brought from town, and so that he would not refuse to eat these foods, she naively concealed the cost from him.

The world bowed down before the great Tolstoy, read him, and revered him. But someone had to feed Tolstoy, make his shirts and trousers, take care of him when he was ill. It was thankless work, and only a faithful, devoted wife like Sofya Andreyevna would have been capable of doing it. One of the reasons for fearing his going away was that she knew his health would break down in different living conditions, and in this, unfortunately, she was proved right.

The death of their youngest son Vanechka was a terrible blow to both of my parents. As the last-born, he was their favorite. His death had a shattering effect on my mother. For seven years the little boy had been the breath of life to her; all her thoughts had been concentrated on him, and his death left her with a feeling of emptiness and with nothing to fill the gap. From that moment she lost her equilibrium and never regained it.

She began to seek outside distraction, and at one time found it in music. At the age of fifty-three she took up the piano again, began practicing scales and exercises, going to Moscow to attend concerts, and, like a schoolgirl, became infatuated with Hofmann, Taneyev, and others. All this was very distressing to my father, but he realized that it was like a drowning man catching at a straw and was very considerate and solicitous of her.

Meanwhile their estrangement, which had begun in the eighties, gradually increased. Continuing in his chosen path, Father had attained inaccessible heights, whereas Mother had not only stopped growing but had lost the incentive for life and was perhaps even regressing. Each in his own way regretted his aloneness, he soaring in solitude at great heights, and she powerless to rise to him, searching for something below. He had already conquered the personal ego, had detached it from himself and from her; she, on the other hand, was tortured by her ego and could find no expression for it. More and more frequently these torments reduced her to a state of exasperation, and he, as the person closest to her, was the victim of it.

Like all people who live in close intimacy, they had formed a pattern of skirmishing. On his part there was a long-suffering silence, and on hers a flood of reproaches and petty criticism. She did the very thing that in her own interests she ought not to have done. She jealously guarded the copyright to the first thirty volumes of his works, caviling over every minor infringement, and threatening him with his last wishes not being carried out because of being illegal.

Another cause of contention that grieved my father deeply was my mother's determined effort to preserve the Yasnaya Polyana forest. In late years the theft of firewood by the Yasenki peasants had increased enormously. When thieves were caught by the warden and brought to the house, Sofya Andreyevna would threaten them with prosecution. Then they would go to Lev Nikolayevich and appeal to him for protection. Sometimes, when they were caught red-handed in the Crown Forest that bordered our estate, they would ask Lev Nikolayevich to say that he had given them permission to cut wood in our forest.

My mother's reaction to these thefts was pathological. She was particularly upset when the pine or fir trees planted by Lev Nikolayevich were cut. "Just imagine," she would say to me almost in tears, "he planted those trees himself, with love, and now they are being ruthlessly destroyed by the peasants!"

For the most part, however, her threats came to nothing. "Sofya Andreyevna often says disagreeable things, but when it comes down to it she never acts unkindly," Father used to say, and it was true. My mother was a kind woman by nature, and she never intentionally harmed anyone.

All these petty differences, which undoubtedly caused my father great anguish, would have had no consequences had it not been for the meddling of outsiders—and Chertkov above all.

My father's adherents were very dear to him. He regarded them as men who had been called to carry on after his death the work to which he had devoted the last thirty years of his life. But to my mother they were interlopers, depriving her of what little remained to her of her husband. She feared their influence and was patently jealous of them. She knew that these so-called friends were highly critical of her and, being incapable of any sort of diplomatic guile, entered into open conflict with them.

That she had grounds for her distrust of Chertkov is proved by the following circumstance. Not wishing to be remembered in a bad light by posterity, she somehow persuaded my father to remove from his diaries everything of a negative character that he had at various times written about her. He consented and entrusted the work to Chertkov, who proceeded to make photographic copies of all the passages to be deleted. Foresightedness worthy of a better fate.

Chertkov had taken up residence on his estate at Telyatinki, about three versts from Yasnaya Polyana, and used to visit my father almost daily. One of the reasons my mother found him particularly objectionable was that he took possession of all my father's manuscripts. She had jealously guarded his manuscripts all her life, and to have this outsider making incursions on her domain was exceedingly distressing to her. But all this was nothing to the indignation and horror that seized her when she sensed that Father and Chertkov shared some secret. This is how she described her feelings about it in her short autobiography:

"Even before this, the influence of outsiders had been gradually insinuating itself and, toward the end of Lev Nikolayevich's life, assumed shocking proportions." And speaking of Father's last will and the influence that Chertkov had on him, she writes: "It was obvious that he was tormented by the pressure brought to bear on him. One of his friends, Pavel Ivanovich Biryukov, was of the opinion that he ought not to make a secret of the will, and spoke to Lev Nikolayevich about it. In the beginning he agreed with this true friend, but he went away, and Lev Nikolayevich succumbed to someone else's influence, although it visibly oppressed him at times. I was powerless to save him from this influence, and there came a terrible time for Lev Nikolayevich and for me, a difficult struggle that made me even more ill. I was heartsick and exhausted, and my reason was clouded by all my sufferings, while on the part of Lev Nikolayevich's friends there was the deliberate, subtle work of many years on the weakened memory and failing strength of an old man. Around this very dear person there was created an atmosphere of conspiracy, with letters and articles received in secret, then sent back after having been read, with mysterious visits and meetings in the woods for the purpose of perpetrating deeds of a nature repugnant to Lev Nikolayevich and which, once they had been committed, made it impossible for him to look me or his sons in the eye with equanimity. This was the first secret in our life together; he had never concealed anything from us before, and it was unbearable for him. Sensing this, when I would ask him whether he had made a will and why he concealed it from me, he either answered in the negative or said nothing. I believed him. But this meant that there was some other secret of which I knew nothing, and I became desperate, constantly feeling that they were assiduously setting my husband against me, and that some dreadful, fatal outcome awaited us. More and more often Lev Nikolayevich threatened to leave home, and this threat was an ever-increasing torment to me, intensifying my nervous, morbid condition." [8]

Indeed, it must be said that my mother's nervousness at one time reached a point where she was not accountable for her actions. Once when she had caught a cold, for instance, the doctor who was living in the house, Dushan Petrovich Makovitsky (a saintly man), gave her a certain medicine. All at once she sprang up, called us all together, and tried to persuade us that Makovitsky had poisoned her.

She bought a toy gun and sometimes at night, for no apparent reason, would shoot it from her window. She became pathologically suspicious, and like all sick people with an obsession, she began to eavesdrop and spy on her husband. Most of the time she simply followed him around, fearful of his more and more frequent fainting spells, but there were also times when she furtively went through his diaries and letters. It was this that gave my father the final impetus to go away. When, at two o'clock in the morning on October twenty-eighth, he saw her rummaging through his papers, he finally made his decision, put a few things together—and left.

I have attempted to shed some light on the facts as truthfully and impartially as possible. If mistakes were made by one or the other, it is not for us to judge. Both of my parents, each in his own way, recognized his mistakes.

"The constant concealment and the anxiety over her is very

oppressive," my father wrote in his personal diary, August 6, 1910. And on August 10, "It is good to feel one's own guilt, and I do feel it." And later, "They are all difficult. I cannot help wishing for death." [9]

Three days before he died, he said to my sister Tanya, "A great deal falls on Sonya; we have arranged things badly." [10] And, in truth, it is hard to imagine the mental anguish she experienced both before and, to an even greater degree, after my father left.

It was deplorable that my mother was not permitted to go to her dying husband. This was his wish and the doctor's advice, but it seems to me now to have been a mistake. It would have been better had she gone to him while he was still conscious. Better for him and for her.

My mother lived for nine years after his death and, like father, died of inflammation of the lungs, and, also like him, at the beginning of November.[11] During her last years she changed perceptibly, becoming more equable and serene, drawing ever closer to my father's world-view. She died reconciled, having touchingly asked forgiveness of all those close to her.

During her final illness, when my sister Tanya asked her whether she often thought of Father, she replied, "Constantly . . . constantly . . ." and added, "Tanya, it torments me that I didn't get along with him better, but before I die, Tanya, I want to tell you that I never, never loved anyone but him."

One would like to believe that in all that happened there was more accusation than guilt. Perhaps if those who stood close to my father in his last years had known what they were doing, everything might have turned out differently.

Notes and Comments

T HE text of this edition is that of I. L. Tolstoy's book *My Memoirs,* published in *Mir,* Moscow, 1933, with corrections of mistakes and typographical errors made from earlier publications (*Russkoye slovo,* 1913, for October, November, and December, and the Sytin edition, Moscow, 1914). Locations of the manuscripts of the memoirs, as well as of the supplementary material sent by I. L. Tolstoy from America in 1928 for this edition of the book, are not known.

All citations and epistolary documents have been corrected according to the latest editions. The text of Tolstoy's letters and the material of "The Postbox" have been collated with the autograph manuscript.

The following abbreviations are used in the notes:

Biryukov—P. I. Biryukov, *Biography of Lev Nikolayevich Tolstoy,* 4 vols., Gosizdat, Moscow, Petrograd, 1922–23.

GMT—The L. N. Tolstoy State Museum.

PS—Correspondence of L. N. Tolstoy and N. N. Strakhov, St. Petersburg; pub. Society of the Tolstoy Museum, 1914.

L. N. Tolstoy—Complete Collected Works of L. N. Tolstoy in 90 vols., Goslitizdat, 1928–59.

Turgenev—Letters. I. S. Turgenev, Complete Collected Works and Letters in 28 vols., series Letters, pub. AN USSR, Moscow, Leningrad, 1961–65.

Turgenev—I. S. Turgenev, Collected Works in 12 vols., Goslitizdat, Moscow, 1953–58.

Fet—Part I, A. A. Fet, *My Memoirs*, pt. I, Moscow, 1890.

YaZ—D. P. Makovitsky, *Yasnaya Polyana Notes.* Typewritten manuscript is in the L. N. Tolstoy State Museum.

Chapter I

1. The Yasnaya Polyana estate was bought by Tolstoy's great-grandfather, N. S. Volkonsky, from S. V. Pozdeyev in 1763. It is presumed that Yasnaya Polyana was originally called "Yasennaya Polyana" (Ash Glade) because of the abundance of ash trees in the local woods.

2. A. P. Ofrosimov, a wealthy Tula landowner, hunter, and horse breeder, friend and neighbor of the Tolstoys, a great lover of gypsy singing. In a letter to her son, Sergei Lvovich, S. A. Tolstaya wrote on August 14, 1888, "We generally have many visitors . . . the Ofrosimovs were here, and Sashenka Ofrosimov sang gypsy songs and danced gypsy folk dances, and his wife played the piano and sang with him. (GMT) Tolstoy portrayed Ofrosimov in *The Living Corpse* under the name of Mikhail Andreyevich Afremov (in the draft versions, Afrosimov). In the play Afremov calls the gypsy song "We walked for versts," about the meeting of the gypsy and the bride, "The Burial."

3. N. I. Tolstoy took part in the Napoleonic Wars: at the end of 1813, on the way back from St. Petersburg to headquarters, to which he was carrying dispatches from General Wittgenstein, he was captured in the town of Sent-Obi, and was held in captivity until Paris was taken by Russian troops on March 19, 1814. There is no information concerning a meeting between N. I. Tolstoy and Napoleon.

4. In his *Reminiscences,* L. N. Tolstoy wrote of his brother, "He was a wonderful little boy and became a wonderful man. Turgenev

said very rightly of him that he was wanting only in the shortcomings necessary for a writer. He lacked the chief defect: vanity, and was not the least concerned about what people thought of him. But the qualities of the writer that he did possess were above all a fine artistic instinct, a perfect sense of proportion, a good-natured joyous humor, a remarkable inexhaustible imagination, and a veracious highly moral world-view, and all this without the slightest self-complacency. His imagination was such that he could recount fairy tales, ghost or humorous stories in the style of Madame Radcliff, uninterruptedly and for hours on end, with such conviction that one forgot that it was invention." (L. N. Tolstoy, vol. 34, p. 386)

N. N. Tolstoy had a literary gift. His sketch *Hunting in the Caucasus,* published in the magazine *Sovremennik* (1857, No. 2), evoked enthusiastic responses from Turgenev, Panayev, and Nekrasov.

5. In his *Reminiscences,* Tolstoy tells of seeing "the American Tolstoy" during his father's lifetime. "I remember his handsome face: bronzed, shaven, but with thick white side whiskers to the corners of his mouth, and white curly hair. One would like to say a great deal about this extraordinary, outrageous, attractive man." (L. N. Tolstoy, vol. 34, p. 393) Tolstoy maintained friendly relations with Fyodor Ivanovich's widow and daughter. In creating the character of Count Turbin senior in *Two Hussars,* and to some extent in the character of Dolokhov in *War and Peace,* Tolstoy used certain facts from the life of "the American Tolstoy," and retained the same name, Fyodor Ivanovich, for both Turbin and Dolokhov.

6. Tolstoy described this sofa in *War and Peace.* In one of the draft versions of *Anna Karenina* there is also mention of the fact that in Levin's study there was an ancient leather-covered sofa "that had always stood in Levin's father's and grandfather's study, and on which all the Levins had been born." (L. N. Tolstoy, vol. 20, p. 403) This sofa is still to be seen at Yasnaya Polyana.

It is not known which "Book of Questions" is referred to.

7. This house was sold in 1854 by V. P. Tolstoy, at L. N. Tolstoy's request, for 500 rubles in currency for transport to the landowner Gorokhov, who made it part of his estate, Dolgoye, which is 17 km. from Yasnaya Polyana. In a letter to T. A. Ergolskaya on October 17–18, 1854, Tolstoy thanks V. P. Tolstoy for his help. "I had lost all hope of such a fortunate sale." (L. N. Tolstoy, vol. 59, p. 279) Tol-

stoy wanted to use the money from the sale of the house for publication of a military journal, but the journal was not permitted, and he lost the money at cards. Later he regretted the sale of the house, and in 1897 traveled to the village of Dolgoye to look at it. "On the 4th I went to Dolgoye," he wrote in his diary. "A very emotional impression of the house, which is falling to pieces. A swarm of memories." (L. N. Tolstoy, vol. 53, p. 169) In 1911 the house was sold to local peasants, and in 1913, by decision of a village meeting, was torn down and used for firewood; the brick was parceled out to the peasant householders. After the house had been at Dolgoye for half a century, several attempts were made to return it to its former location. The first to try to do this was P. A. Sergeyenko. In 1898 he informed S. A. Tolstaya of his intention. "Sergeyenko asked me what could be given to Lev Nikolayevich for his seventieth birthday on August 28," she noted in her diary on February 19, 1898. "He was thinking of buying the house and having it moved to Yasnaya, restoring it to its former location in the same condition in which it had been." (S. A. Tolstaya, Diaries, pt. III, p. 33)

In August of that same year, 1898, Sergeyenko and Andrei Lvovich visited the old house. Tolstoy's son wrote of this to O. K. Dieterichs, August 16, 1898: "Yesterday went with Sergeyenko (you remember the very tall writer) to look at the house where I was born and where my father grew up; he wants to buy it and present it as a surprise to Father on August 28. I know that *papa* will be very pleased, as he told me that recently he was terribly moved when he went into the house and recalled all his childhood and adolescence, which he had spent there." (Cf. A. L. Tolstoy, *About My Father*, Yasnopolyansky collection, Tula, 1965, p. 134) For some reason, Sergeyenko was unsuccessful in his efforts. At the end of 1913, a Moscow patron of the arts, A. Shakhov, tried to redeem the house and return it to its former location, but was not able to do so as the ramshackle house had been dismantled in the summer of 1913.

Chapter II

1. Stepan Andreyevich Behrs.

2. L. N. Tolstoy's letter of October 26, 1872; cf. L. N. Tolstoy, vol. 61, No. 414.

3. Tolstoy's adversary in this quarrel was apparently Ivan Petrovich Borisov (a relative of Fet, and a friend of Tolstoy and Turgenev), a fierce defender of the Prussian side. Turgenev wrote to him half-jokingly on August 12, (24), 1870, "By now you could have demanded and obtained the bottle you won from L. N. Tolstoy, most esteemed Ivan Petrovich, since the last blows, inflicted in fact by the Prussians, have decided the issue. . . . I can well understand why Tolstoy supports the French side," Turgenev further explained, "a French phrase is repugnant to him, but he hates still more the ratiocination, system, and science of the Germans." (Turgenev, Letters, vol. VIII, p. 269–270.

4. T. A. Ergolskaya and N. P. Okhotnitskaya.

5. I. L. Tolstoy's words are correct only with regard to certain chapters of the novel. Tolstoy reworked only individual chapters repeatedly; the novel as a whole was neither rewritten nor recopied. Sofya Andreyevna loved this work of Tolstoy's very much and conscientiously assisted him in the capacity of copyist. "I have now begun to feel," she wrote on November 14, 1866, "that this is your, and therefore my, offspring, and releasing this packet of pages of your novel to Moscow I have indeed let a baby go, and am afraid they may do it some harm. I have grown to love your work. I will hardly grow as fond of any other work as I have been of this novel." (S. A. Tolstaya, Letters to L. N. Tolstoy, pub. in *Academia,* Moscow, Leningrad, 1936, p. 70)

6. Four *Russian Books for Reading* were issued in a separate edition in 1875. S. A. Tolstaya took a very active part in copying the *ABC Book,* the *New ABC Book,* and *Books for Reading.* She was also actively engaged in copying *Anna Karenina.* Despite the fact that she had helpers, she remained the chief copyist of the novel. "We are finally writing *Anna Karenina* properly, that is, without interruptions," she wrote to her sister T. A. Kuzminskaya on December 9, 1876. "Lyovochka, animated and content, adds a whole chapter every day. I copy energetically, and even now, under this letter, the pages of a new chapter, which he wrote yesterday, lie ready." (GMT)

7. Hannah Tarsey was governess to the Tolstoy children from 1866 to 1872.

8. Tolstoy resumed work with the peasant children in January 1872, while he was working on the *ABC Book.* He wrote to Fet on

February 20, 1872: "I have again set up a school, and my wife, the children, all of us teach and are satisfied." (L. N. Tolstoy, vol. 61, p. 271) The school was in existence until the end of April 1872.

9. K. A. Islavin.

Chapter III

1. The name was taken from the title of the comedy *Froufrou*, popular at the beginning of the seventies of the last century. Its authors, Henri Meilhac and L. Halévy, were well-known French dramatists and librettists. In *Anna Karenina*, Tolstoy gave Vronsky's horse the name *Frou-Frou*.

2. Tolstoy mentions his funeral rites in his will, written in the diary March 27, 1895 (cf. L. N. Tolstoy, vol. 53, pp. 14–15), but does not specify the place of burial. In his *Reminiscences*, written in 1903–06, Tolstoy recalls the story of the "green stick" that Nikolenka had told his brothers, saying, ". . . this stick is buried near the road, at the edge of a ravine in an old forest reserve, where, since my corpse must be buried somewhere, I have asked them to bury me in memory of Nikolenka." (L. N. Tolstoy, vol. 34, p. 386) In his testamentary instructions, dated 1908 (a diary note of August 11, dictated to N. N. Gusev and taken down in shorthand), Tolstoy repeats his request that they bury him in a wooden coffin, and "whoever wishes to can bear it or drive it to the forest reserve opposite the ravine, at the place of the green stick." (L. N. Tolstoy, vol. 56, p. 144)

3. It is well known that Tolstoy was always enthusiastic about engaging in physical labor; at the age of eighty, he took pleasure in mowing for long periods with the Yasnaya Polyana peasants. In his diary for 1884 (July–August), there are many entries concerning mowing. On June 19, 1884, he notes, "The peasant Grigory Bolkhin, the Kaster-master, and Pavel the shoemaker are mowing the meadow. I started working with them at about eleven, and mowed till evening. The children—Ilya, Lyolya, and Alcide—also worked. Everyone was very happy. In the evening we went bathing." (L. N. Tolstoy, vol. 49, p. 106) Ilya Lvovich often took part in the peasant field work with his father. "When Lev Nikolayevich worked in the field and tried in every way to be useful to the peasants and to the

people around him," writes Ilya Lvovich's daughter, Anna Ilyinichna Tolstaya-Popova, "my father always took a great part in his
work, being a very powerful and agile young man. They made boots
together, mowed and plowed. My father knew how to work and
loved it." (*Memoirs of A. I. Tolstaya-Popova.* GMT)

Chapter IV

1. Tolstoy set out on foot for the Optina Monastery on June 10,
1881, with S. P. Arbuzov and a teacher at the Yasnaya Polyana
school, D. F. Vinogradov. He and his companions arrived there
toward evening on June 14, and returned to Yasnaya Polyana June
19. This trip is described in detail by S. P. Arbuzov, who mistakenly
dated it 1878. (Cf. *Memoirs of S. P. Arbuzov, former servant of
Count L. N. Tolstoy,* Moscow, 1904, pp. 65–104)

2. *Embouchure,* the way of using the lips for blowing into wind
instruments.

3. Tolstoy took part in the Crimean War, 1854–55. He arrived in
Sevastopol on November 7, 1854, and was attached to the 3rd Light
Battery of the 14th Artillery Brigade. From April 5 to May 15, 1885,
he served at the 4th Bastion. On August 27, 1855, he was in the last
battle of Sevastopol. On September 1–2, he was engaged in preparing reports of the last bombardment of Sevastopol and the capture
of allied forces. (Cf. L. N. Tolstoy, vol. 4, pp. 299–306) On September 4, 1855, in a letter from Sevastopol to T. A. Ergolskaya, Tolstoy
wrote, "I wept when I saw the city enveloped in flames and the
French flag on our bastions; this was altogether a very sad day."
(L. N. Tolstoy, vol. 59, p. 335)

Chapter V

1. In a letter to his brother Sergei Nikolayevich, informing him
of the death of N. N. Tolstoy, September 24–25/October 6–7, 1860,
Tolstoy wrote, "I only thought of making his portrait and death
mask on the second day; the portrait failed to capture his wonderful
expression, but the mask is fascinating." (L. N. Tolstoy, vol. 60,
p. 354)

A marble bust of N. N. Tolstoy was made from this mask by the sculptor Geefs in 1861. It is at Yasnaya Polyana. Carved on the left shoulder is the inscription: "Gme. Geefs, *Statuaire du Roi, Bruxelles,* 1861" (Guillaume Geefs, royal sculptor, Brussels, 1861).

2. In 1875, during the writing of the novel *Anna Karenina,* Tolstoy underwent a severe spiritual crisis and, like Levin, "was so close to suicide several times that he hid cords from himself so that he wouldn't hang himself, and was afraid to go out with a gun for fear of shooting himself." (Part 8, chapter IX) In *Confession,* Tolstoy wrote of his spiritual crisis, "I was rushing away from life with all my strength. The thought of suicide came to me as naturally as thoughts about improving life had come to me formerly. This thought was so tempting that I had to use guile against myself, so as not to bring it to fulfillment too hastily. . . . And I, a man favored by fortune, used to hide a rope lest I should hang myself on the crossbeam of the bookshelves in the room where I undressed alone every night, and gave up hunting with a gun lest I should be tempted by so easy a way of delivering myself from life." (L. N. Tolstoy, vol. 23, p. 12) Also cf. p. 172 of the present publication concerning this.

3. This photograph was made by the photographer Levitsky on February 15, 1856. Tolstoy initiated this group photograph. He was in his officers' uniform, as he had only left the army on November 26, 1856. The photograph is in Tolstoy's home at Yasnaya Polyana, and is autographed by the writers it portrays. "I was looking at pictures of my writer friends made in 1856," Tolstoy wrote in his diary, January 14, 1907, "all of them are dead." (L. N. Tolstoy, vol. 56, p. 6)

Chapter VI

1. A letter to L. I. Volkonsky, May 3, 1856. (Cf. L. N. Tolstoy, vol. 61, letter No. 111)

2. L. N. Tolstoy's quarrel with S. I. Turgenev occurred on May 27, 1861, at A. A. Fet's Stepanovka estate. It was provoked by Tolstoy's harsh remarks on Turgenev's story about how the governess

made his daughter mend pauper's rags with a didactic purpose in mind. Irritated by what Tolstoy said, Turgenev replied rudely. After leaving Fet's, Tolstoy wrote a letter to Turgenev demanding a written apology. (Cf. L. N. Tolstoy, vol. 60, No. 210) Without waiting for a reply (it did not reach him) Tolstoy sent a second letter challenging him to a duel. After receiving a letter of apology from Turgenev, Tolstoy renounced the duel. Relations between the two writers were broken off and resumed only seventeen years later, when Tolstoy sent a warm friendly letter to Turgenev on April 6, 1878. (Cf. L. N. Tolstoy, vol. 62, No. 419)

3. By order of V. A. Dolgorukov, chief of gendarmes, on July 6–7, 1862, a search was made at Yasnaya Polyana. Colonel of gendarmes Durnovo carried out the search with a Krapivensky District police chief and a district police official. The floors of the stable were torn up and fishing nets cast in the pond. They were looking for a secret press, for prohibited manuscripts, etc. L. N. Tolstoy was in the province of Samara at the time, but his sister M. N. Tolstaya and her children and T. A. Ergolskaya were in the house. The gendarmes found nothing they could charge him with except a portfolio that contained forbidden books, and a photograph of Herzen and Ogarev; the maidservant Dunyasha succeeded in snatching it and throwing it into a ditch. When he learned of the search, Tolstoy returned in a state of extreme indignation. "Now the longer I am at Yasnaya," he wrote to A. A. Tolstaya, "the more painful becomes the insupportable insult and the more unbearable our whole rotten life." (L. N. Tolstoy, vol. 60, p. 435) Tolstoy was on the point of leaving Russia. On August 22, 1862, he wrote a letter to Aleksandr II; he wanted to know "whom to blame for all that has happened," and to demand "that the guilty be, if not punished, at least exposed. . . ." (Ibid., p. 441)

4. The portrait was painted in September 1873, at Yasnaya Polyana. Its extraordinary likeness to Tolstoy was noted by all who knew him. This portrait by Kramskoy was the first done of Tolstoy, and will remain one of the best. V. V. Stasov wrote in 1877, "All those superior distinctive elements that characterize the person of Count Tolstoy: originality, profundity of intelligence, the phenomenal power of his creative gift, goodness, simplicity, and unswerving will—all this Kramskoy has depicted with great talent." (V. V.

Stasov, Articles and Notes, vol. II, pub. in *Iskusstvo,* Moscow, 1954,
p. 123)

Chapter VII

1. To Ilya Lvovich's story about the mummers can be added S.
A. Tolstaya's description, in a letter to T. A. Kuzminskaya, of their
New Year's celebration, 1872. A jolly masquerade was held at Yasnaya Polyana, the mistress of the house herself dancing the *Russ-
kaya;* but the greatest impression was made by the masked figures:
D. A. Dyakov, K. A. Islavin, Tolstoy's nephew Nikolai Tolstoy, and
finally Lev Nikolayevich himself, who, on this occasion was disguised not as a bear trainer, but as a goat. "All the men disappeared
too," S. A. Tolstaya wrote, "and suddenly reappeared in the guise
of two bears, a trainer, and a goat. Dmitry Alekseyevich was very
funny as the trainer, Uncle Kostya executed a perfect bear dance,
Lyovochka danced like a goat, and Nikolenka was the other bear."
(GMT)

2. It is not clear what novel is intended.

3. S. L. Tolstoy wrote concerning the origin of these sayings,
"After he had picked up some absurdity or comic occurrence from
life, he (L. N. Tolstoy—Ed.) epitomized it, gave it an appropriate
name—something in the nature of a title—and brought up analagous
cases. Thus he, and through him, his family, developed a series of
characteristic expressions or sayings understood only by those who
knew the anecdotes from which they had originated. Such expressions as "Anke cake," "It's the architect's fault," "The peasant
woman is washing," "They're feeding," and others. (S. L. Tolstoy,
*Humor in L. N. Tolstoy's Conversations, Pamyatniki tvorchestva i
zhizni,* 3, 1923, p. 12–14)

4. On October 17, 1886, Tolstoy wrote to T. A. Kuzminskaya, "We
are all happy and very quiet. From your letters, I see that you are
too, and the whole of Russia and Europe as well. But don't trust
this silence. The smoldering battle against 'Anke cake' has not
ended, it is growing, and here and there can be heard the rumbling
earthquake of the exploding cake. I live only because I believe that
the cake is not eternal, but man's reason is eternal." (L. N. Tolstoy,
vol. 63, p. 393)

Chapter VIII

1. The reference is to three M. I. Glinka romances: "To Her," a mazurka for voice and piano (verse by A. Mitskevich, translated by S. Golitsin), "The Murmuring Forest" (V. Zhukov's verses), and "I recall the wonderful moment" (Pushkin's poem).

2. From M. I. Glinka's romance, "I recall the wonderful moment."

3. This remark of Tolstoy's was first quoted by P. I. Biryukov in the words of S. A. Tolstaya, "I took Tanya, ground her together with Sonya, and got Natasha." (P. I. Biryukov, vol. 2, p. 16)

4. He means the family's move to Moscow in the autumn of 1882, to their own house in Dolgo-Khamovinchesky lane. K. A. Islavin helped not only Sofya Andreyevna, but Lev Nikolayevich, who asked his advice about the arrangement of the house. Tolstoy wrote his wife on September 17, 1882, "Today I'm going to Sukharev Tower to look at redwood chairs and furniture for the salon. I'll take Kostenka. If he approves, I'll buy." (L. N. Tolstoy, vol. 83, p. 360)

5. No verification of I. L. Tolstoy's assumption has been found. From the correspondence that has been preserved, it appears that when, in his seventies, Tolstoy began to subject official Christianity to criticism and to depart from it, S. S. Urusov strove to turn him back to the church. Countless heated arguments arose between them in connection with this effort. A great many of Tolstoy's letters to S. S. Urusov on the subject of this polemic were not kept: according to S. L. Tolstoy's version, Urusov, angered by Tolstoy's rejection of the church, burned his letters. Relations between the two men were resumed toward the end of the eighties, and in the spring of 1889, Tolstoy visited Urusov at his Spasskoye estate.

Chapter IX

1. I. L. Tolstoy is mistaken. There were no horse races in the summer of 1873, and the races later described by him were organized for the second visit of the Tolstoy family to their Samara estate, August 6, 1875.

2. On June 28, 1875, Tolstoy, with his wife and older children, went to a fair in the city of Buzuluk. At that time, they visited a

hermit at the hermitage of the Spaso-Preobrazhensky Monastery near Buzuluk. S. A. Tolstaya remembered that "The hermit, who impressed us all, lived in underground caves. . . . This elderly hermit looked like a man of conviction who had no doubt that he was living as he ought to. He conducted us through the caves. . . . Lev Nikolayevich talked to him about religion. . . ." (S. A. Tolstaya, *My Life,* vol. 2, p. 438, GMT)

3. Tolstoy traveled with his family to the province of Samara for the first time in June 1873. The Tolstoys' were shocked by the picture "of the terrible disaster that had befallen the people as a result of three years of crop failure." (L. N. Tolstoy, vol. 62, p. 35) In order to determine for himself the extent of the famine, Tolstoy drove to all the hamlets and villages within a radius of 70 kilometers. In July 1873 he addressed a letter to the publishers of *Moskovskie vedomosti,* in which he wrote of the peasants' disastrous predicament in the regions of crop failures in the province of Samara. For greater persuasiveness, he included a description of the property status of every tenth peasant farmstead in the village of Gavrilovka, compiled by the people themselves and authenticated by a village elder and a priest. The progressive press took the letter as an important social phenomenon. It resulted in a flood of donations for the benefit of the famine-stricken Samara peasants; 1,867,000 rubles and 21,000 poods of bread were received in all. (L. N. Tolstoy, vol. 62, No. 29)

4. Tolstoy used this expression in the First Peasant's speech in his play *The Fruits of Enlightenment.*

Chapter X

1. Tolstoy read Jules Verne's novels to the children in November 1873 and January 1874. On January 9, 1874, Sofya Andreyevna wrote to T. A. Kuzminskaya, "After tea Lyovochka tells the children very interesting stories from a French book with pictures. Perhaps you have heard of or seen Jules Verne's *Cinq semaines en ballon,* or *Les enfants du capitaine,* or others?" (GMT) There are fifteen illustrations for the novel *Around the World in Eighty Days* in the Tolstoy archives. The art critic A. A. Sidorov notes that in Tolstoy's drawings "one is struck by the originality of his vivid touches." (A.

A. Sidorov, *The Drawing of the Russian Masters*. Second half of the XIX century, pub. AN, USSR, Moscow, 1960, p. 126)

2. On April 2, 1879, A. K. Solovyov, a member of the Narodnaya Volya, made an unsuccessful attempt on the life of Aleksandr II. Tolstoy read the news in *Moskovskie vedomosti* for April 3, 1879 (No. 82).

Chapter XI

1. The poem referred to is by William Cowper (1731–1800), *The History of John Gilpin* (1782–1783?).

2. Tolstoy told of the origin of the legend of the "ant brothers" in his *Reminiscences*. One day his eldest brother, Nikolenka, announced to his younger brothers that he had "a secret that will make all people happy when they discover it . . . all will love one another, all will become ant brothers." Tolstoy supposed that "it was the Moravian Brethren, about whom he [N. N. Tolstoy—Ed.] had either heard or read." (L. N. Tolstoy, vol. 34, p. 386) The Moravian Brethren were a religious sect which originated in Bohemia in the fifteenth century. It was founded by Peter Chelcic, who created his own "doctrine of justice." Tolstoy was interested in the doctrine.

3. N. N. Gay introduced Tolstoy to K. P. Bryullov's expression, "Every art begins with almost." Tolstoy repeatedly uses the phrase in letters and diaries, and in chapter XII of *What Is Art* he devoted several pages to a development of Bryullov's ideas. In the article *Why Do People Stupefy Themselves?* he wrote, "This maxim is strikingly true, and not only in relation to art, but to all life. It can be said that true life begins just there, where almost begins, where the infinitely small changes occur that seem to us no more than almost." (L. N. Tolstoy, vol. 27, p. 280)

Chapter XII

1. *Toroka*, the Russian word used here, means the small straps on the back of the saddle pommel for fastening the game. The hare is

strapped to the saddle by its hind legs, and the fox and wolf by the neck.

2. Tolstoy actually gave up hunting and became a vegetarian in the mid-eighties.

3. Cf. vol. 83, pp. 445–46.

Chapter XIII

1. I. L. Tolstoy is mistaken. The last name of Bibikov's house-keeper was Pirogova.

2. The novel was published in the journal *Russky vestnik* at three different periods: the beginning of 1875, 1876, and 1877 (in the first four books). Tolstoy, in fact, worked a great deal on corrections, but the printing was interrupted for other reasons: in the summer, he stopped working on it; in 1874 and 1875 he suffered the death of two of his children and of T. A. Ergolskaya. During these same years he became enthusiastic over his school. "I have promised to publish my novel in *Russky vestnik*, but till now have been unable to tear myself away from living people and occupy myself with imaginary ones," he wrote to A. A. Tolstaya on December 15 . . . 30?, 1874. (L. N. Tolstoy, vol. 62, pp. 130–31)

3. This was the Russo-Turkish War of 1877–78.

4. The last chapters of the novel were to be published in *Russky vestnik*, May 1877; however, Katkov was not in agreement with Tol-stoy's negative attitude, as set forth in the epilogue, toward the vol-unteer movement for the Serbs, and therefore refused to print it. On Strakhov's advice, Tolstoy published part 8 of *Anna Karenina* as a separate booklet. The edition carried the following note: "The last part of *Anna Karenina* has come out in a separate edition instead of in *Russky vestnik*, because the editor of that journal was unwill-ing to print this part without certain deletions, to which the author did not agree." (Cf. L. N. Tolstoy, vol. 20, p. 363) In the May issue of *Russky vestnik*, Katkov made the following announcement from the editor: ". . . the novel, properly speaking, ended with the death of the heroine. According to the author's plan, there was to be an epilogue of a couple of pages, in which the reader would learn that Vronsky, in his agitation and sorrow after Anna's death, sets out for Serbia as a volunteer, that all the others are alive and well, but that

Levin remains in his village and rages against the Slavic Committee and the volunteers. The author will perhaps develop these chapters for a special edition of his novel." (*Ibid.*) Tolstoy, indignant at this "exposition" of Katkov's, wrote a letter to the editor of the newspaper *Novoye vremya*, but did not send it. S. A. Tolstaya's letter with a detailed explanation of the reason for the epilogue's not appearing in *Russky vestnik* was published in *Novoye vremya* (1877, No. 463, June 14). Katkov replied in an article in *Russky vestnik* entitled *What Happened on the Death of Anna Karenina*, concerning part 8 of the novel, in which he attempted to justify himself for not having published the epilogue in his journal, by saying that in his opinion, "the novel was left without an ending in the eighth and last part."

5. Cf. letter of January 25 . . . 26, 1877 (L. N. Tolstoy, vol. 62, No. 311).

6. Cf. letter of August 25, 1875 (L. N. Tolstoy, vol. 62, No. 197).

7. Cf. letter of April 8 . . . 9, 1876 (L. N. Tolstoy, vol. 62, No. 258).

Chapter XIV

1. I. L. Tolstoy supposes that the "Postbox" at Yasnaya Polyana was still in operation in the mid-seventies. Among the manuscripts from the "Postbox" there is only one, the poem "On August Twenty-eighth," written for L. N. Tolstoy's birthday, that can be dated, approximately, 1878. S. A. Tolstaya recalled that she and her sister had started the "so-called Postbox" in the summer of 1881. (S. A. Tolstaya, *My Life*, vol. 3, p. 687) Tolstoy's biographer, P. I. Biryukov, attributed its beginning to 1882. N. K. Gudzy is of the same opinion. (L. N. Tolstoy, vol. 25, p. 869) S. L. Tolstoy, in *Sketches of the Past* indicated a fourth date, 1883, as the inception of the "Postbox." Some of the works that have been preserved are of this date. Dates on other works and entries in Tolstoy's diaries mention the existence of the "Postbox" at Yasnaya Polyana in 1883–85 and 1887.

T. A. Kuzminskaya wrote to P. I. Biryukov concerning the origin of the "Postbox," "Since both our families were large, and there were many young people between the ages of fifteen and twenty, and all sorts of events—and still more because we often felt like laughing at something, or extracting secrets, and praising or condemning—a pact was made with the young people that during the week everyone would write whatever he liked, and not sign his name, of course. And then on Sunday evening at the tea table, someone would read aloud all the week's efforts." (L. N. Tolstoy, vol. 25, p. 869) S. A. Tolstaya recalled, "V. V. Treskin wrote verse well; my sister and Seryozha tried, but it was more careless and absurd. Sometimes Lev Nikolayevich wrote interestingly and cleverly." In her opinion, "all this bad writing characterized summer life at Yasnaya Polyana rather accurately. . . ." (S. A. Tolstaya, *My Life,* vol. 4, p. 85)

2. The text of the question is written in an unknown hand.

3. The answer is written by L. N. Tolstoy. Farther on, in an unknown hand is added, "No, you've gone mad."

4. From the words, "An answer is requested, Pyotr, etc.," this is written in V. V. Nagornova's hand. The original text read "Ustyushka," "Mashka," and is corrected in Tolstoy's hand.

5. The text breaks off at this point.

Chapter XV

1. Ilya Lvovich cites a fragment from L. N. Tolstoy's *Reminiscences.* (L. N. Tolstoy, vol. 34, pp. 387–88)

2. In July 1866 two officers of an infantry regiment stationed in the village of Novaya Kolpna appealed to Tolstoy to appear in defense of the soldier Shibunin, who was subject to a military court-martial for striking an officer who had insulted him. Tolstoy appeared in court and spoke in defense of the soldier. Nevertheless, he was sentenced to death. Tolstoy at once wrote a letter to A. A. Tolstaya, who was close to Court circles, with a plea to petition the Tsar for mercy. He forgot to designate the regiment in which Shibunin had served. The Minister of War, Milyutin, used this oversight as an excuse to refuse to petition the Tsar on Shibunin's behalf. Tolstoy sent a second letter with the required information. But it was too late. The sentence was confirmed and executed. Recalling the affair later, Tolstoy wrote to Biryukov in May 1908, "This incident had a much greater influence on my entire life than all the seemingly more important events: loss or improvement of status,

success or failure in literature, or even the loss of those close to me."
(L. N. Tolstoy, vol. 37, p. 67)

3. The "historic concert" refers to lectures on the history of music
at which A. Rubenstein appeared in Moscow in the winter of 1885,
1886, and 1888–89. The composer accompanied the readings with a
performance of musical works of various periods.

4. Cf. p. 41 of this text.

5. The reference is to the tract *The Kingdom of Heaven Is
Within You,* in the twelfth chapter of which Tolstoy cites a section
of A. I. Herzen's work, *From the Other Shore.* (L. N. Tolstoy, vol.
28, pp. 284–85)

6. Cf. Fet, part 1, p. 296.

Chapter XVI

1. Cf. Fet, part 1, pp. 105–6.

2. Cf. letter of February 23, 1860. (L. N. Tolstoy, vol. 60, No.
163)

3. A letter to Fet, May 11, 1870. A. A. Fet's poem *A May Night* is
discussed in the letter. "It is one of those rare poems in which not
a word can be added, deleted, or changed; it is a living thing and
delightful," Tolstoy wrote in this letter. (L. N. Tolstoy, vol. 61,
p. 235)

4. Cf. letter of April 28 . . . 29, 1876. (L. N. Tolstoy, vol. 62,
p. 272)

5. Cf. letter of October 17 . . . 18. (L. N. Tolstoy, vol. 62, p. 287)

6. Reference is to the poem *Junker Schmidt* by Kozma Prutov.

7. At Tolstoy's request, his friend the literary critic and philosopher N. N. Strakhov supervised the publication of the *ABC Books,
Anna Karenina,* and *War and Peace* for the Collected Works of
1873. Strakhov's articles on *War and Peace* were first published in
the magazine *Zarya,* Nos. 1, 2, 1869, No. 3, 1870. Comments on *Anna
Karenina* are contained in his letters to Tolstoy and in the article *A
View of Current Literature* in *Rus,* January 1883.

8. A letter of April 14 . . . 15, 1872. (L. N. Tolstoy, vol. 61,
No. 372), in which Tolstoy replied to N. N. Strakhov's letter, which

has not been kept, containing his opinion of the story "A Prisoner in the Caucasus."

9. Tolstoy's letter to Strakhov, April 23 . . . 25, 1876 (L. N. Tolstoy, vol. 62, No. 261), was in reply to Strakhov's letter of April 1876, in which he said, "I wrote to you concerning my understanding of the idea of your novel, and asked whether I was correct, but you have said nothing about this idea (or whether I was wrong). I firmly adhere to it, however." (PS p. 81) This letter by Strakhov was not preserved. He repeatedly expressed his opinion of *Anna Karenina* in letters to Tolstoy.

In his article *A View of Current Literature*, Strakhov wrote, "The general idea of the novel, though not realized throughout the work with the same power, is very clear; the reader cannot escape the inexpressibly painful impression, despite the absence of any gloomy persons or events, despite the abundance of absolutely idealistic scenes. Not only does Karenina resort to suicide without obvious external cause or suffering, but even Levin, in all respects happy and leading a normal life, feels drawn to suicide toward the end, and is saved from it only by the religious thoughts suddenly awakened in him when the peasant tells him that one must remember God and live for the soul. This is the moral teaching of the novel, which he formulated for the introduction to the story *What Men Live By*." (Collection *Critical Articles on I. S. Turgenev and L. N. Tolstoy*, SPb, 1885, pp. 447–48)

10. Cf. letter of September 13, 1871. (L. N. Tolstoy, vol. 61, No. 351)

11. He refers to the article *On the Moscow Census*, which was first published in the newspaper *Sovremennye izvestiya*, No. 19, January 20, 1882.

12. Cf. T. L. Tolstaya-Sukhotina, *Friends and Guests at Yasnaya Polyana*, Moscow, 1923, p. 39.

13. The portrait of S. A. Tolstaya with her daughter Aleksandra in her arms was painted by N. N. Gay in 1886. It hangs in the L. N. Tolstoy Museum at Yasnaya Polyana.

14. N. N. Gay painted Tolstoy's portrait in January 1884. S. L. Tolstoy found it "the best of all the portraits of Lev Tolstoy for its likeness and facial expression, despite the sunken eyes. I consider

this portrait particularly successful," he wrote, "because my father did not pose for it, and was so absorbed in his work while Gay was painting it that he forgot about the painter's presence." (S. L. Tolstoy, *Sketches of the Past*, 1965, p. 361) The portrait hangs in the Tretyakov Gallery.

Chapter XVII

1. Cf. note 2, chapter VI.

2. From a letter dated September 13/25, 1856. (Turgenev, *Letters,* vol. III, p. 13)

3. From a letter dated October 29 (Nov. 10), 1854. (I. S. Turgenev, *Letters,* vol. II, p. 237)

4. From a letter dated December 5/17, 1856. (I. S. Turgenev, *Letters,* vol. III, p. 52)

5. From a letter dated February 17–22 (March 1–6), 1857. (I. S. Turgenev, *Letters,* vol. III, p. 95)

6. From a letter dated September 13/25, 1856. (I. S. Turgenev, *Letters,* vol. III, p. 13)

7. From a letter dated November 25 (December 8), 1857. (I. S. Turgenev, *Letters,* vol. III, p. 170)

8. T. L. Sukhotina-Tolstaya, *Friends and Guests at Yasnaya Polyana,* Moscow, 1923, pp. 23–26.

9. From a letter dated July 9, 1861. (Fet, part I, Moscow, 1890, p. 378)

10. From Turgenev to A. A. Fet and I. P. Borisov, February 22–29 (March 5–12), 1860. (I. S. Turgenev, *Letters,* vol. IV, p. 44)

11. I. L. Tolstoy cites selections from I. S. Turgenev's letters to L. N. Tolstoy, October 19/31 and December 15/27, 1882. (I. S. Turgenev, vol. 12, pp. 564–65, 575)

12. At Turgenev's request, Tolstoy sent him *Confession* by his friend A. G. Olsufyeva, who visited the ill Turgenev at Buzhival and fulfilled Tolstoy's commission.

Turgenev read it and asked A. G. Olsufyeva to return the next day to discuss it with him. In her *Memoirs,* Olsufyeva wrote, "Turgenev met me in a state of agitation. 'Well, how can he, how can he

abuse his talent in this way? It's simply a sin!' he began almost before we had sat down at the fireplace. 'I read it yesterday—read it
and was inwardly enraged. Tolstoy, who is such a great artist, such
a subtle psychologist, who knows so well how to enter into our
hearts, and to write such nonsense!' Turgenev muttered." (*Istori-
chesky vestnik,* March 1911, pp. 860–1)

Olsufyeva advised Turgenev to write his opinion to Tolstoy. Turgenev did not carry out his intention of writing Tolstoy about *Confession,* but to Grigorevich he wrote, "I read it through with great
interest, a remarkable thing for sincerity, honesty, and power of
conviction. But it is all based on false premises—and in the end
leads to the most dismal denial of every kind of human life. . . . It
is a kind of nihilism. . . . Nevertheless, Tolstoy is just about the most
remarkable man in contemporary Russia. . . ." (I. S. Turgenev,
Works, vol. II, pub. *Pravda,* p. 317)

13. In fact, Turgenev visited Yasnaya Polyana four times: August 8–9, 1878; September 2–4 of the same year; May 2–4, 1880; August 22, 1881.

14. I. S. Turgenev read his story "The Dog," which was written
in April 1864. The story was published for the first time in the newspaper *Peterburgskie vedomosti,* No. 85, March 31 (April 12), 1866.

15. The episode of the dancing relates to Turgenev's visit to Yasnaya Polyana on August 22, 1881, not 1878, as the author of these
memoirs states. L. N. Tolstoy wrote in his diary that day, "Turgenev
did the cancan. Sad." (L. N. Tolstoy, vol. 49, p. 57)

16. The author is in error. The last time Turgenev returned to
Russia was in May 1881. In June of that year Tolstoy wrote to him
about a prospective trip to Spasskoye to see him. "I feel only now,
after all the ups-and-downs of our friendship, that I can be more
intimate with you, and that I will feel closer and closer to you. . . .
I want very much to visit you between July 5 and 20." (L. N. Tolstoy, vol. 63, p. 70) Tolstoy spent July 9 and 10 at Turgenev's Spasskoye estate. On August 22 of that year Turgenev visited Yasnaya
Polyana for the last time.

17. In his last letter to Tolstoy (end of June 1883), Turgenev
called him "great writer of the land of Russia." (I. S. Turgenev, *Letters,* vol. 12, p. 580)

18. From a letter of June 28, 1867. (L. N. Tolstoy, vol. 61, pp. 171–72)

19. In the aforementioned letter to A. A. Fet, October 7, 1865 (cf. L. N. Tolstoy, vol. 61, p. 109), he writes about Turgenev's story *Enough,* which Tolstoy had read in September 1865. (Cf. *ibid.,* p. 106) The story was first published in Turgenev's *Works* (1844–64), part V, pub. Salaev, 1865.

20. In October 1883, a public meeting in memory of I. S. Turgenev was planned in Moscow by the Society of Lovers of Russian Literature. S. A. Yuryev, president of the society, asked Tolstoy to attend this meeting. Recalling the occasion, Tolstoy said, "When Turgenev died, I wanted to deliver a lecture about him. Especially in view of our past misunderstandings, I had a desire to recall and recount all the good things about him, of which there were so many, and which I loved in him. The lecture was never given. Dolgorukov did not permit it." (A. B. Goldenweiser, *Close to Tolstoy,* Goslitizdat, Moscow, 1959, p. 62)

The director of the press department and the Ministry of the Interior feared Tolstoy's appearance at the meeting. The head of the press department, E. M. Feoktistov, wrote to D. A. Tolstoy, Minister of the Interior, "Tolstoy is a madman, from whom one can expect anything; he can say incredible things—and there will be a considerable scandal." Feoktistov suggested that the Minister warn the Governor-General of Moscow to examine all speeches to be delivered at this meeting. (Yu. Nikolsky, *The Affair Concerning I. S. Turgenev's Funeral.* Byloye, 1917, No. 4, p. 153)

The Governor-General of Moscow, V. A. Dolgorukov, ordered S. A. Yuryev to use some "plausible excuse" to announce that the meeting was "postponed indefinitely." (Department of Police Affairs, 1898, No. 349, *Concerning the Writer Count Tolstoy,* Byloye, 1918, No. 9, p. 207)

S. A. Tolstaya wrote to T. A. Kuzminskaya on October 29, 1883, ". . . Lyovochka didn't want to write his speech, he only wanted to talk; he would probably have drafted it the day before, but since it is forbidden, it will be neither written nor spoken. He would have mentioned Katkov, but only in the sense that not all thinkers and writers are free from fawning on the authorities and the government, but that Turgenev was a completely free and independent man and served only one cause, and that cause was literature; free thought and free speech, from which there would be no deviation. ..." (GMT)

21. From a letter dated September 30, 1883. (L. N. Tolstoy, vol. 83, p. 397)

Chapter XVIII

1. V. M. Garshin's story, *Four Days,* was first published in the magazine *Otchestvennye zapiski,* 1887, No. 10, with the subtitle *One of the Episodes of War.*

2. V. M. Garshin visited the Tolstoys on March 16, 1880. S. Durylin, in his work on Garshin, says that I. L. Tolstoy is mistaken in quoting Garshin as having said, "I went through the whole campaign," and that Garshin could not have said this, as he was at the front in the Russo-Turkish War for only four months (May 5–September 4, 1877). But the picture of Garshin's arrival, and the impression he made on the Tolstoy family, was accurately described as far as Durylin could establish. (S. Durylin, *Vs. M. Garshin. From Notes of a Biographer.* In *Links,* issue 5, 1935) In the foreword to de Maupassant's works, Tolstoy recalls that Turgenev was the first to acquaint him with Garshin's work. From then on he read everything that Garshin published; he valued him highly as a writer. Garshin's stories *Signal* and *The Legend of the Proud Aggey* were published in *Posrednik,* as were *Bears* and *Four Days on the Battlefield.* Garshin was on friendly terms with V. G. Chertkov. Their correspondence was published in the collection *Links,* 1935, No. 5. When Garshin fell seriously ill, Tolstoy tried to find out through A. M. Kuzminsky ". . . whether Garshin is in the Kharkov insane asylum," and was prepared to go to him. (S. A. Tolstaya's letter to T. A. Kuzminskaya, February 8, 1881, GMT)

3. V. Garshin, *Stories,* SPb 1882; V. Garshin, *Second Book of Stories,* SPb. 1885.

In his article, *The Death of V. M. Garshin,* G. I. Uspensky speaks of two small volumes of Garshin's stories, in which ". . . the whole content of our lives is exhausted, *in conditions in which Garshin and all his readers had to live. . . .* Precisely everything of the greatest importance that our life gave to his mind and heart—everything, to the last line, is experienced and felt by him with the most poignant emotion, and that is exactly why it could only be said in two books, two very small books." (G. Uspensky, *Collected Works*, vol. 9, Moscow, 1957, p. 147–48)

Chapter XIX

1. It is known that S. A. Tolstaya learned about the assassination of Aleksandr II on her way to Tula on March 2, 1881, and that she wrote to T. A. Kuzminskaya about it on March 3, 1881. (GMT) "On March 1, Aleksandr II was assassinated; we learned of it the following day from a poor little Italian boy who had wandered into Yasnaya Polyana," recalled S. L. Tolstoy. (*Sketches of the Past,* Tula, 1965, p. 83)

2. From L. N. Tolstoy's letter to Aleksandr III, March 8–15, 1881. (L. N. Tolstoy, vol. 63, p. 45)

3. From L. N. Tolstoy's letter to P. I. Biryukov, March 3, 1906. (L. N. Tolstoy, vol. 76, pp. 113–14)

4. Tolstoy's letter to Aleksandr III was written in connection with the impending death sentences for the participants in the assassination of Aleksandr II, members of the Narodnaya Volya Party: A. I. Zhelyabov, N. I. Rysakov, T. M. Mikhailov, N. I. Kibalchich, S. L. Perovskaya, and G. M. Helfman.

N. N. Strakhov delivered the letter to Pobyedonostsev, who read it and returned it, refusing to give it to the Tsar. Through Professor K. Bestuzhev-Ryumin, N. N. Strakhov then gave the letter to the Grand Duke Sergei Aleksandrovich for transmission to the Tsar.

S. A. Tolstaya recalled, "Aleksandr III ordered that a reply to the letter be sent to Count L. N. Tolstoy to the effect that he could have pardoned them had an attempt been made on his own life, but he did not have the right to forgive his father's murderers." (S. A. Tolstaya, *My Life,* vol. 3, p. 668)

The death penalty was carried out on April 3, 1881. Many years later, remembering his appeal to the Tsar, Tolstoy wrote, "I will not say that this response to my letter had an influence on my negative attitude toward authority and the state. It had begun and become established in my soul long ago, during the writing of *War and Peace,* and was so powerful that it could not have been intensified, but only made clear. When the penalty had been carried out, I felt an even greater aversion to the authorities and to Aleksandr III." (L. N. Tolstoy, vol. 76, p. 114)

5. The reference is to Abram Bunde, who had come to see Tolstoy in the spring of 1892. L. N. Tolstoy described his appearance as follows: ". . . Three days ago an old man of seventy turned up at the house, a Swede who has lived in America for thirty years, and has traveled in China, India, and Japan. Long yellowish-gray hair, beard the same, small of stature, wearing a huge hat; ragged, looks a little like me, a preacher of life according to the law of nature. Speaks English beautifully, is very intelligent, original, and interesting. Wants to live somewhere, was at Yasnaya, and to teach people how one can feed ten men as if they were one with 400 sazhens of land, with no draft animals, and with only one spade. . . ." (L. N. Tolstoy, vol. 84, p. 146) Tolstoy even thought about "collecting his ideas, filtering them and expounding them." (L. N. Tolstoy, vol. 87, p. 149) After living for a short time at Yasnaya Polyana, and then at T. L. Tolstaya's estate at Ovsyannikovo, Abram Bunde went to Petersburg and then apparently returned to his native country.

6. T. L. Sukhotina wrote to M. S. Sukhotin concerning this visitor: "What amazing people are staying with us! Yesterday a gentleman arrived who is a vegetarian, besides which he eats only every second day. Yesterday was his fast day, and he did not eat a single meal, but walked eight versts with us without the least sign of weakness. He is forty-seven years old, and has followed this regime successfully for several years. *Papa* was very fascinated by him as he always is with anything that is out of the general run of things." (GMT)

7. The reference is to D. E. Troitsky.

Chapter XX

1. Cf. note 7, chapter XVI.

2. M. S. Gromeka's study, *Last Works of Count L. N. Tolstoy*, was first published in *Russky mysl* (1883, Nos. 2, 3, 4, and 1884, No. 11). Tolstoy had a high opinion of Gromeka's article. "He explained what I had unconsciously put into the work," he said to G. A. Rusanov. (L. N. Tolstoy, in *Reminiscences of Contemporaries*, Goslitizdat, Moscow, 1960, vol. 1, p. 295)

3. The beginning of work on *The Decembrists* dates from November 1860. Tolstoy wrote Herzen on March 14/26, 1861, "Four months ago I started a novel in which a returning Decembrist is to be the hero." (L. N. Tolstoy, vol. 60, p. 374) The novel remained unfinished: only the first three chapters were written. At the end of 1877, Tolstoy resumed work on his project of a work on the Decembrists. He collected and studied historical materials, undertook a large correspondence with, and met some of, the Decembrists and people who had known them. Synopses and outlines of the novel were made. He was occupied with work on the novel until January 1879. It was never completed.

4. Tolstoy reread Gogol's *Selected Passages from Correspondence with Friends* several times. In 1851 he quoted Gogol in his diary: "In order to be good, every work must be, as Gogol says of his farewell tale ('it was sung from my soul') sung from the soul of the author." (L. N. Tolstoy, vol. 46, p. 71)

In 1887, according to Tolstoy, he read Gogol's *Selected Passages* a third time. "Each time I read it," he wrote to V. G. Chertkov, on October 10, 1887, "it made a powerful impression on me, but this time most of all. Selected passages from his correspondence and his short biography must be published in *Posrednik*. It is a wonderful life." (L. N. Tolstoy, vol. 86, pp. 89–90)

5. Tolstoy became acquainted with A. P. Bobrinsky, one of the founders of the religious Society for the Encouragement of Spiritual-Moral Readings, and in 1876 began corresponding with him. Bobrinsky came to Yasnaya Polyana in 1876, and discussed religious questions with Tolstoy. In 1874, Granville Radstock, an English preacher-evangelist, came to Petersburg; he was the founder of a religious doctrine according to which a man can cleanse and save his soul not by "good deeds," but only by faith in the atonement by the blood of Christ. Radstock found many followers among the Russian aristocrats, one of whom was A. P. Bobrinsky.

Tolstoy was interested in Radstock's personality. In March 1876, he inquired about him in a letter to A. A. Tolstaya. "Do you know Radstock? What sort of impression did he make on you?" (L. N. Tolstoy, vol. 62, p. 260) In his novels *Anna Karenina* and *Resurrection* Tolstoy depicted followers of Radstock's teaching. They were members of high society—Lydia Ivanovna, in *Anna Karenina,* and Katerina Ivanovna Charskaya and the preacher Kisevetter in *Resurrection.* In his diary for 1891, Tolstoy explains Radstock's popularity in fashionable society: "Why Radstock's success in high society? Because he doesn't demand changes in one's life, acknowledgment of its injustice, doesn't demand renunciation of power, property, and the prince of this world." (L. N. Tolstoy, vol. 52, p. 45)

6. L. N. Tolstoy visited the Optina Monastery four times: in 1877, 1881, 1890, and October 1910. Cf. note 1, chapter IV, and note 7, chapter XXVIII.

7. Cf. P. I. Biryukov's biographical work, *Biography of Lev Nikolayevich Tolstoy,* Moscow-Petrograd, 1923, vol. 2, part IV, chapter XIV.

8. Cf. *Confession.* (L. N. Tolstoy, vol. 23, p. 12) Cf. note 2, chapter V. I. L. Tolstoy cites the *Confession* in M. K. Elpidin's edition, Geneva, 1889.

9. Cf. letter of December 16, 1882. (L. N. Tolstoy, vol. 63, p. 106)

10. Cf. L. N. Tolstoy, vol. 23, p. 32.

11. Tolstoy speaks of the allocation of "stretches" of time in his tract *What Then Must We Do?* "It seemed to me that every man's day is divided into four parts, or four stretches, as the peasants call it, by his meals: (1) until breakfast, (2) from breakfast to dinner, (3) from dinner to supper, and (4) from supper to evening. Man's activity, for which, according to his very nature, he feels the need, is also divided into four types: (1) muscular activity, the work of arms, legs, shoulders, and back—heavy toil, from which you sweat; (2) the activity of fingers and hands, the work of dexterity of craftsmanship; (3) the work of the mind and imagination; (4) the work of personal intercourse." (L. N. Tolstoy, vol. 25, p. 388)

12. I. L. Tolstoy is not entirely accurate in his account of the story *What Was Told by the Shore of the Ganges* (1884). (Cf. Rabindranath Tagore, *Collected Works in Twelve Volumes,* vol. 1, Goslitizdat, Moscow, 1961)

Chapter XXI

1. Cf. L. N. Tolstoy, vol. 25, p. 191.

2. Tolstoy's first meeting with V. S. Solovyov was apparently on May 10, 1875. "My acquaintance with the philosopher Solovyov," Tolstoy wrote to N. N. Strakhov on August 25, 1875, "gave me much

that is new, raised the philosophical yeast in me, and greatly confirmed and clarified the ideas most needed for death and for the remainder of life, which for me are so comforting that, if I had the time and knew how, I would try to convey them to others." (L. N. Tolstoy, vol. 62, p. 197)

Tolstoy and Solovyov, who was a follower of official Church Christianity, drifted apart, chiefly because of their religious views. Solovyov did not accept Tolstoy's teaching of the "nonresistance to evil through violence," and in his books, *The Justification of Good*, and *Three Conversations*, as well as in a letter to Tolstoy, which was never sent (pub. in *Problems of Philosophy and Psychology*, 1905, No. 79), he condemned his world-view.

Chapter XXII

1. Cf. L. N. Tolstoy, vol. 63, p. 184.

2. Cf. L. N. Tolstoy, vol. 66, p. 21.

3. The reference is to V. G. Chertkov; he came to Yasnaya Polyana in August 1885. L. N. Tolstoy mentioned his arrival in a letter to S. A. Tolstaya, August 17, 1885. (L. N. Tolstoy, vol. 83, p. 506)

Chapter XXIII

1. From a letter to T. A. Ergolskaya, January 12, 1852. (Cf. L. N. Tolstoy, vol. 59, pp. 159–62) I. L. Tolstoy's translation.

2. From a letter to S. N. and I. L. Tolstoy, September 1884. (L. N. Tolstoy, vol. 63, p. 118)

3. From a letter to I. L. and S. L. Tolstoy. (L. N. Tolstoy, vol. 63, p. 382)

4. The letter was presumably dated 1886. (L. N. Tolstoy, vol. 63, p. 449)

5. A letter of October 1887. (L. N. Tolstoy, vol. 64, pp. 115–16)

6. A letter to I. L. Tolstoy, October 1887. (L. N. Tolstoy, vol. 64, p. 117)

7. From a letter to I. L. Tolstoy, October 1887. (L. N. Tolstoy, vol. 64, p. 119)

Chapter XXIV

1. D. A. Khilkov, mentioned in a letter of Tolstoy's, March 1888 (cf. vol. 64, pp. 159–60), was one of his adherents in the second half of the eighties and in the nineties. In 1884, he gave up a military career, retired, gave his land to the peasants, and kept only a small plot in the Sumsky district in the province of Kharkov, on which he worked himself. Tolstoy met Khilkov in 1887, and corresponded with him for many years. In March 1888, Khilkov married Cecelia Vladimirovna Weiner in a civil ceremony.

2. A letter dated end of April–May 6, 1888. (L. N. Tolstoy, vol. 64, pp. 167–68)

3. Letter of December 25, 1888. (L. N. Tolstoy, vol. 64, p. 208)

4. In November 1932, because the cemetery at Nikolskoye near Pokrovsko-Streshnev outside Moscow was abolished, the remains of the children were removed to the Kochakov cemetery.

5. Cf. L. N. Tolstoy, vol. 84, pp. 288–90.

6. From a letter to I. B. Feinerman, May 16, 1895. (L. N. Tolstoy, vol. 68, p. 96)

Chapter XXV

1. Tolstoy's work in helping the starving peasants continued from September 1891 to July 1893. On his last trip to Begichevka, he wrote to N. N. Strakhov, July 13, 1893, "I now feel like writing about the condition of the people, and summing up what has been discovered during these two years." (L. N. Tolstoy, vol. 66, p. 367)

2. From a letter to N. N. Gay (father) and N. N. Gay (son). (L. N. Tolstoy, vol. 66, p. 81)

3. Tolstoy became acquainted with I. I. Rayevsky in the fifties at a gymnastic school in Moscow. After his death, Tolstoy wrote an obituary article "In Memory of Iv. Iv. Rayevsky," in which he said, "This was the very finest man I ever met." (L. N. Tolstoy, vol. 29, p. 262)

4. E. M. Persidskaya and N. N. Filosofova.

5. A letter of January 13, 1892. (L. N. Tolstoy, vol. 66, p. 137)

6. I. L. Tolstoy's work in giving aid to the starving in 1898 evoked an extremely vigilant attitude on the part of the local authorities. In the Orel archive there is a "File concerning permission given to Count Ilya Lvovich Tolstoy to open a soup kitchen in the Mtsensk District to aid peasants suffering from crop failure of spring, 1898," which contains a series of documents that reveal the workings of the government agencies. Simultaneously with permission to open the soup kitchen, on May 4, 1898, a "Strictly confidential" order was sent under seal of the Governor of Orel "with a view to avoiding the possibility of notorious propaganda"; a Mtsensk district police official was ordered to carry out "a constant secret surveillance of everything that takes place . . . in this soup kitchen," that is, in the one opened in the Mtsensk District. Another kitchen had been opened in the village of Lopashino. A police official went there and talked to a certain Benderskaya, a landowner. The record of this conversation has been preserved in the Governor's files. Benderskaya reported that she had seen L. N. Tolstoy arrive in the village before the opening of the soup kitchen. "He wore an old overcoat, ragged footwear, and carried a knapsack on his back; he went into the peasant huts, inquired about their needs, drew up a list of the needy, and announced that they would be fed in a soup kitchen that he was going to open. To the plea of peasants of other communities that he feed them too, the answer was, 'Let your landowners bestir their brains.' " (Novy Mir, 1956, No. 7, p. 275) Tolstoy's diary entry concerning this visit was, "I walked to Lopashino, made a list." (L. N. Tolstoy, vol. 53, p. 191) Here is the description of supper in the soup kitchen in the village of Lopashino, in the report of the same police official: ". . . In the peasant Gordei Alekhin's hut, forty children and eight adults were gathered; they ate pea soup, and almost everyone had a piece of bread. Present at the supper was Count I. L. Tolstoy's daughter, a girl of about twelve, and her governess. The governess explained to me that the soup kitchen was opened for fifty-seven people, that Count Ilya Lvovich is in charge of it, and that his wife is in charge of distributing from their home the produce brought from the Count's estate; they serve hot food twice a day, which varies: potato soup, pea soup, kasha, kvas." (Ibid.) Tolstoy's activity in helping the starving called forth the displeasure not only of the government, but of the local landowners as well. According to the statement of the landowner Benderskaya, Tolstoy's assistance to the starving peasants promised her and those like her

"joys" from which only the powers that be could protect them: "(1) we ourselves will be plowing, cooking, and milking cows; (2) waiting for the false murmur of divine punishment—total famine, and, (3) most important of all—there will be insurrection and plunder if the administration does not come to our defense. Today my cook left the servants' quarters, says she's sick, that I can't tie her to me by force, that they'll feed her for nothing. And thanks to the Count and his means and methods of action, disaster is inevitable." (File in Orel Governor's office, f. 580, ed. xr. 2426, stol. 2 Gos. arxiv. Orel obl.)

7. Letter of June 7–10, 1898. (L. N. Tolstoy, vol. 71, p. 376)

Chapter XXVI

1. The Tolstoys left Moscow for the Crimea on September 5, 1901. They returned to Yasnaya Polyana June 27, 1902. S. A. Tolstaya wrote of their stay in Gaspra: "The house in which we live resembles a medieval castle. . . . Everything is so comfortable, luxurious, and beautiful that one could wish for nothing better. We all live in the upper part of the house; downstairs we use only the dining room, but not the bedrooms, study, or drawing room, for fear of something being damaged. . . . *Papa* is well; he rode horseback on two successive days, on a docile horse that belongs to the German steward. He likes it here very much, is delighted with everything, admires everything. . . . *Papa* and Masha are very strange. It's as though they suffered every sort of deprivation in life, and having voluntarily endured this on principle, now want to make up for lost time; they are enjoying all the good things of life with the utmost enthusiasm: they eat marvelous sweet grapes all day, go for walks and drives, sleep in wonderful beds, and enjoy living in this luxurious villa. . . ." (S. A. Tolstaya, letter to O. K. and A. L. Tolstoy, September 14, 1901, GMT) More detailed information about Tolstoy is found in a letter from M. L. Obolenskaya to T. L. Sukhotina, at this time. ". . . *Papa* is unusually happy. I'll tell you about our day. *Papa* gets up at six o'clock or earlier. He dresses, then goes out onto his beautiful balcony, which has an awning, but is flooded with sunlight and has an incomparable view of the sea and of Ai Petri. He walks about, eats grapes, and enjoys himself. Sometimes he goes

down and takes a stroll. Now he can easily walk to the sea and back, and the hills are not hard for him. Since coming here, his pulse has not once been irregular. When he comes back, he has coffee and sits down to work in his huge pleasant room (where he also sleeps) or on the same balcony. Then he has lunch, sleeps, and again goes for a walk or rides the steward's horse, goes to Alupka or somewhere, and *maman* or one of us goes with him. When he returns toward sundown for dinner, *papa* always tells us where he has been, how he went, and what he saw. We have dinner and afterward sit in the drawing room; *papa* lies down on the sofa and *maman* and I do needlework. Kolya reads aloud or Goldenweiser plays. Around nine o'clock *papa* sighs and says, 'Well, we're burning the midnight oil tonight,' and we all hasten to drink our tea and go off to bed. By ten o'clock the whole house is asleep, except for *maman,* who is wide awake. . . . We have a huge bouquet of flowers on the table every day, mostly roses, and the garden here is full of them. Frightful luxury! *Papa* says it's too good for him, even shameful. You can understand what a joy it is to see how well he is!" (GMT)

2. As early as October, that is, a month after his arrival, Tolstoy had said that "he wants terribly to describe all that he feels here, all his impressions, but that it is very difficult and complicated, with such an abundance and variety of impressions, and the beauty of nature, which entrances and moves him so that while he is walking in solitude, he sighs and exclaims 'How lovely!' And then the impressions of these immense luxurious estates of rich men and grand dukes, which were taken from the Tatars, and the Tatars themselves with their religion and poverty, and the depravity of rich Russians." (Letter from M. L. Obolenskaya to V. S. Tolstaya, October 6, 1901. GMT) Despite his serious illness, Tolstoy was working on articles, *On Religion,* and an insertion he dictated for his article *On Tolerance,* a foreword to *The Soldiers'* and *The Officers' Memorial.* At the same time he was planning an address *To Youth,* and *To the Clergy,* and *To the Working People,* as well as an article *On the False Meaning Ascribed to Christianity,* among others. "The power of his thought is still so great," wrote S. A. Tolstaya, "that although he is ill, and one can scarcely hear him, he dictates corrections for his latest article to Masha, and makes notes concerning his illness in a notebook." (S. A. Tolstaya's letter to T. A. Kuzminskaya, February 3, 1902, GMT) Recovering slowly, still

feeling very weak physically, Tolstoy nevertheless felt a great surge of creative power at this time. By June–July 1902, he was working a great deal, sometimes until five o'clock in the afternoon. S. A. Tolstaya wrote, "He's thin, all bent over and walking with a stick, but he does a great deal of mental work." (S. A. Tolstaya's letter to P. A. Sergeyenko, July 3, 1902, GMT)

3. *Circle of Reading*, vol. 42, p. 232.

4. V. G. Chertkov.

5. I. L. Tolstoy's conclusions are based on established facts of the time when Chertkov persuaded Tolstoy to make changes in his publicist and literary works. In a series of letters, he advised him to change his treatment of the figures of the revolutionists in the novel *Resurrection,* considering it unnecessary to "show the other side of the coin" for "an understanding of the life of a revolutionist." (L. N. Tolstoy, vol. 33, p. 383) Tolstoy in fact reworked this section of the manuscript, but because, as he wrote to Chertkov, he had had this intention earlier. (Cf. vol. 88, p. 158)

Having written another "ending" to the story *The Candle* at Chertkov's suggestion, Tolstoy wrote to him, "But all this is not good, it can't be any good. The whole story was written with that 'ending' in mind." (L. N. Tolstoy, vol. 85, p. 276) In the publication *Posrednik,* the story *The Candle* was printed with this artificial ending, but after 1886 Tolstoy repudiated it.

The pressure brought to bear by the "Tolstoyans" was indeed great. As P. I. Biryukov wrote to V. G. Chertkov, October 19, 1885, "We will ask Lev Nikolayevich to change only those places where these moral principles suffer, which we and Lev Nikolayevich recognize, and from which he sometimes deviates nominally, carried away by the art of exposition." (GMT) In the majority of cases, however, and especially in his literary creations, Tolstoy rejected the encroachments of his followers; I. L. Tolstoy's assertion is therefore clearly exaggerated.

6. On October 22, 1907, N. N. Gusev, L. N. Tolstoy's secretary at the time, was arrested and put in the Krapivensky jail. In a letter to D. A. Olsufyev on November 8, 1907 , Tolstoy explains the reason for the arrest: "Someone informed against him, saying that he abuses the Tsar; they searched him and found my pamphlet, *The One Thing Needful,* with words of harsh criticism of Aleksandr III and Nikolai II penciled in the margin." (L. N. Tolstoy, vol. 77,

p. 238) The words of criticism were Tolstoy's, and Gusev had only transferred them from a London to a Petersburg edition, in which they had been omitted. The arrest upset Tolstoy. He appealed to D. D. Kobeko, Governor of Tula, for his release, sent a letter to Count D. A. Olsufyev asking for help through the Minister of the Interior for Gusev's release. At the same time he was visiting N. N. Gusev in prison and taking the correspondence with him. On November 19, 1907, D. A. Olsufyev informed Tolstoy by letter that he had succeeded in seeing Stolypin, who promised to "suppress" the Gusev case. On December 20, 1907, Gusev was released.

7. M. M. Kholevinskaya was the zemstvo doctor until 1884 in the Krapivensky District; later she worked in Tula.

She met Tolstoy in 1884 and often visited Yasnaya Polyana. She was arrested in 1893 for the dissemination of Tolstoy's banned works. By L. N. Tolstoy's petition through A. F. Kony, she was released in January 1894, but in February 1896 was again arrested on a charge of possessing and distributing Tolstoy's banned writings.

At T. L. Tolstaya's request, Kholevinskaya gave Tolstoy's book, *What I Believe,* banned in Russia at the time, to the worker I. P. Novikov; her entire guilt consisted in this. Tolstoy's letter to I. L. Goremykin, Minister of the Interior, and to N. V. Muravyev, Minister of Justice, remained unanswered. M. M. Kholevinskaya was exiled to Astrakhan.

8. From a letter dated about April 20, 1886. (L. N. Tolstoy, vol. 69, pp. 83–86)

9. From a letter of March 12 . . . 13, 1908. (L. N. Tolstoy, vol. 78, p. 88)

Chapter XXVII

1. N. N. Gusev, L. N. Tolstoy's secretary from 1907 to 1909, kept a diary, which was published in *Posrednik* in 1912 under the title *Two Years with L. N. Tolstoy. Notes of L. N. Tolstoy's Former Secretary.* V. F. Bulgakov was L. N. Tolstoy's secretary in 1910. His diary, *L. N. Tolstoy in the Last Year of His Life,* was published in 1911.

D. P. Makovitsky, L. N. Tolstoy's house doctor from 1904 to 1910, kept detailed daily notes, *Yasnaya Polyana Notes,* published only in part. The manuscript is in GMT.

Stenographic notes were kept by N. N. Gusev, and at times by D. Makovitsky.

2. In a letter to T. A. Kuzminskaya, December 3, 1906, S. A. Tolstaya describes the burial of Maria Lvovna as follows: "I accompanied Masha to the stone pillars, where my strength failed me, and Lyovochka went to the edge of the village, then we returned home." (GMT) In another of her letters, S. A. Tolstaya describes Maria Lvovna's illness and death. "Masha fell ill on November 20; in the evening she had a sharp pain in her left shoulder and a severe chill. Soon her temperature was over 40° and she was consumed by fever all week. The inflammation turned out to be in the left lung, a very serious pneumonia. No remedy lessened the intensity of the pain. She was delirious, rarely regained consciousness to say something affectionate to one of us; she was meek and gentle. . . . On the day of her death, the twenty-sixth, she suddenly began to weep, embraced her husband, but said nothing. Only later, and almost inaudibly, she murmured, "I am dying." In the evening her breath came at longer intervals and with greater difficulty; she lifted her arms and they put her back. It is impossible to forget the sight of that touching creature; her head was bent to one side, her eyes closed, the expression of her face so tender, meek, spiritual, and outwardly gracious. . . . *Papa* held her hand. I stood nearby; the whole family was assembled in two rooms—she died in the room under the vault—all the servants were there too. Masha was buried in our churchyard; our Yasnaya Polyana people bade her a touching farewell." (Letter to O. K. Tolstaya, December 7, 1906, GMT)

3. Of all his children, M. L. Obolenskaya was closest to Tolstoy and loved him "without reasoning, without criticism, and completely." (S. A. Tolstaya's letter to L. I. Veselitskaya, December 7, 1906, GMT) The sensation of "the importance and joy" of her "position with Father" brought her immense satisfaction. Her constant concern about him, about his health and his affairs, was the chief thing in her life. She had a great understanding and sympathy for Tolstoy's spiritual quest and the ideas he held. She herself believed that it would be good for her father to be with her, not because she was better than the others, but because she loved him, sympa-

thized with his world-view. "The main thing is that one suffers doubly—both for oneself and constantly for *papa* and with *papa*." (Letter to V. S. Tolstaya, October 6, 1901, GMT)

4. From a letter of October 24–25 (November 6–7), 1860. (L. N. Tolstoy, vol. 60, pp. 353–54)

5. The reference is to *Diary for Myself Alone*. From July 29 to September 22, 1910, Tolstoy kept two diaries. One, his customary diary, which he had kept from 1847 and which was accessible to those close to him, who could make notes or copies from it; the other, *Diary for Myself Alone*, which Tolstoy did not permit anyone to read. In it he made notes concerning his family life, his relations with his wife, children, friends, and his difficult spiritual state. (Cf. L. N. Tolstoy, vol. 58, pp. 129–143)

6. No information about this article has been discovered.

7. The 28th was indeed a special date in Tolstoy's life. He was born on August 28, 1828; the censor's permission for *Childhood and Youth* was signed on May 28, 1856; S. L. Tolstoy was born on June 28, 1863; I. L. Tolstoy married Sofya Nikolayevna Filosofova on February 28, 1888; and on October 28, 1910, L. N. Tolstoy left Yasnaya Polyana for the last time.

Chapter XXVIII

1. Maria Nikolayevna Tolstaya died on August 4, 1830, five months after the birth of her daughter. In his *Reminiscences*, L. N. Tolstoy writes that his mother died "as a result of the birth" of his sister, M. N. Tolstaya. (L. N. Tolstoy, vol. 34, p. 354)

2. Fet, part I, chapters 8 and 9.

3. M. N. Tolstaya lived with her husband at the Pokrovsky estate in the Chern District of the Province of Tula, twenty versts from I. S. Turgenev's estate, Spasskoye-Lutinovo. Maria Nikolayevna's acquaintance with Turgenev (October 1854) soon ripened into friendship and they kept up a lively correspondence. M. N. Tolstaya's image was evoked by the story Turgenev dedicated to her, *Faust*. According to a family legend, Turgenev, like the hero of his

narrative, read in the summerhouse with Maria Nikolayevna, only it was not *Faust* that they read, but *Eugene Onegin.*

4. From a letter of March 3, 1909. (L. N. Tolstoy, vol. 79, p. 100)

5. M. N. Tolstaya, in a letter to D. P. Makovitsky, December 10, 1908, expressed her regret that Tolstoy had destroyed his letter to Bishop Germogen and had not sent her a copy. She would have pointed out certain things to him, and it would have "opened his eyes."

Tolstoy's letter was written in reply to the appeal of Germogen, the Saratov bishop, to the clergy and the people, in which he exposed as "a morally illegitimate enterprise" the desire of a certain segment of society to celebrate Tolstoy's Jubilee. He demanded that Tolstoy be banished "beyond all state boundaries."

Tolstoy did not send his letter to Germogen (cf. L. N. Tolstoy, vol. 78, No. 252), but he later sent a copy of it to M. N. Tolstaya to be given "to certain people" to read, but not copied.

"I did not send the letter" [to Germogen—Ed.], Tolstoy wrote in the letter cited by Ilya Lvovich, "because it's not worth it, and principally because *le beau rôle* (the advantage) is too much on my side." (Cf. L. N. Tolstoy, vol. 78, p. 284)

6. A. L. Tolstaya and V. M. Feokritova.

7. In August 1896 (10–15), L. N. and S. A. Tolstoy went to the Shamardino Monastery, and from there to the Optina Hermitage. This trip was described in detail in S. A. Tolstaya's unpublished notes, *My Life.* (S. A. Tolstaya, *My Life*, vol. 7, pp. 49–55) On their arrival at the Optina Hermitage, the Tolstoys visited the grave of Lev Nikolayevich's aunt, A. I. Osten-Saken, who had died at the Optina Hermitage, and that of E. A. Tolstaya, T. A. Ergolskaya's sister. S. A. Tolstaya went to confession with Father Gerasim.

According to Sofya Andreyevna, Tolstoy "found both the inner and outer spirit of the Optina Monastery greatly deteriorated."

In A. S. Suvorin's diary, there is mention of the fact that Tolstoy met Father Joseph, prior of the Optina Hermitage. In his entry for November 10, 1896, Suvorin quotes from M. A. Stakhovich's story about the Tolstoy trip to the Optina Monastery: ". . . He [Tolstoy—Ed.] and the Countess went to the Optina Hermitage, where she fasted and repented. He did not fast, but attended a service and spent some time with the old monk, Joseph. . . ." (*Diary of A. S. Suvorin*, pub. L. D. Frankel, Moscow, Petrograd, 1923, p. 133)

Chapter XXIX

1. *The first will* was made by Tolstoy in the form of diary notes, March 27, 1895. (L. N. Tolstoy, vol. 53, pp. 14–16) Tolstoy asked that his wife, V. G. Chertkov, and N. N. Strakhov "look through and sort" his papers. He asked that his heirs transfer publication rights to his works to the public domain.

The second will was in the form of a letter to V. G. Chertkov, May 13/26, 1904 (cf. L. N. Tolstoy, vol. 88, pp. 327–29) in which he entrusted to V. G. Chertkov and S. A. Tolstaya the sorting and "disposition of his papers" as they saw fit.

A diary note of August 11, 1908 (cf. L. N. Tolstoy, vol. 56, p. 144), dictated and taken down in shorthand by N. N. Gusev, is Tolstoy's *third will*. He expressed the wish that all his writings should be placed by his heirs in the public domain ("If not all, then certainly those necessary for the people, such as the *ABC Books,* and *Books for Reading*").

In July 1909, Tolstoy conceived the idea of drawing up a *legal will*. He turned for advice and assistance to the lawyer I. V. Denisenko, who drew up a plan of the will and sent it to Tolstoy. For some unknown reason this draft did not reach him.

The fourth (the first legal) *will* was written by Tolstoy on September 18, 1901 (cf. L. N. Tolstoy, vol. 80, p. 267), at the time of a visit to V. G. Chertkov. According to this will, none of his works could be anyone's private property, and could be "published and copied by all without compensation. . . ." All of Tolstoy's manuscripts were placed at the disposition of Chertkov. This will was not acceptable to lawyers, because, according to law, property can only be willed to a specific person, and not to the public at large, as the will had specified. Therefore, on November 1, 1909, Tolstoy's *fifth will* was made (cf. L. N. Tolstoy, vol. 80, pp. 268–89). V. G. Chertkov, a Moscow attorney N. K. Muravyev, and F. A. Strakhov took part in drawing up the will. Tolstoy named his youngest daughter, A. L. Tolstaya, as his legal heir, but did not specify to whom his literary inheritance was to pass in the event of her death, and the will could be considered invalid from the legal standpoint.

On July 22, 1910, in the woods near the village of Grumont, Tolstoy's *sixth will* was written (cf. L. N. Tolstoy, vol. 82, p. 227). The text was composed by N. K. Muravyev and copied by L. N.

Tolstoy. His manuscripts and all his papers were bequeathed out-right to A. L. Tolstaya, and, in the event of her death, to T. L. Sukhotina.

On November 16, 1910, in an open session of the circuit court of Tula, Tolstoy's will was certified for execution.

Chapter XXX

1. A legend was circulated among some of the Tolstoyans concerning Tolstoy as Socrates, victim of Xanthippe—Sofya Andreyevna. It is possible that I. L. Tolstoy has in mind P. A. Sergeyenko's play *Socrates*, about which M. S. Sukhotin wrote in his diary, "Incidentally, Sergeyenko's Socrates and Xanthippe are drawn from Lev Nikolayevich and Sofya Andreyevna, of course." (*Tolstoy in the Last Decade of His Life*, from the Diary of M. S. Sukhotin, *Literaturnoye Nasledstvo*, vol. 69, book 2, p. 222)

2. Cf. vol. 57, p. 99.

3. I. L. Tolstoy has misquoted the Gospel text cited by L. N. Tolstoy in the collection *For Every Day*, cf. vol. 43, p. 254.

4. Tolstoy's children, T. L. Sukhotina, Sergei, Ilya, and Andrei Lvovich, assembled at Yasnaya Polyana on October 29, 1910, and wrote a letter to Tolstoy, which his youngest daughter, Aleksandra, took to him. With the exception of Sergei Lvovich and Tatyana Lvovna Sukhotina, they all thought that their father ought to return. Sergei Lvovich, however, considered that Tolstoy had been right to leave Yasnaya Polyana.

"I think," he wrote, "that *maman* is nervously ill, and for the most part not responsible for what she does, and that you had to separate (should perhaps have done so long ago), however painful it may be for both. I think, too, that even if something should happen to *maman*, which I do not expect, that you must not reproach yourself for anything. The situation was hopeless, and I believe you chose the right way out." Ilya Lvovich wrote, "I know how difficult life was for you here. Difficult in many respects. But, after all, you looked on this life as your cross. . . . I am sorry you did not bear this cross to the end. . . ." (S. L. Tolstoy, *Sketches of the Past*, Tula, 1965, p. 263)

All these letters are published in S. L. Tolstoy's book, *Sketches of the Past*, Tula, 1965, pp. 262–65. L. N. Tolstoy's letter to S. L. Tolstoy and T. L. Sukhotina, cf. vol. 82, pp. 220–21.

5. Entries for July 30 and August 2, 1910. (L. N. Tolstoy, vol. 58, pp. 129, 130)

6. T. A. Kuzminskaya, *My Life at Home and at Yasnaya Polyana*, I–III, Moscow, 1925–26.

7. Cf. notes 5 and 6, chapter II.

8. S. A. Tolstaya's autobiography was published in the magazine *Nachala*, No. 1, 1921.

9. Cf. L. N. Tolstoy, vol. 58, pp. 131, 132.

10. These words of L. N. Tolstoy were written down by T. L. Sukhotina. Cf. Biryukov, vol. 4, p. 251.

11. S. A. Tolstaya died on November 4, 1919, at Yasnaya Polyana.

Index